MIXED FAMILIES

JOYCE A. LADNER is associate professor of sociology at Hunter College, City University of New York, where she teaches courses on the family, child welfare, and race and ethnic relations.

A native Mississippian, she received her Ph.D. degree in sociology from Washington University, St. Louis, in 1968. She has taught at Southern Illinois University and Howard University. She conducted research on the role of women in community development in Tanzania, East Africa, in 1970.

The recipient of several research grants, she has published numerous articles in scholarly journals and in popular publications. She is the author of *Tomorrow's Tomorrow—The Black Woman* (1971) and the editor of an anthology, *The Death of White Sociology* (1973).

Ms. Ladner lives in New York City with her husband, Walter Carrington, and their two-year-old son, Thomas.

JOYCE A. LADNER

MIXED FAMILIES

Adopting Across Racial Boundaries

1977
ANCHOR PRESS/DOUBLEDAY • GARDEN CITY, NEW YORK

To my husband, Walter Carrington,
the eternal humanist and optimist.
With love.

To our son Thomas, who symbolizes
that future generation of vital,
creative individuals in whom we place
our hope for a better world.
With love.

ISBN: 0-385-12792-8
Library of Congress Catalog Number 76-44053
Copyright © 1977 *by Joyce A. Ladner*
ALL RIGHTS RESERVED
PRINTED IN THE UNITED STATES OF AMERICA

Contents

Acknowledgments

It is difficult for me to acknowledge gratitude to the many individuals and organizations who assisted in making this book possible.

This research was supported by grants from the Howard University Faculty Research Project, the Russell Sage Foundation, the Cummins Engine Foundation, and by a special grant from the Social Science Research Council's Committee on Grants to Minority Scholars for Research on Racism and Mental Health. The Metropolitan Applied Research Center under the direction of Kenneth Clark and Hylan Lewis provided me with a stimulating environment in which to complete the research. To all of these organizations I am deeply grateful.

I wish also to thank Andrew Billingsley, who perhaps more than anyone else provided me with the ongoing support and encouragement to initiate and complete this work. Hylan Lewis and Andrew Billingsley critiqued the entire manuscript. Robert Staples, Walter Stafford, and Alphonso Pinkney critiqued selected chapters of the draft. I wish to express my thanks to them.

Several research assistants aided in the collection of the data. To Wilma Perry, Jyl Hagler, Tamara Lieberman, William Martin, Gerald Gill, and Dorie Churnet, I am appreciative of their cooperation.

Josie Johnson, Wendell Rivers, and Robert Williams were especially helpful in providing me with contacts in Missouri and Minnesota. I am deeply indebted to Lillian-Anthony Welch, who arranged appointments and, in her characteristically unselfish manner, accompanied me to Minnesota and Connecticut and was of invaluable assistance in the data-collection process.

Without the unqualified co-operation of the adoption agencies and parents, this study would not have been possible. I shall forever be indebted to the parents for their willingness to be interviewed. The St. Louis, Minneapolis-St. Paul, and Washington, D.C., chapters of the Council on Adoptable Children and the Open Door Society provided invaluable assistance by making available to me rosters of their memberships and by agreeing to allow me to come to their meetings, which were valuable sources of data.

My husband, Walter Carrington, gave me the emotional support and understanding, and he served as an intellectual sounding board for many of the ideas I have developed in this book. It goes without saying that I thank him also.

My editor at Doubleday, Loretta Barrett, deserves special thanks for having the vision to understand the potential of this research. I thank her for her continued support and the invaluable assistance she gave to this project. I also owe special thanks to Angela Iadavaia-Cox for her editorial assistance.

Of course, ultimate responsibility for the contents and point of view expressed in this book is my own.

Introduction

The act of adoption has become progressively fraught with anxiety in the centuries since Pharaoh's daughter plucked the infant Moses from among the bulrushes. Up until recently, to the extent that the couple and the child had "matching" characteristics, peer and parental objections were blunted, and the stranger's stare was avoided. Then supply began to fall behind demand with the increased use of contraceptives and legalized abortions. The changing values of young women—more aware of and concerned about the consequences, for themselves and for their children, of having a child out of wedlock—also contributed to the decline in such births. These consequences—economic, social, and psychological —assuming greater importance, were symptomatic of massive changes occurring in the American family. Adoptable white babies became scarcer and scarcer in America, sending white adults, tired of waiting at home for long periods, to the quadrants of the earth in search of children to adopt. But no journey took them farther psychologically than that which finally led them to the abandoned offspring of the black community in their own country.

This book is about white Americans who adopt black children and about the controversy the adoptions created. It delves into the private lives of these couples, examining why they adopted and what their experiences have been. It examines the kinds of goals the adoptive parents have for their children and their expectations of the child's motivational and intellectual capacity. Do the parents' expectations of their black children differ from those of their white children? What are the parents' attitudes regarding their black child's racial identity?

This book also records and examines the reactions of grand-parents, other relatives, friends, and neighbors, as well as the relationship between adoptive and biological children. It explores the roles these parents, their children, and other significant persons play and how they influence the developing black adopted child. Of critical importance too, it looks at the role the adoption agency plays in the family drama.

Because these adoptions have created a storm of protest and controversy, it is impossible to view these parents or their families as typically middle-class American. Their lives have been strongly affected by the controversial nature of the family formation process they engaged in; for not only did the parents decide to shape their family by the accepted but atypical act of adoption, but they also crossed color barriers to do so. The controversial and atypical character of these families will be seen throughout this analysis, as will the ways in which they have responded and adapted to challenges created by family dynamics and outside forces.

The motivations for adopting any child, regardless of race, ethnicity, religion, or nationality, are similar. They vary from the desire to have offspring despite infertility to the wish to rescue an orphaned or otherwise homeless child. Some individuals adopt because they want an additional child, to serve as a companion to an only child, or to round off their family in terms of sex. Others adopt to replace a dead child, to have an heir, or to bring stability to a troubled marriage.[1]

This book will attempt to bring an understanding and clarity to the motivations of parents who adopt across racial boundaries. In exploring the inner sanctums of the lives of these parents who have followed such an unorthodox path for establishing their families, myths will be shattered, painful truths will be revealed, and, it is hoped, the reader will share the writer's ambivalences, antipathies, and occasional awe for those few who have made a vocation of parenthood.

Transracial adoption, as will be shown, is an extremely complex phenomenon. Such complexity defies simplistic explanations and pat solutions.

I first became interested in transracial adoption in 1969 when I noted the increasing amount of human-interest coverage given the phenomenon in newspapers, magazines, and on television. The question of motivation particularly intrigued me. Why were more and more whites adopting black children? After compiling a bibliography of the works published in professional journals and the popular press, my curiosity remained unslaked. The literature was sparse and uneven. Only a few doctoral dissertations had been written. The majority of the journalistic articles praised the couples for their "courage and commitment." Few raised serious questions about why they adopted or whether white parents could raise psychologically healthy black children in this racially polarized American society.

In 1971 I heard the first organized rumblings against these adoptions by black social workers. They bitterly criticized adoption agencies for not recruiting black parents and seriously questioned the ability of white people to rear black children.

This study also grew out of my interests in child socialization and in race and ethnic relations. I had conducted extensive research on the socialization of young black girls and their concepts of womanhood.[2] When I decided to study transracial adoption, I saw it as a logical extension of my earlier work. What, I wondered, were the problems white parents faced in socializing black children? Were they different from those experienced by other parents?

This book addresses a serious methodological concern. Can a black sociologist effectively conduct sensitive research among white subjects? There has been a lot of controversy over the extent to which researcher bias distorts social analysis. I had been very much a party to that controversy. I had argued that it was difficult for white researchers, who represent the dominant culture and point of view, to understand blacks and give the same interpretations and meanings to their lives as blacks would. This was especially true when white middle-class social scientists studied lower-class blacks. Racial and class biases often prevented the researcher and informant from interpreting social reality in the same context. I was, therefore, quite sensitive to the potential hazards. I anticipated that some of my informants would be skeptical and curious about the research and my motives.

Many readers are likely to challenge whether or not I have elicited accurate responses as to why the individuals in this study choose to adopt across racial boundaries. I am aware that assessing motives is difficult.

All too often one is dealing with both the conscious and unconscious factors. It is indeed difficult, if not impossible, for the sociological researcher to study unconscious motivation because he or she does not have the qualifications. For the most part, the researcher must accept, with some healthy skepticism, the reasons parents *say* they adopted, while being aware of the discrepancies between their stated reasons and their behavior.

Neither can I say I was qualified to challenge their stated reasons for adopting. Somewhere there must exist a thin, gray area that both separates and joins together the truth and falsity. Bearing this in mind, it is not productive to go beyond the limitations of my data.

This research brought with it many self-discoveries. My initial feelings were mixed. I felt some trepidation about studying white people, a new undertaking for me. Intellectual curiosity notwithstanding, I had the gnawing sensation that I shouldn't delve too deeply because the findings might be too controversial. I wondered too if the couples I intended to interview would tell me the truth. Would some lie in order to cover up their mistakes and disappointments with the adoption? How much would they leave unsaid? Would some refuse to be interviewed because of their preconceived notions about my motives? Would they stereotype me as a hostile black sociologist who wanted to "prove" that these adoptions would produce mentally unhealthy children? And how many were simply tired of allowing their family's privacy to be invaded further after they had been featured in newspaper and magazine stories?

Readers are likely to question my motives. Was the father in Washington, D.C., correct when he refused to be interviewed because, according to him, "Everyone out at Howard University [where I then taught] is a black racist and you couldn't possibly understand our position correctly." Prior to starting the interviews I admit to having been skeptical about whether the adoptions could work out well. Because I was reared in the Deep South, with all of its rigid racial segregation, transracial adoption represented, for me, an inexplicable departure from custom and tradition. I would have thought it just as unorthodox for a black couple to adopt a white child. Racial polarization in America sensitizes everyone to the potential hazards in this kind of "mixing" of the races. On the other hand, I was also unwilling to accept the facile clichés the critics used to describe the motives of the adoptive parents. I wanted to find out for myself what kinds of people were adopting and why they did it. What were their day-to-day experiences? How did the adoption affect their biological children? How were the children coping? It was also important to find out the reactions of their families, friends, and neighbors; their philosophies on race relations and black identity; their experiences with the adoption agencies; and their hopes and expectations for their children's future.

The study was conducted in Georgia, Missouri, Washington, D.C., Maryland, Virginia, Connecticut, and Minnesota. The majority of the 136 parents were selected from the rosters of the local chapters of the Open Door Society (ODS) and the Council on Adoptable Children (COAC), organizations that promote transracial adoption. Additional parental contacts were made through personal contacts and referrals from adoption agencies and adoptive parents.

An in-depth interview was conducted with each set of parents, each of whom had adopted at least one black child. Repeated interviews were done with a few parents. The interviews were carried out in an informal atmosphere in the couples' homes. The children usually provided the backdrop as they played in the background. Meetings of the Open Door Society and the Council on Adoptable Children, which I attended in several cities, were rich sources of data, as were the group discussions I conducted with the parents. The interviews were semistructured and open-ended. I encouraged the parents to give detailed responses, and I taped and transcribed all interviews and group discussions.

The researcher is always faced with the dilemma of whether to select a small number of subjects and study them intensively or select a large sample and gather less intensive data. Although the former is personally appealing and is a method I have used in the past, I decided to survey a larger cross section of adoptive parents, hoping to be able to generalize my findings more than would have been possible with the smaller sample.

There are limitations to the one-shot in-depth interview. The researcher cannot check for accuracy and validity. The format is not conducive to the development of rapport between the researcher and informants, which could facilitate communication. It was also impossible for me to get to know the children and to find out, in the majority of cases, what they were thinking. Unlike field studies where intensive observations about what goes on in families are recorded, this study was designed in such a manner that this was, for the most part, impossible. There were some notable exceptions: One evening after a discussion with some parents, several asked if I would have a private meeting with their children. The parents suggested that I talk to the children about what it means to be transracially adopted.

There was another built-in limitation. Many of the COAC and ODS members have developed strong friendships with one another. It is not unusual for some of the activists in these groups to know individuals who have adopted black children in distant cities. They see each other at conventions or learn of a member's activities through newsletters the chapters publish. A few have acquired national reputations. Although these couples are initially brought together by the fact that all have transracially adopted, they often find that they have other interests in common. The grapevine keeps these people in fairly close contact with each other. Hence, one of the problems I faced as I interviewed them was not wanting to risk offending them because my questions were too blunt. I knew that if I, for example, badgered a couple for some of the intimate details they were unwilling to reveal or discuss, I might have easily acquired the reputation for being hostile or insensitive. Some individuals who were not sure they made the right decision to adopt a black child revealed a fragile emotional state. Many also carried unhealed wounds caused by unkind family, friends, and neighbors who opposed the adoption. It wasn't unusual for some of the parents to freeze up when I asked questions concerning things about which they were acutely sensitive. Because I knew how effective the grapevine was, I decided to avoid the potential for having someone who was offended by my questions or my manner pass on a negative impression to others whom I hoped to interview. In order to keep doors open I had to remind myself constantly to be at my congenial, understanding, and empathizing best.

A fairly typical comment made by parents, when contacted by phone and asked for an interview, was, "Mary Williams told me about the interview you did with her and James. I was expecting you to call." Thankfully less typical was the hostile father who told me over the phone, "So you're the one who is doing this study to prove how racist we are!" Although he and his wife agreed to be interviewed, he did not conceal his cynicism and hostility. I later learned that he thought I was secretly allied with the black social workers and that I intended to pass my data on to them for their own use. This close social network of the adopting couples was an inhibiting factor for the collection of data.

The network also had its advantages. Many of the parents, after being interviewed, transmitted a positive attitude to their friends and encouraged them to participate in the study. A few were downright enthusiastic and quite helpful. They also had their own ideas about how the study could be used. For example, a young woman who was very active in one of the organizations prodded me to interview a couple who had adopted several black children. When I asked why she thought I should, she explained that she and some of her friends were convinced that the couple had adopted the children to fulfill some racist fantasies. Although I eventually conducted the interview, I did not, of course, comply with her request to report my impressions to her.

I am very concerned about protecting the privacy of these families. Therefore, all names and other identifying materials in this book are fictional. There was also the recurring concern I had for my relationship to them, how they defined my role, and how they thought I would interpret their values and behavior. As I grappled with this problem I quite consciously avoided making quick judgments and forming strong opinions about these adoptions and allowed the events to unfold and the facts to speak for themselves. In spite of my initial trepidation, the majority of the parents were straightforward and honest. I was rather surprised that the characteristic demeanor for many was that of not only a willingness but also an enthusiasm to co-operate. Some seemed to have a need to tell their story openly and willingly. The interview appeared to act as a catharsis for some. They were able to discuss troubling issues and to do some brainstorming with a relatively anonymous, unthreatening, but informed interviewer. In some cases, it obviously helped that the interviewer was black because it allowed the couples to inform this symbolic representative that they were sincere in their intentions and did not knowingly or intentionally adopt the child to bring harm to his psyche. As one father told me, "Maybe you will let the black people know what kinds of people we *really* are." Could the black interviewer be serving as a sounding board for what other blacks think about a white couple having adopted a black child? Some parents seemed to think so. Ordinarily one would expect the parents to talk over these concerns with their families and friends. Some did, while others could not because family and close friends had expressed disapproval for what they had done.

Supporters of transracial adoption have often exalted the adopting parents by pointing to their virtues. They have been referred to as charitable, good-hearted, decent, and noble. Some think they are more concerned with child welfare than the average parent. In my pursuit for clarification, I sought to find out if these parents lived up to such lofty descriptions and, if so, *why* they chose this rather risky path. Weren't there other ways for expressing their concern for the plight of homeless black children? As one cynic put it, "Why don't they contribute to the NAACP's legal defense fund for the South Boston busing case instead of seizing parenthood from blacks?" Other well-meaning critics suggested countless ways in which they could make more acceptable contributions. They suggested that the white parents try to influence changes in adoption-agency policies to make it easier for blacks to adopt, or that they lobby in state capitals for quality child-welfare legislation, thereby aiding in the reduction of the number of adoptable children. Why did the white parents have to assume this most basic responsibility for these black babies? Were the white parents guilty, as their critics accused them, of having rescue fantasies? Did some of them feel that only they could adequately provide permanent homes for these children, or that, if they didn't, no one else would?

Also I wanted to find out to what extent these children were merely pawns in a quasiconspiratorial system involving "decent" white parents, insensitive or racially biased adoption agencies, and dissenting, hostile black social workers. Were the children only incidental to a political and ideological confrontation being waged between blacks and whites? Indeed, I wondered if these children were being lost in the tug-of-war between these antagonistic groups.

As the interviewing progressed, I realized that I should also hear the point of view of the black social workers who had expressed vehement opposition. It was also necessary to focus on the people who create adoption-agency policies, because they bore the responsibility for turning these children over to white parents instead of black ones. I had easy access to the activist black social workers. I knew a few of them on a personal basis, and they referred me to others. I traveled to different parts of the country to interview some of the more outspoken critics. They were quite cooperative and candid. I sought to find out more about them as a group. How did they get involved in the adoption controversy? What led them to conclude that it amounted to "genocide against black people"? Were the white parents at least partially correct in their characterization of them as black racists? Were the critics only interested in putting a stop to the adoptions, or did they also intend to find black homes for the children? Did their position represent a broader political strategy? How many of them worked in child welfare and, closer to the point, how many worked in adoptions? Had any of them adopted? How important was their notion that whites are incapable of transmitting a *black* identity to black children? This fundamental problem had widespread implications for the adoption of foreign children and children whose ethnic backgrounds were different from their parents —for example, native American, Asian American, Chicano, and Puerto Rican. The question was: Could *any* child of a different race, nationality, or ethnic group develop into an emotionally healthy individual with a strong and positive sense of identity if he or she is reared by parents outside his or her ancestral group?

The critics' chief target was the adoption agencies. For so long these agencies had faithfully abided by the "matching" concept, in which children are assigned to parents with similar physical features. For example, a blond couple was given a blond child. I sought to find out how this unusual practice of making transracial placements got started. I selectively interviewed adoption workers in most of the cities where the parents in the study lived. From these interviews I was again able to fit together additional pieces of this ever-expanding picture. Each agency usually had its highly individualistic philosophies and characteristics. I found it valuable to understand and interpret the philosophies of the people who were making these important decisions about the lives of these children.

All of the subjects in this study—the parents, their children, the black social workers, adoption workers, and others—are playing critical roles in one of the most important developments in American families in this century. The writer hopes to provide some insight into this complex and controversial approach to family formation.

A NOTE ON STYLE: Throughout this book, you will come across what will seem to be an inconsistent and improper use of the pronouns "they," "them," and "their." We use these pronouns not only to represent the individual plural but also the indifferent singular. This was done to avoid the use of gendered pronouns "he" and "his."

A Personal Note

In 1975, four years after I began the interviewing for this study, my husband Walter and I adopted a six-month-old son, Thomas. Happily, our experience differed markedly from that of so many black parents whose unfortunate or negative experiences with adoption agencies I will have occasion to criticize in this book. We were treated with courtesy and dignity by an adoption caseworker who was sensitive to our needs and reflected her agency's paramount concern for the welfare of the children entrusted to its care.

Our decision to adopt was made only after long and careful consideration of the responsibilities and rewards of becoming parents. It was especially important for us that we quite early came to the realization that *parenthood*—adoptive and biological—has more universal similarities than differences. For the purposes of this book, I gained new insight into the infinitely more complicated nature of the conflicts white couples who adopt black children must resolve.

While I have attempted to analyze the data I collected with objectivity, I can make no claim to being entirely "value free." However professionally I might have wished it were otherwise, I know that much that I have written has been colored by my deeply rooted belief that every child has the right to a permanent home and loving parents.

Joyce A. Ladner

Themes in Black and White

"If we can give our black son a secure sense of himself, we feel confident that he can make it in the white or black worlds," said a white father. His wife agreed: "Black identity isn't important at all because if you don't have any self-confidence, or human identity, you cannot expect to develop any of these other identifications. If Jamie wants any black identity I'm sure he can get it on his own when he gets grown."

A black social worker who would rather see black children placed in permanent foster care, adopted by welfare families, or placed in institutions than be adopted by whites said: "Our children must remain in the black community, they belong to us, and it is our responsibility to take care of them—to give them a black identity and black survival skills. We have to teach them what it means to be *black* men and women."

A young white couple who had adopted two black children moved from their predominantly white suburban home to a neighborhood about two thirds black and one third white. Their new home is smaller and older than their previous one. They joined an integrated church and went out of their way to make black friends, especially families with young children. "We knew we'd have to change our lifestyle if we were serious about giving our girls a black identity. We also did it for our two sons because their expanded world will make them better human beings." How would it change their children? The father replied, "Because we are now an integrated family. None of our children will grow up with the parochialism that my wife and I experienced as youngsters." His wife added: "It is wrong for some of these people who adopt black children to keep them stuck out in those white suburban enclaves and not expose them to black culture. How else are they going to develop a black identity?

"The only effective thing the black social workers have done was to express their anger," said a black psychiatrist. "I am not aware of any programs they've organized to increase black adoptions. Sure, they have talked a lot about black identity, but their concern was more political than anything else. I seriously doubt they ever intended to go any further than calling attention to the problem."

A young white couple who adopted two black children said they have a friend who frequently uses the word "nigger" in their children's presence. "We overlook it because we know he doesn't mean any harm by saying it. It's just a habit," said the mother. How do the children react? "Oh, they don't pay him much attention. Besides, if they have to hear someone use that word we'd rather they heard it from a friend instead of someone else who might be hostile." This couple say that their black children have a lot of rhythm and can dance "really super." "You know," said the father, "that's because all black people can dance real well. Our children inherited this from their people."

1

THE FAMILIES
A Look into Their Private Worlds

The experiences of couples who adopt across racial boundaries are as varied as the couples themselves.[1] This diversity makes it impossible to pigeonhole couples on the basis of transracial adoption alone. Their lives exhibit all the joys and happiness, as well as the disappointments and despair, that exist in typical American families. Their attitudes toward transracial adoption; their motivations for having crossed the color barrier in order to create their families; and their expectations for the future are, in many ways, no different from those of ordinary middle-class parents. Yet, as will be shown, they differ significantly from their counterparts.

In this first chapter we enter the private worlds of four families who adopted. We do so at some risk: While to some degree each of our four case studies represents a major category of transracially adoptive parents, we must be careful not to paint the portraits with too broad a brush. The details of the thousands of couples who have embarked on this "high risk" venture make each composite picture unique, like so many snowflakes.

All the interviews were conducted in the casual comfort of the families' homes, in most cases in the kitchen, the true heart of any house, with the coffee pot perking constantly in the background. Reminiscences, questions, answers, all were punctuated by the children's voices—playing in the backyard, pestering Mommy for advice, begging Daddy for adjudication of squabbles, vying with siblings for the interviewer's attentions. Normal family life, in every way.

While salient points about the families' attitudes toward transracial adoption and its effects have, of course, been left intact, certain details have been changed to mask the privacy of the case-study couples who were gracious enough to submit to very frank and candid interviewing. The first couple are college-educated and widely traveled; before settling down in a large eastern city they spent time in Africa. The second family lives the communal life in a rambling house in a large southern city. The third pair are raising their children in a suburb outside an eastern city and have no biological children. The last case history deals with a working-class couple in a border state.

"The idea that a white family cannot give a black child the proper psychological preparedness for a racist society is one kind of objection I've heard expressed by black social workers. But I don't agree with it," Peggy Scott says emphatically. Sitting in the Scotts' spacious suburban home in a predominantly white neighborhood near a large eastern city, Peggy asserts over and over that she and her husband, Warren, are more than qualified to raise their four-year-old daughter June. Peggy and Warren are young, college-educated, and widely traveled. The couple spent several years teaching in Africa before returning to the United States to settle down and have a family.

A highly articulate woman of stern bearing, Peggy currently teaches in a public school with a very small black student enrollment. Warren, a very proud and somewhat reserved person, is a university professor. Both Peggy and Warren strive very hard to gloss over the fact that the child they adopted (at the age of six months) is of Negroid ancestry. "We didn't start out to adopt a mixed-race child," Warren says. When the adoption agency suggested that the couple consider adopting a racially mixed child because of the acute shortage of adoptable white babies, however, Peggy and Warren both felt race would make no difference to them because they wanted a child badly and certain medical problems made it difficult for Peggy to have her own. "We would have had to wait a long time to get a healthy white infant and we didn't want to wait," Peggy explains.

The Scotts' decision to adopt transracially was shared by their parents before they got the baby. Peggy's parents, described by her as "well educated, highly intelligent, and successful," were delighted. "My family was pleased," she says, "not because we adopted a black child, but because we were adopting a child, period. They are not terribly politically aware one way or the other . . . just ordinary American-type people. They did not perceive the adoption as any kind of cause, and neither did we." Peggy emphasizes that she and Warren *informed* his parents and did not ask their permission. "They raised objections, not on a racial basis but out of a protective instinct for their son," explains Peggy. "His mother said, 'It's hard enough to be parents, so why take on the problems of the world?'" Since the adoption, however, Warren's parents have adjusted and have never regarded June as anything less than a granddaughter.

June's natural mother appeared to be American Indian, although the woman's father was Oriental and her mother was American Indian, Caucasian, and, according to Peggy, "any number of other things." Little June's father was "visibly Negro." This is a point of confusion for the Scotts. Because June's natural mother is of mixed non-Negroid ancestry, Peggy and Warren don't see why the child should automatically be classified as Negro.

Peggy and Warren were apprehensive before the adoption. Peggy was especially concerned that people might focus too much attention on them as a mixed-race family. This concern continues and has caused the Scotts to consider carefully the kind of lifestyle they will live, the friends with whom they will associate, the neighborhood in which they will live, the kind of school June will attend, and the kinds of jobs they will accept. Their preoccupation with the fact that June might appear to be "different," and that she could face many problems because of it, has caused the Scotts to concentrate on assuring their child what they consider a "problem-free life."

To accomplish this, Peggy and Warren avoid people, places, and things that might bring emotional or physical harm to their family. For example, Warren speaks of receiving a job offer in the South. After going for an interview, he decided against investigating the job further because he felt regional racial attitudes would not provide a friendly atmosphere in which to raise June.

As Warren leaves the interview for a business appointment, Peggy explains that they have placed June in a racially mixed day-care center where, according to Peggy, "she does not stand out." After pausing a moment, Peggy continues, "This is certainly one of the things I wanted to make sure of. I didn't want to make June feel noticed."

With obvious strain in her voice, Peggy talks about the some-times patronizing public reaction her daughter evokes. It is common, Peggy says, for strangers—frequently elderly women—to approach and congratulate them on what a good deed or noble act they had done by adopting a black child. "It is really bad to have someone act like it's some kind of cause on your part," Peggy asserts. "What it really is is a form of prejudice on their part." Well-meaning as Peggy feels these people are, she thinks their actions serve only to focus attention on the transracial aspects of the adoption.

The favoritism June and other transracially adopted children often encounter is also a source of annoyance to Peggy. "Teachers bend over backward to be nice. It may not be a negative form of prejudice but it is still relating color to your actions," Peggy remarks. "I'm glad I'm aware of it because it will be easy for me to say to a teacher to stop giving June treatment different from the others in the class." Peggy's ideal for her daughter is for her to blend into her environment without drawing special attention, positive or negative, to herself or her parents.

Peggy Scott vehemently opposes the position that black social workers and other critics have taken against whites adopting black children. "I cannot say there is a uniqueness about blackness. I don't fully appreciate that," she notes. "I just feel that all this talk about people in terms of their differences is relatively immaterial. I also question one of the major tenets of the black social workers —that whites are incapable of transmitting black survival skills to their black child. I'm more concerned about the black community discriminating against her because she has white parents, and labeling her as an outsider. Are they going to claim she is not being raised as a proper black?" she asks.

In order to protect June, Peggy does not want her to identify solely as a black child. "I reject this whole business that says the black child has to be raised in a black family because only the black family can give her a feeling of self-worth," Peggy says. Seriously questioning whether black families are transmitting strong self-concepts and "black identity" to their children, Peggy asserts, "I feel that one of the problems black youngsters have is that the *parents* don't have strong feelings of self-worth. They are so defensive that they have turned into black racists," she says. "If they really believe that they are equal, then their children will grow up feeling equal. That's the kind of preparation I think they need for life."

Peggy Scott's voice is etched with sarcasm as she continues. "I wonder if June is not in fact going to know more about black history than the black child reared in the black home. We make sure she is exposed to both black and white history. My prediction is that if June wants to know more about black history, she will be perfectly capable of getting it." Peggy feels that there is too much concern raised today about black culture. "What does it really mean?" she asks. "Our only concern is that June grows up as an individual who knows her strengths and weaknesses and is realistic about society." As an afterthought Peggy adds, "After all, when you get down to it, it's about human identity and human relations. But if it ever becomes necessary for us to give June a black identity, we can do it better than most blacks I've met. After all, we spent two years in Africa."

Quite unlike most transracially adoptive parents, Peggy took the offensive during the interview and never relented. Reflecting the rage she felt at the audacity of strangers who question their ability to rear their black daughter, Peggy at one point said, "All this theorizing by the black social workers is ridiculous. No stranger, regardless of his credentials, could presume to inform us on child-rearing practices and the social and psychological factors involved in a white family rearing a child that society regards as black!"

Admitting that all of June's playmates are white, except for a young black boy whom she occasionally sees when the parents visit, the Scotts say that there is absolutely nothing wrong with this arrangement. "After all," says Peggy, "June is not all-black anyway."

Jeff and Erica Talbot share an attitude on rearing a black child that differs totally from that of the Scotts. Jeff is critical of many whites who adopt black kids. "There are a lot of people from middle-class backgrounds, who live in all-white communities, who proceed with the belief that all they have to do is to love the child in order for him or her to make it as a person. I don't believe that's enough!" he says. "More has to be done with combating the social and institutional implications of racism and black education, black culture, black history. A lot of these people have their heads in the sand and are bad news as far as I am concerned," he adds. Jeff reflects a moment, then says, "These parents love the kid but they don't translate that into a *corporate* influence."

The Talbots are convinced that a lot of whites are adopting black children because of the unavailability of healthy white infants—the so-called "blue-ribbon" baby. "I'm not sure how much guilt is involved," Jeff continues. "I don't think they're overt racists after they adopt these black kids. But I do think they are *naïve*." He adds, "I've seen people who love their kids, but they also watch them freak out on drugs. I've worked with them. Love just wasn't enough."

Jeff, at thirty, is a social worker with black youth in a large southern city. He and his wife, Erica, twenty-nine, are fairly recently settled into a rambling old frame house that serves as a commune. They share the commune with eleven adults and several children. While Jeff goes about his chores in the commune, Erica breaks from her daily routine—taking care of four little ones —for a moment to relate her feelings about adopting a black child. As she prepares tea, she explains that two of the four are her biological children—Meg, six, and Randy, eighteen months. Faith, a Korean, was adopted two years after the birth of their oldest child; Phillip, the offspring of a black father and a white mother, was adopted sometime later. He is now two years old.

The communal household in which the Talbots live lends itself to an unusual family arrangement. The Talbot children constantly interact with the others as an extended family. All adults participate in all decisions, and action is taken by consensus. The Talbot children are, therefore, exposed to a form of the counterculture lifestyle.

When asked why they adopted, Erica says, "We did so because children need homes and because one does not need to reproduce his own children because there are plenty already available." Jeff and Erica's first exposure to the idea of adopting transracially took place in 1967 when they were living on the East Coast. There they met a couple, former missionaries in South America, who had adopted several children across racial lines. Impressed by the couple, the Talbots decided they would like to know more about their experiences in rearing their adopted family. The two couples grew close, and Jeff and Erica decided that adopting transracially seemed to be a very positive thing to do. As a social worker at the time, Jeff began to pay closer attention to the transracial and international adoption movement, and he read the literature available to him. The Talbots went through many soul-searching conversations about the subject, which motivated them to take some action.

Because they had adopted Faith, their Korean daughter, through Pearl Buck's Welcome House, the couple decided to return to that agency to adopt across racial boundaries. They received excellent co-operation from the agency but they were warned that they would face a great number of problems—more, in fact, than they had faced after adopting Faith, a Korean. It appeared that it is not as politically volatile to raise an Asian child in this society because racial attitudes toward Orientals (at least cute little Asian girls) are not as hard and fast as those toward blacks. Jeff and Erica did not have much concern on the problematic aspects of international adoptions. On the other hand, they were quite preoccupied with being white parents to a black child. By this time, though, the Talbots had joined an active parents group and felt that their participation in the group would be invaluable in helping them adjust to possible problems. The group included a collection of very dedicated and professional adults who had adopted black and foreign children. At their monthly meetings, the members invited psychologists and other professionals to address them on problems associated with adopting multiracial children.

When the Talbots were told of Phillip's availability for adoption, they decided to proceed. Erica confesses that she "had some apprehensions about adopting a black child. Because of my own prejudices, I wondered if I would love the child, and if I would be able to cope with the problems. I also thought I might not be able to give him a lot of black cultural heritage." Erica now says her fears were not justified. "I have no trouble loving Phillip," she says. "He's as much mine as any of our children. The adoption helped me to realize that I can relate to any child, and it doesn't matter what he is or who he is." The Talbots feel that part of the success of Phillip's adoption is due to his having come to them when he was a few weeks old. Faith was nine months old when Jeff and Erica adopted her, and, because of her relatively late placement, Faith still expresses a lot of insecurities she developed in foster care.

Jeff and Erica's own parents were not overjoyed with either adoption. Erica remembers that her father resented that Meg, their natural daughter, would have a black brother. "I told him that we disagreed because we thought it would be a very healthy thing for Meg to have a brother who is part black," said Erica, "and we felt really good about the decision we had made to adopt Phillip." According to Jeff, his parents have always been very cautious of saying or doing anything that might offend him; so they were hesitant to speak their feelings. Erica and Jeff think that Phillip has been at least partially accepted by their parents because he is from mixed ancestry. "He is not real black in color and he does not have Afro hair as such," says Jeff. "These are the things that would have especially offended my father." Observing the favoritism his father shows toward his biological grandchildren, Jeff has had to sharply remind his father that he and Erica will not countenance any discrimination toward their adopted children.

The children are curious about adoption. Erica explains, "Faith is just beginning to get into the questioning period where she wants to know why her mother didn't keep her and what her mother looked like." The children are fully aware that there are two ways to acquire children. Since Jeff and Erica discuss adoption openly in their presence and attempt to answer their little questions about adoption, the children take it as a natural state of affairs and feel there is nothing abnormal about being adopted. The Talbots recognize, though, that Faith is a bit insecure, and they try to give her the necessary reassurance. "I think Faith is a little insecure about that fact that you are not her mother like you are Meg's mother," Jeff says to Erica. "She would like to have been in your stomach like Meg was." Erica agrees. "The girls talk about that a lot. Our children don't think in terms of discrimination, and it is incomprehensible to them that someone would be mean to a person because of his color or because he was adopted," she says. "So they don't understand the reactions of hostile people we meet in public." Jeff adds, "You know something? Their not being racists has certainly helped me."

While Jeff and Erica are quite concerned about racial identity, they also want others to know that they consider themselves normal parents who live with the same mundane tasks associated with childrearing as other families. They emphasize that they try to relate to each child according to their individual needs. Much like any typical informed mother who is currently a housewife because the children are still young, Erica reads literature on childrearing and child development, and, with Jeff, considers childrearing to be a succession of trials and errors. As each of the couple's children gets older, Jeff and Erica feel they are better prepared to transmit new ideas, use new methods, and generally improve their childrearing skills.

With four young children underfoot, Jeff and Erica say they have had to make many adjustments as a family. These adjustments—and tensions—have nothing to do with race or national boundaries, but with ages and numbers of children. Life in the commune "is ideal for the children because of the type of people they are surrounded by," says Erica. With the exception of a black college student, all other adult members of the commune are white. However, the neighborhood is 80 to 90 per cent black, and all the Talbot children are in constant contact with black children and adults in the neighborhood. The adults in the commune are quite friendly with their black neighbors, and Phillip, according to Erica, "is a social butterfly. He is known for miles around because he goes up and down the block trying to talk to people."

In their neighborhood, the Talbot family is not exposed on a daily basis to a lot of hostility and curious stares. For the most part, their black neighbors treat them in an accepting manner. But Jeff and Erica are certain that if they lived in a white neighborhood, their neighbors would be less than friendly.

When asked what role adoption agencies can play in helping families who adopt transracially, both Jeff and Erica were very critical of the fact that the agency did not follow up on the placement after placing Phillip in their home. Upon moving to the South, the couple helped to organize a group similar to the one they were associated with on the East Coast. (Most of the parents, however, have adopted Asian children.) The Talbots feel the parents have to take it upon themselves to be social activists and wake up the agencies from their slumber.

The agencies, according to Jeff, are letting many people adopt without seriously questioning them about the kind of neighborhood they intend to rear the child in. "They shouldn't let the applicants get away with their trite and pat responses—about how much they want the child and how much they will love him," he says. "They will end up with white children who have black skins. They won't be accepted by the blacks because they have been reared in all-white suburbia." For Jeff and Erica, the answer to the dilemma lies in the child's being reared by parents who are as honest and as open as possible, and who accept the fact that they have adopted a child who will be regarded as *black* first (regardless of his complexion), and not a *human being* without racial identification. If the child is caught between white and black worlds, Jeff feels, he will not develop a healthy personality and self-concept.

The Talbots are aware, though, that there are many blacks who do not approve of their having adopted him. "When black folks see Phillip with us, they have several reactions in succession," Jeff says. "First they have negative feelings about the fact that a black parent gave him up. Second, they wonder why the black community is not fulfilling its responsibility to adopt these children. Third, I have encountered some people in my job who see it as sad news for a white to be raising a black child."

A man with great personal convictions, Jeff is more concerned about changing institutional policies than with reshaping individual racial attitudes. He views the adoption agencies as "operating in the dark" because their staffs do not have the proper education to understand today's social problems, making them unable to be more selective and discriminating in making their transracial placements. "I can't think of any organizations or groups in America that are effectively combating racism," says Jeff, "and the adoption agency is one of them." Erica reminds him that their local parents group has "forced the adoption agencies to reach out into the black community." She continues, "For a long time they were saying the black community doesn't respond, that they don't adopt. But what they hadn't done was make blacks aware that these children were available and they could qualify to adopt them, even if they didn't have an expensive house and a separate room for the child."

While Jeff and Erica are obviously devoted to children, they do not divorce their childrearing attitudes from the way they feel about and respond to the world in general. They do not believe they should shield and protect any of their children from the realities of life. Jeff's intensity is also expressed in his active role against what he refers to as "institutional racism." Adoption agencies, according to him, "simply reflect other racist institutions in the society. I know a lot of black people who are as much a hardship on their race as white racists are," he says. "And I know a lot of women who retard the women's liberation movement as much as male chauvinists do. So let's face it. The adoption field has its tired old employees who have been in the agency thirty-five years. They come from a stone racist background and they haven't moved five feet on their racism in their entire lives." He adds emphatically, "Yet *they* are in charge of placing black children in homes!"

Jeff and Erica do not perceive themselves as counterculture crusaders. Both emphasize that although they are more aware than most transracially adoptive families of the necessity to transmit to Phillip a black identity, ultimately the child's ability to function as a healthy black child with white parents—as a human being—will be determined by multiple considerations, only one of which is related to his racial background. All their children, the Talbots maintain, are being reared in an open and honest way. Since Jeff and Erica do not value the acquisition of a lot of material possessions, their children will be taught similar values. Jeff says, "What you put into a kid is what you get out of him. I want for Phillip the same that I want for our other children. I want him to be a healthy human being who is concerned about his brothers and sisters. I don't expect anything from him, but at the same time I want a lot from him."

Unlike Jeff and Erica who have a combination of adopted and biological children, some couples decide to adopt all their children, even though they are physically able to produce offspring. For the most part, these couples are young, middle-class, flexible in lifestyle, more concerned about homeless children than most adoptive parents, and committed to curbing population growth. They seem to have no need to reproduce their very *own* biological children. They withstand pressure from their own parents to carry on the family bloodline. Occasionally, they themselves are adopted, as illustrated in the following case study.

Vicky and Harold Katz are remarkable people who appear mature and very sure of themselves and about what they want to do with their lives. Their decision to adopt all their children was not whimsical; it reflects the influences of their own lifestyles and upbringing before they were married. Vicky, a diminutive twenty-seven-year-old blonde, was reared a Catholic; Harold, thirty-six, is Jewish. After seven years of marriage, they have four adopted children and live in a racially integrated suburb of an eastern city.

Vicky was born in an orphanage in a large midwestern city. She assumes that her birth was out of wedlock, knows nothing about her biological parents, and has no interest in discovering her biological roots. She and her sister, younger by two years, were adopted by a Catholic couple who had been childless ten years. Vicky's adoptive father, an engineer, and her mother, a housewife, had always longed for children. "Mother always regretted that they waited so long to adopt us," Vicky recalls.

Vicky describes her adoptive family as being in the *"Catholic Worker* tradition. My parents strongly believed in racial equality and the rights of the poor. I grew up knowing a lot about social welfare, since it was discussed at the dinner table. I guess my sense of egalitarianism and justice comes from the values of my parents." Vicky relates, "As long as I can remember, I knew about the problems of homeless children. You see, our parents never treated adoption as something abnormal. They discussed it openly and honestly, and we knew there were lots of other kids who weren't as fortunate as we to have such loving parents."

Although Vicky acknowledges that the primary influence on her decision to have all adopted children came from her "wonderful, understanding, and devoted parents," she was also impressed by neighbors who, in addition to having six or seven biological children, were also foster parents to numerous youngsters with physical and mental handicaps. "These were my second parents," Vicky explains. "They turned their home into an orphanage. You should see how these so-called hard-to-place children come alive when the mother works with them. Whenever she speaks before groups she tells them, 'Every child has something to give.' I guess I have been guided by that philosophy too, since two of our children were medically handicapped." Vicky has grown even closer to her "second parents" in recent years. Both her parents and her sister have died, all within the past six years.

Vicky's husband, Harold, grew up on the East Coast. His father was a successful entrepreneur until his retirement, and for a time Harold worked with him in the family business. His mother, a housewife, was never very child-oriented, Harold says. "She never got up in the morning to send us off to school when we were young," Harold reports. He also recalls going off to class with mismatched socks because of his mother's indifference. It is his opinion that she gave birth to two children because it was expected of her. Vicky and Harold constantly remind her to stay out of their private lives. Harold's sister, who is thirty-four, moved away from home only a year ago.

The Katzes met in Vicky's hometown, where both worked in a large department store. She had just dropped out of a nursing program after two years. Soon after their marriage they moved back to his hometown to an integrated neighborhood, where Harold entered business with his father. Only six months after they were married, when Vicky was twenty, they went to a Jewish adoption agency and applied for a child. "The agency was really surprised," Vicky says. In fact, the agency seriously questioned the Katzes' motives for wanting to adopt before having children of their own. "We finally convinced them that we knew what we were doing," Vicky reports. But still there were problems: Legally both adoptive parents had to be twenty-one. But the Katzes were willing to wait, and, Vicky says, "Shortly after my birthday we brought Pam, of Jewish parentage, home. She had a serious heart defect," Vicky said. "The agency had classified Pam as hard to place because of it. They were told that cardiac surgery would cost about ten thousand dollars and that Pam's chances for surviving the operation were about 15 per cent. "We figured 15 per cent wasn't that bad, but the ten thousand dollars knocked us for a loop,"

Vicky explains. After telling the agency that they wanted Pam but couldn't possibly afford the surgery, the agency told them, "Fine, we'll pay the bill." Pam now receives a medical subsidy from the state, which covers any recurrent medical problems she might have. Although a bit shy, the girl is now in good health and is developing on the level with the average six-year-old.

Because Harold had been married previously and carried the pain of the death of his only child, Vicky says she did not have to convince him to adopt so soon after they were married. "Harold had strong feelings about the need of kids to be in a permanent home," Vicky explains. "He also didn't have such a strong male ego that he felt he had to reproduce himself again. Actually, we were in this together from the beginning." After the first adoption the Katzes decided to adopt all of their children.

Harold and Vicky are not certain Harold's parents even understand *why* they are doing this. The entire process seems to be more than the older Katzes can comprehend. "What's wrong with our genes that you don't want to have our grandchildren?" Harold's father reportedly asked his son. Harold's parents' major concern is "adoption versus biological children," according to Vicky. "They aren't opposed to transracial adoption, but they are against our not giving them their biological grandchildren. Still, they long for the day they will have their very own grandchild, and they are pressuring us more than ever since my sister-in-law still hasn't married."

The Katzes adopted their second child, Charles, from the same agency that placed Pam. "When we asked for a second child, we told them we wanted a child who would be hard to place," said Vicky. "They called us in and said, 'We have a child whose father is unknown. Do you think you can handle that?'" Harold and Vicky decided to adopt Charles because they weren't concerned about what he might look like when he got older. After the adoption, out of curiosity, they thought of every conceivable combination of ancestry for their new son. He had olive complexion with straight hair and a broad nose. "A lot of babies have broad noses, so that never bothered us," says Vicky. As Charles grew older it soon became apparent to the Katzes that he was of black and white parentage. "I had been exposed to a lot of mixed-race kids through my parents and in high school," Vicky explains. "So when Charles's hair and complexion started changing, we knew his father was black."

Charles is a very self-sufficient, even-tempered child who likes to play by himself. There is also a lot of sibling rivalry between him and his two older sisters. With a smile Vicky says, "He takes great delight in smashing the games his sisters have carefully assembled."

By the time Harold and Vicky were ready to adopt a third child, their only specification to the agency was that it be an older child in the hard-to-place category. Sex and race were unimportant. This time they went to a public agency because the private agency's fees were, they felt, exorbitant. Judy, whose mother and father were black, was two-and-a-half when the Katzes adopted her, and had been rejected by a black couple, Vicky was told, because she was too dark. Judy had been in foster care since birth, and her chances for adoption were decreasing as she got older.

Vicky and Harold were given the unusual privilege of visiting her foster home before the adoption. The foster parents lived in a small town with their nine biological children. Since Judy's foster mother did not drive and did not take Judy out very often, the child was, at first, afraid of cars. "We drove to pick her up and she wasn't crazy about getting into our car," Vicky recalls. "The day we left to bring her home she was hysterical. The social worker wasn't the least bit consoling." Angrily Vicky adds, "She just crammed the child into our car, arms and legs flinging everywhere."

Seeing that the child was frightened by her new surroundings, the Katzes worked very hard to make Judy feel more at ease. They were successful to a great degree, but Judy's adoption has had many ups and downs. "When she first arrived, she had impeccable table manners for a child her age," Vicky says. "Her foster mother had toilet-trained her at fifteen months, so she was extremely self-sufficient. She acted like a little lady." Shortly after coming to live with the Katzes, though, Judy regressed in her toilet training and began wetting and defecating in her panties, grinding her bowel movements into the floor tiles. "We allowed this behavior to go on for about two weeks and it was driving Harold and me up the walls," Vicky exclaims. "Pam, who is a year older than Judy, started to tease her by calling her a baby. That only made matters worse.

"After I had had it up to here," Vicky says, laying her index finger against her throat, "I sat her down and told her, 'Look, I'm tired of standing downstairs scrubbing underwear. If you want to be a baby, fine!'" Vicky says she "got out the Pampers and put them on her. Judy couldn't take that at all, so within two days she went back to her toilet training." Vicky chuckles. "She's a smart little cookie. I think part of the problem was that she knew her foster mother had taken a lot of pride in toilet training her so early. So Judy decided to use this as a weapon to punish us for having taken her away from her other parents.

Now Judy is in a neighborhood nursery that is racially mixed and operated by the local synagogue, and her behavior has improved remarkably. "We were concerned that she not be discriminated against because of her race, and we didn't want her to get any special treatment, either," Vicky says. "We were assured by the school principal that neither would happen." When asked if her schoolmates see her as different from themselves, Vicky replies, "I don't think the kids see Judy as different, but she sees herself as different." Vicky describes Judy as being able to take care of herself and as not being the type to be easily battered around by other kids.

At age four Judy has begun to exhibit behavior that reflects deep-seated problems. Although she gets along quite well with her sisters and brother, she goes into complete withdrawal whenever her parents discipline her, simply refusing to talk to them. Judy is also nonverbal. Vicky says in an almost defeated tone, "I just don't know about the success of adopting older children. I'm just not sure any more." She continues, "Judy's withdrawal is driving us up the wall. We can only hope it will change when she goes to school this fall. Then she'll have her own play group, and she can achieve on her own without being in constant competition with her older sister. If that doesn't work, then I guess we'll have to look to other solutions."*

A year ago the Katzes adopted Barbara, a fourteen-month-old

---

* This is an example of the many unexplained things that occur in the earlier lives of children—the outcome of which people who adopt them later have no control. Since they are frequently unaware of what these familial and environmental shaping forces have been, the adoptive parents are at a loss to unravel and solve the problems that have been produced.

white girl who has Down's syndrome (mongolism) and is retarded. When adopted, Barbara failed to respond to any stimuli in her environment, acting like a newborn infant. With obvious pleasure Vicky now reports, "In the year since she was adopted we feel so rewarded because she is now cooing and chattering away. She has progressed so rapidly that it is unbelievable."

Somewhere in the distant future Harold and Vicky might consider adopting a fifth child, but only after the others have grown up a bit. They are also considering the possibility of a foster child. So absorbed is Vicky with children that she says she can be walking down the street and see a child whom she wants "to snatch up." "Some people are devoted to their careers and some are devoted to their hobbies, but my thing happens to be kids."

Because of their philosophy of child welfare and their personal convictions, one is not surprised that all of the Katzes' children were classified by adoption agencies as hard to place. The transracial placements are but a minor theme that fits into their general family pattern of providing homes to such children. That the children were black or mixed racially was irrelevant. That they needed homes was most important.

All of the older Katz children know the meaning of adoption. "For a long time," Vicky notes, "Pamela thought the adoption agency kept babies in a file drawer in the office." Now they have come to understand what it means. "They walk around the house saying, 'Mommy's adopted, I'm adopted, Daddy's not adopted.'" When an adult family friend, who was adopted, came for a visit, the children joined in a chorus and repeatedly said, "Ron was adopted!"

Having been adopted enables Vicky to understand her children's curiosity on the subject. She and Harold are already anticipating the teen-age years, when their children, they expect, will be seeking answers to questions about their adoption and trying to adjust to other problems of adolescence. "At that period they are concerned with who they are, where they came from, and why they're here," she notes. "My parents handled the questions my sister and I had so positively that I can now pass this understanding on to our kids without any great problems." The healthy attitude she and Harold have is already reflected in the way their very young children speak frankly about having been adopted.

With their characteristic assuredness, Harold and Vicky handle the black identity problem as confidently and as openly as one would expect. Their three older children are quite aware of the differences in their colors. Pamela, their older white daughter, knows that Judy is brown. "Pamela doesn't like the word 'black' because black to her is very dark, and Judy isn't black, she's brown," Vicky comments. "Pam throws her black crayons out. She won't use them. She just has a thing about that color."

Since they didn't set out with a plan to adopt black children, but hard-to-place children, the Katzes are not preoccupied, as some parents are, with the racial status of their children. They don't go out of their way to let others know that they adopted black children, nor do they try to conceal the fact. They take it in stride as simply another factor of childrearing meriting serious attention. They are quite aware of the black social workers' opposition, but they feel that they did not deprive black families of the opportunity of adopting these children. Harold and Vicky are not at all defensive about having adopted; neither do they attack the black social workers. They feel strongly that their black children must be exposed to those things that will help them to develop solid black identities. "It's very nice to think that because a child is half black and half white he should be raised as a 'black-white' child," says Vicky. "But even though Charles has a white mother and a black father, society doesn't see him as an 'integrated' or a 'black-white' child. By state law he's black, and I feel he and Judy should be prepared for anything that arises in the future, whether it's total polarization, total integration, or whatever." Vicky adds, "We are very concerned about raising little brown kids who think they are white. This is something we are going to try to avoid. My in-laws have this terrible fear that one day our black children are going to march out of the house at age sixteen or eighteen and join the black community." Vicky ponders the problem. "If they do that, I'll feel that I've raised a positive person—a person who can feel that he *can* join the black community."

While four young children underfoot can make the average mother cry out in exasperation on occasion, Vicky takes this responsibility in characteristic, matter-of-fact fashion. She and Harold share child care and house cleaning. Harold feels strongly that childrearing is a serious responsibility, requiring devotion from both parents. Whenever Vicky gets tired from overwork, Harold stays with the kids while she takes weekend trips alone to a nearby resort. "When I go away from my family I can lie in bed and order a pizza at midnight and eat it all by myself if I want to —and that's a good feeling," she says. For a change of pace, Vicky occasionally goes into work in their business while Harold stays home and cares for the children. She also bowls one morning a week, accompanied by the children. A male friend of the Katzes, who is a single parent and who lives nearby, exchanges baby-sitting with them, making errands and occasional outings possible. A lot of day-to-day responsibility for the children's care is assumed by Harold, since he arrives home fairly early each day.

Fully aware that many mothers who have chosen to form their family the way the Katzes have would smother their children and feel that they are indispensable to their children, Vicky has no such feelings about her children. "They are being raised to be as self-sufficient as possible," she explains. With this in mind, she is looking for a job, and for a housekeeper who can drive the family car to shuttle the children to and from school.

Many will undoubtedly agree that this is a most unusual couple.

"All of our family and friends were thrown for a loop when we adopted two colored children," says Gloria Henderson, a gregarious, overweight young woman. With her husband, Mel, she adopted Mel, Jr., who is now three years old, and Alice, who is two. Gloria, who jokingly describes herself as "pleasantly plump," explains, "A few of our friends stopped coming to visit without ever saying why, but I guess we knew the reason. One of my girl friends back in my hometown—a girl I've known all my life—told me she couldn't understand why any decent white person would want to raise a 'nigger child.' She still talks to me whenever we go down there, but she won't touch the children."

Gloria and Mel Henderson do not fit the stereotype of those who adopt across racial lines. They are lower-middle-class, high school graduates, relatively uninformed on social and political issues, and very deeply religious; both were born and reared in small southern communities. Although they have heard about black social workers' displeasure with transracial adoptions, Mel concedes that, "We don't know that much about it, since we stick pretty much to ourselves." The Hendersons do not belong to one of the transracially adoptive parents' groups, although there is one in their area.

When the Hendersons learned they could not have children because of a chronic health problem of Gloria's, they decided to adopt. Gloria, twenty-four, says, "My doctor gave me the name of an adoption agency to call the same day I was told I couldn't get pregnant. When I called they said they didn't have any little babies right then, and we could apply, but it would probably take quite a long time." After talking it over with her husband, the couple decided to call other agencies. Going through the Yellow Pages, Gloria called every agency in town and in the process was told by all that they had older white children or children with handicaps available but no healthy infants. Of course, they could get on the waiting list if they wanted to. One agency said they would get priority treatment since they didn't have children already. Asked what this meant, the worker told Gloria, "anywhere from one to two years, maybe a little longer." Two agencies mentioned the possibility of transracial adoption. Gloria, whose desire to experience the joys of mothering a little healthy baby were quite strong, explains, "Mel and I decided we didn't want an older kid, and we certainly couldn't deal with handicaps. So we were willing to see what some of these 'interracial' babies looked like." Mel, who is about six feet tall and very thin, added, in his typically timid manner, "I knew a boy back in my hometown whom everyone said had a black mama and a white daddy. He looked almost white. So I figured the 'interracial' babies the agency mentioned might look like him." Their adoption worker obliged their curiosity by showing them photographs of mixed-race children who had been placed by the agency.

The Hendersons were married when she was twenty and he was twenty-three. She worked as a secretary and he as a draftsman at the same business firm. Both had migrated to a midwestern city, where they had relatives. Mel served a two-year stint in the armed forces after high school, where he learned his profession. They now live in an all-white working-class neighborhood in a small frame house with a large, well-kept backyard. During the summer they have cookouts in the yard. They also erect a small portable swimming pool for the children.

Gloria describes herself as a "natural mother." "I am one of the few women I know who still *love* being a housewife and mother. I wouldn't want it any other way," she says. "I have no desire to ever go back to work, and Mel and the kids like it this way." Mel confirms, "There is no life for Gloria without kids. She used to come home upset every time she went to a baby shower for one of her girl friends. It was really hard on her to see all of her friends having babies when she wasn't," he says, looking tenderly at Gloria. Now Gloria's entire life revolves around meeting the needs of her family. Both children are immaculate, with polished shoes and not a strand of hair out of place. Their spotlessly clean, modest three-bedroom home also reflects her devotion to being a good housewife.

Devout Baptists, the Hendersons attend church services every Sunday and are active in several church groups. Much of their social life revolves around church-related functions, and most of their friends attend their church. According to Mel, "Our faith is the only thing that keeps us going. Gloria and I would be lost without our belief in God." Gloria agrees, "My faith in God and belief in my fellowman are the two most important things in my life. Our children go to Sunday school, and they are being taught what we believe in already." Although Gloria and Mel attend an all-white congregation, they say the adoption of two visibly Negro children has not caused them much difficulty with the congregation. Although there are still a lot of stares, the Hendersons' minister has been supportive. "He counseled us and encouraged us to go through with it," says Gloria. "He told us that all men are equal under God."

When the Hendersons applied to the first adoption agency, they were assigned a black social worker. "She was so hung up on being a Negro that she couldn't think about anything else. Every question she asked us was concerned with 'How do you feel about what colored people think?' or 'How are you going to give the child a black identity?' After the second interview, we'd had it with her. So we told the director of the agency we were withdrawing our application." When the quiet, soft-spoken Mel is asked his impression of the black social worker, he replies, "She was very hostile toward whites. I don't think she likes white people. She seemed to want to drive us away." As an afterthought he says, "She made me nervous." Gloria turns to him, showing a bit of surprise, and says, "Mel, you never told me she made you *nervous*. I just thought you didn't like her questions. I must confess that I didn't understand half the stuff she was talking about . . . with all those questions about 'black' things."

After this experience, the Hendersons went to another agency, which eventually placed both children. They had a very fulfilling experience with the social worker assigned to them. Gloria feels that the single most important influence on them adopting was their social worker, who was white. "She was delighted that we wanted to give a home to a part-black child," recalled Gloria. "She gave us all the help we needed. Any time I have a problem now I can call her and she will give me advice," she adds, giving the impression that she regards this middle-aged social worker as a "mother figure."

Initially, family opposition to the adoptions was very negative. All four grandparents, who still live on their small farms in the South, were opposed. With the passage of time, however, three of the grandparents have come to accept the children. Mel's father still refuses to have anything to do with the children. "My daddy said I brought shame to him by doing this," Mel says in a rather sad tone. "But I don't think he has been very understanding about *why* we adopted our kids. He's pretty selfish. He wanted me to have children, and we couldn't. So I guess he'll stay angry with us the rest of his life. I hope not, though." Gloria adds, "We put it in the hands of the Lord. He'll eventually come around." Because of Mel's father's negative attitude, the Hendersons have never taken the children to Mel's hometown. His parents have been to visit them once since they got the children, and his mother adores the children.

Gloria's parents' attitudes have softened a lot. "My mom really loves them. She takes them everywhere when we go down there," Gloria says. "My dad surprised me because, although he loves them a lot, he still doesn't treat them as good as he does the other grandkids," she adds. "But Mama sews them clothes and bakes cookies for them. She's always sending them boxes in the mail. The kids love her a lot, too." Gloria comes from a very large family, but Mel has only one sister.

Neither has had many problems with their other family

members. Of course, they were all curious, but Gloria feels that once the relatives learned she couldn't have children, they accepted their transracial adoptions. "They all felt kind of sorry for me and they wanted so much for us to be able to have children," she explains.

The Hendersons know very little about "black identity" and have not given much thought to how they will cope with racial identity problems that Mel, Jr., and Alice might have as they grow up. According to Gloria, "That's something [identity] you can't teach them. They'll get it, but we haven't figured out the angles yet." She continues, "We went to a black culture exhibit downtown, but I didn't understand any of that stuff. I didn't like it either. Maybe if I learn more about it I'll understand and appreciate it."

The Hendersons have no black friends and have no intentions of making any. They are not hostile toward blacks; it's just that their world naturally excludes them. For all of their lives they have lived in an almost completely segregated world. Thus it is not surprising that they express a bit of white paternalism toward their very own children. In speaking about possible difficulties the kids might encounter because of their race, Gloria remarks, "We feel terribly sorry for them, the pitiful little things. But they shouldn't carry any bitterness in their hearts toward white people." She continues, "We're trying not to teach them about hostility. We're going to try to teach them that there are some wrong things done by our great-grandparents but that we didn't do the wrong." Mel adds, "Our generation hasn't done wrong toward Negroes. I pray that by the time they are older all the bitterness Negroes have about white people will be gone."

Gloria and Mel, in an expression of their stereotypes regarding blacks, attribute their son's musical ability to his being of Negro descent. "Mel, Jr., has a lot of rhythm," his adoptive father says. "You should see him when the music comes on. That's because he's part Negro." In her motherly fashion, Gloria says she longs for the day she can buy flashy clothes for Alice. "I want her to dress pretty like the colored girls dress when she gets to be a teen-ager," Gloria says, "and not dowdy, like the white girls."

2

FAMILY DYNAMICS

Adoption across racial boundaries is considered in adoption circles to be in the high-risk category. The problems parents may encounter can be numerous. By definition, the transracially adoptive family does not conform to the traditional and idealized model of the white middle-class family. Rather, it represents one of the new pluralistic family forms that are becoming more prevalent and acceptable in American society.[1] Because most of these forms are not universally accepted as *normal*, those who choose to form their families in this way are often stigmatized. Thus the adults who adopt black children are regarded by many Americans as deviant.

In spite of the almost inevitable problems associated with transracial adoption, especially those problems related to the socialization process, and to parent-child relations, and to the relationships between the adopted child and his or her white nonadopted siblings, parents most often emphasize and value the positive attributes of the adoption. When I asked one couple if they would discuss their positive feelings about the adoption of their six-year-old black daughter, Mrs. Horton, a young housewife with two biological children, read a poem titled *The Answer to an Adopted Child* to me:

> *Not flesh of my flesh,*
> *Nor bone of my bone,*
> *But still miraculously*

> *My own.*
> *Never forget*
> *For a single minute:*
> *You didn't grow under my heart,*
> *But in it.*[2]

She explained, "This poem can tell you better than I can in my own words what having Carol has done for us." Mr. Horton, an engineer, said, "We love all our children and we see each of them as special individuals. But Carol is special in a different way. We chose her, and although she is not of our flesh, she bears so many similarities to the other members of our family. I guess there's something to the statement that 'association brings about assimilation.'"

The controversy and politics of transracial adoption often overshadow its more intimate aspects. Many of the critics of transracial adoption know little and sometimes nothing about specific families who have adopted black children and how the adoptions are working. Their biases are based upon their general opposition to racial integration, and the historic racial discrimination extant in the United States. As a black social worker put it, "It is not necessary for me to know something about the individual whites who are adopting black babies. I know enough about white people—enough to make me know that I don't think they know how to raise black children."

The advocates of transracial adoption are equally blind in their devotion to the cause. They are often unwilling to ask the serious questions about *all* facets of the black adopted child's welfare. So convinced are they that any parent who voluntarily assumes such a serious responsibility toward a child can only be a sincere humanitarian, they consider it an irrelevant and unkind act to question the motives of such people, to question what kind of parents they are, and to question whether the child's interests are equally being served. (This controversy will be explored in Chapter 5, "Values in Conflict I: Black Autonomy.")

Neither of the conflicting parties is always acting in the best interests of the child, since such doctrinaire attitudes preclude a rational approach to understanding the internal family dynamics —that is, the interaction and relationships between the adopted child and members of his or her nuclear family. Some of these internal family dynamics that the black child experiences are illustrated in the following case study—one that is typical of other such adoptive families.

When Marie Cooper was thirty-nine and her husband, Robert, was forty-six, they suddenly realized how fast their three children were growing up. "We had always talked about having four children before we were married, and like a lot of people, we thought of having a lot of children eventually. But when the youngest one was old enough to be nothing like a baby anymore [she was five], I got the usual female feelings about having a baby around the house and at that very moment there was a poster from the Open Door Society in the school where our little girl was going. It said if you have room for one more child you should adopt. We didn't actually have 'room for one more' physically, since there wasn't an empty room in the house. But I kind of wanted one more, and adoption seemed like an awfully good idea. Furthermore, we had friends who married across racial lines, and they had children also. So I thought that this would be very easy for us to do. It seemed easier at first than later, when we got to talking to an adoption worker. But it did at first seem to be just the easiest thing in the world, so we decided, 'Why not do it?'"

As Marie and I talked over iced tea on the veranda of her Tudor-style home on a sweltering hot day, Alice, twelve, Mark, ten, and Catherine, seven, and some of their playmates were passing Timmy, their six- or seven-month-old adopted black son, from one arm to another. He was on center stage. Marie said, "The children were just delighted by the idea [of adopting transracially], and with their enthusiasm we were really impelled to go ahead with our plans to adopt. And among the older family members, their reaction was the opposite of what we expected. We decided not to talk to our family, our older family, about the adoption because they would be forced into having an opinion, and then they would feel that they would have to get their opinion across, and we didn't want them to participate in it. So when it was all decided and the baby was almost here, then we told a few of our closest relations, but it really wasn't until after the baby was here that we told our family. Looking back, we did exactly the right thing. They were very calm."

A strikingly handsome woman with a rather mild manner, Marie grew up in an aristocratic family in one of the border states. She was a Junior Leaguer and also studied abroad. She is an intellectual—a quick thinker—and an activist and patron of the arts. Their home is very modestly but tastefully decorated. Robert, who is a prominent attorney, is very busy with his practice but does make a special effort to spend time with the children. Marie is quite candid in stating that it was initially her idea to adopt a black child. However, Robert was quick to agree that it was a good idea.

"One of the things that worried me was that we might encounter some negative responses from our black friends. I went to one black friend whom I felt most respectful of his opinion and we had a long talk to get his opinion. He really surprised me. He asked me, 'Are you strong enough to take the kind of opposition that you are going to get more and more of, from the community as a whole, from the blacks and the whites?' I assured him that I was, and it didn't seem to me that anybody had an inborn right to live without opposition of some kind. He said, 'Well all right, and if you think that's what you want to do, then do it.' He and his family have been very supportive, and his wife is one of Timmy's godparents. Now, what he didn't say and what I was afraid he'd say is that adoption of black children by white families is a denial of the child's racial heritage permanently. I heard this stated at a conference by the black social workers. They had just had their own meeting [in Nashville, Tennessee] and had come out with a very strong statement against transracial adoptions. There were a number of white social workers there too who felt the same way. I do not believe that a black child living with a white family can't get or have a black identity, but I think they [social workers] are entitled to say it and to think it. Timmy will meet many people who feel that he really can't be black because he has a white family. And then there will be many people who will feel just the opposite. This will be his permanent problem. It will be harder for him, I think, because problems will come from people whose primary reaction will be to the color of his skin."

The Coopers live in a racially integrated neighborhood, and she is active in numerous predominantly black organizations, especially those involving the arts. "Our children attend integrated schools and have many black friends, and our own lives, as I said earlier, have become very involved [in integrated activities]."

To a great extent the household seemed to revolve around Timmy, a gregarious, plump, brown-skinned baby with soft features. When the neighborhood children came to play, they asked Marie if Timmy, who was crawling on the veranda as we talked, could join the older children on the lawn.

Recalling their experience when Timmy finally arrived (at three weeks old), Marie said, "It's like the transition you make between knowing you're pregnant and having the child you've delivered in your hands. The most beautiful moment was when the agency called and told us they had found a child for us. At last all this uncertainty was over, and there was going to be a real baby that we could love, that we could squeeze and cuddle. We have never had the occasion to question whether we did the right thing by adopting Timmy. We know we did."

In an interview with the black friends to whom the Coopers turned for advice on whether they should adopt, their assessment was that this adoptive placement had turned out exceptionally well. Martin Davis, the Coopers' black friend, said: "Timmy is a well-adjusted, bright little boy. He doesn't have any of the hang-ups you might expect him to have. He's just a very ordinary kid who likes to play, he makes friends easily, and he fits perfectly into his family. He and his sisters and brother get along real well. He knows he's black. That is one thing Marie and Robert have taken seriously. He understands that he's a black kid and that the rest of his family is white, but he isn't hung up about it because of the way his parents handled the subject of black identity. He's around blacks all the time because of his parents' lifestyle. Marie is involved in all kinds of activities in the black community. I don't think Timmy is going to have any major hangups about himself as he grows up. No more than the average middle-class kid."

Another black who knows the Cooper family quite well has a different reaction to Timmy's relationship with his family. The attention the family lavishes upon Timmy caused her to quip,

"They treat him just like a pet dog. You'd think they just got a new pet that they can't wait to show off." She also commented, "As Timmy gets older the Coopers continue to treat him like he is *too* special. They don't treat him like a human or an average child." Of course, Timmy responds warmly to the attention shown him. One simply cannot predict what the effect of this type of "special child" treatment will be in later years. One could also question whether the attention lavished on Timmy is any different from that which any new baby in a family would experience.

Several studies have examined the characteristics of those whites who choose to adopt across racial boundaries. The profile that emerges from these studies, including my own data, portrays a well-educated, economically successful, middle-class suburban American couple who already have children of their own. The husband, who falls in the thirty to forty age group, most often holds a professional or highly technical job, with a majority having completed college. Although the males work in practically all occupations (including farmers, postal clerks, policemen, etc.), a large percentage work in various educational fields, and many are college professors.

The females, who are usually between twenty-five and thirty-five years old, are usually housewives, owing perhaps largely to the young ages of their children, although some work part-time or as volunteers. A majority of these women have had some college education.

These parents are adherents to a religious faith and attend church regularly. The largest number are Protestant, the second largest number are Catholic, and a considerably smaller number are Jewish. Politically, they are usually Democrats or Independents, although a small number indicate they are Republican or on occasion vote for a particular Republican candidate.[3]

A striking characteristic is that they usually possess a high degree of self-confidence, self-awareness, and inner-directedness. As one parent remarked, "We follow our own counsel instead of listening to others, especially when it involves making a decision that might be controversial." The parents are also more socially and physically distant from their own families. This social distance maintained from their family allows them to remain relatively immune to the criticism of their parents who usually express initial objection to the adoption. (See Chapter 10.)

Nutt and Snyder, in a survey of 564 families, found that in 1968 the age of parents who adopt transracially dropped a full five years. The median age for parents in 1970 was about 30 years. This major shift since 1970 is also characterized by the motivations of those who adopt.[4] Nutt conducted a study of 40 families in the Boston area and found 2 distinct groups who adopted transracially. He classified them as "patients" or "resource" couples. The traditional couples who applied to an agency for a child, usually due to infertility, were viewed as "patients," since they differed little from the typical applicant who expects to be evaluated and judged by the agency. On the other hand, the "resource" couples were those applicants who approached the agency to adopt a "hard to place" child. They usually had children of their own, and instead of placing themselves at the mercy of the agency, they tried to help the agency solve the problem of finding homes for these children.[5]

While many biological children have been the result of unplanned pregnancies, adopted children by definition never arrive in the family by accident. Their new parents have made special, planned efforts to include them in. A black child adopted by white parents is regarded as a child of "special value" because his or her parents have defied a racial tradition in the society—that of including a child who is not only of another bloodline, but also of another race.[6] Their color, by society's definition, sets them apart from their family and causes attention to be drawn to them and their adoptive family. This necessitates that these parents must in many ways have different qualities for parenting than parents who adhere to the traditional models of family formation. Numerous studies have found that they are generally very autonomous and often make decisions independent of the advice and counsel of friends and family.

The strong wills, independent minds, and spiritedness of many of these white parents is most apparent when one observes how they cope with problems related to the adoption. Only an unusually self-reliant couple has the capacity to enter into and endure this kind of adoptive process in the first place. It is fair to say that those individuals who succumb to outside pressures, and who rely upon the approval of significant others, are not such likely candidates for this type of parenthood. Thus it is common to hear the parents express the view that their own families considered them a bit strange, different, and "not like the rest of the family" long before they adopted, an indication of their nonconforming lifestyles. Yet some of these parents found that they lacked the necessary coping strength when confronted with rejection from their families. One of the negative outcomes of the adoption for some is the strain it placed on their relations with their families, and the persistent stares and hostile reactions of strangers. While they keep the black child and never seriously consider returning him or her to agency care, it has, on occasion, turned out to be more than they bargained for.

While most parents in this study always emphasized the positive aspects of the adoption and often denied they had ever had second thoughts about the adoption, numerous negative outcomes were cited. In spite of the self-confidence and inner strength they display, these parents do sometimes fail in successfully parenting the black child they adopted. One child was adopted by two college professors and they decided to return him to the agency because they thought he was "too slow" and did not possess the high intellectual capacity of the other family members. Their alienation from this young child, who was adopted in infancy, was evidenced by the minimal physical contact they had with him. They relegated practically all of the child-care tasks to hired nonfamily members. Another couple showed their rejection of the child when his skin turned very dark. Although they didn't return him to the agency, they minimized his contacts with the outside world by rarely taking him on family outings. Such problems become more pronounced as the child matures. (See Chapters 7 and 8.)

Childrearing in transracially adoptive families is a more conscious and calculated process, especially in the early stages after the child has been placed. It also involves a long-term sensitivity to certain facets of the child's development that are not factors in in-race adoptions and for parents who have biological children only.

Parents are careful, thoughtful, and deliberate in the most minute day-to-day routines of socializing their children. Seldom does a day pass when the black child's white family members are not reminded that they do not look like other "normal" white families and that they have chosen a pluralistic model of parenthood and family formation that frequently draws harsh condemnation and criticism. Therefore, parenthood for whites who adopt black children is usually more difficult than in those families where parents and children are of the same racial background. Because of the questioning and negative attitudes of some elements in the society (see Chapter 5), these parents make a more conscious effort to make the adoption work—in part to prove that they made the right decision when they adopted across racial boundaries. In doing so, they often appear to observers to be model parents to *all* their children. However, this is not always the case.

In spite of the constant attention that is focused on the family by outsiders, it is noteworthy that most appear to have been able to transcend and overcome the barriers of race. Instead of concentrating on the problematic aspects of the adoption, these parents, for the most part, viewed it as a highly satisfying experience that expanded their family's horizons and gave more purpose to their lives.

This highly fulfilling experience is a reflection of their strong value for and attachment to the family, especially their concern for children. The majority of the parents in this study (80 per cent) had children born to them prior to the transracial adoption. A father in the Midwest articulated a sentiment common to other parents who adopted transracially: "We are really hung up on the family unit and how powerful it is. In our opinion, being parents is a job. You've got to do your research, you've got to do your homework, and you've got to plan. You don't just have babies and expect Mommy to stay at home while Daddy goes out to work and look for all of them to grow up and live happily ever after. It doesn't work that way. Probably the two greatest ripoffs in our society today are marriage and children, because anybody can get married and anybody can have children. You don't need any education or permits or anything else. But the irony is that one of the hardest things to do in your life is to raise a family, and society does not prepare you for it." His sentiments accurately reflect how many of these parents feel about the seriousness of having a family.

In spite of the months of preparation one has gone through, meeting the adopted child for the first time is one of the most memorable experiences they will ever have. While aware of their fears, anxieties, and oftentimes their motives for adopting a black child, the first meeting between parents and child often evokes intense emotional reactions. Some parents say that when they first saw their black child they wanted to laugh and cry at the same time. Others described a joyful sensation which, as one mother described, "just swept us up." For most, there was the immediate feeling that the child was their own, and of course, they began treating him or her the same. A typical reaction was described by one mother who said that the moment they saw their infant daughter in the agency, she immediately picked her up and said, "Hi, Bonnie [the name they had talked about but had not decided upon until that moment]. Mommy and Daddy are ready to take you home." Quickly dispensing with the agency regulations designed to give parents the opportunity to decide "if" they wanted Bonnie, Mrs. James said, "All I wanted to do was to sign the papers as quickly as possible and take our little girl home. We knew she was ours from the moment we saw her." Thus the long period that adoptive parents spend discussing a hypothetical child is culminated in receiving a real Bonnie or whomever. As one parent commented, "As soon as Joshua was in our arms, that just put the whole human perspective into it. He was ours." Also, a father explained their first meeting with their baby: "Our social worker called us and said we could come in and see the child they had selected for us, and make up our minds if we wanted him. We walked into the room where Malcolm was and looked at him, then at each other. We wondered why they would ever doubt that we were going to adopt him for one moment. The feeling we got from having him with us made us feel very close."

According to Colette Taube Dywasuk, an adoptive mother and the author of *Adoption—Is It for You?*, "To you the child will be yours the day you take him home from the adoption agency. You will be full of warmth and tenderness for this vulnerable stranger whom you know you will grow to love. Yet you will be amazed to discover how quickly and completely the child becomes a very important part of your life."[7]

Usually the adopted child has a tremendous impact upon the family. Not only does he or she cause the parents to begin to frequently call themselves an "integrated" family, but they also are credited with having brought a dimension of growth and development to them that would otherwise not have been possible. Thus there is a tendency for them to ignore or minimize any problems the adoption creates. Even when problems can no longer be ignored, their tolerance level for understanding and solving them is great. A mother echoed the feelings of many parents when she said, "We're very happy and glad that we adopted Jimmy. We can't conceive of this family without him since he is so much a part of us." Admitting that the adoption had created unanticipated problems, the majority of parents said they were, nevertheless, sure they had made the right decision to adopt. When I asked a couple in Washington, D.C., what were the satisfactions they had received from the adoption, Mrs. Pierce replied, "Miriam is an asset. She is a delightful child." According to Mr. Pierce, "She is a strong-willed little person and has a very bright, easygoing personality. . . . She is just another wonderful person in the family." Another mother described their three-year-old as being a "real joy to the whole family. There's just no way of describing how much fun we've had with that boy." When asked what has been the impact of the adoption on him, a father remarked that "the gain of loving another person is loving yourself more . . . just by sharing my love with my black son has enhanced my view of myself and my behavior around other people."

Some parents said that they had different and more valuable feelings about adopting that they did not feel with giving birth. As one mother said, "It's just different. I can't explain it, but I know I felt different." A father in the South made the same point when he told the interviewer, "I just think there is something about adopting a child, no matter what kind of child it is, that helps you understand a new dimension to life. I don't know if I can verbalize it. There are certain good feelings that come . . . you know, certain good feelings about kind of grafting somebody into your family. It's kind of humbling. It is definitely positive." This warm and endearing feeling permeates these parents' relationships with their adopted children. It has made most of them a closer-knit family, as indicated by one father who said: "We were a very happy family before we got Jason. It's just that now all of us, including our three older children, are that much happier." Perhaps one father summed it up when he said, "I think there is a real distinction between giving birth and parenting a child. Giving birth is an important experience, but it is not parenting. It's being the parent that really develops a relationship." This differentiation he is making is often referred to as the distinction between biological and sociological parenthood; the latter is considered by family scholars as the more important.

In most cases, the black adopted children were the youngest children in the family, since parents frequently adopt after they have children of their own. Being the youngest in the family, adopted, and racially different placed the child in the special position of being the protected and endeared baby or youngest sibling upon whom affection was showered by the parents and siblings. Parents also gave numerous accounts of the adopted child being the focus of attention of neighbors, teachers, and friends. A St. Louis mother said of her five-year-old: "Dwight is a social butterfly in the community. He has so many friends that he even introduces his older sister and brother to new kids. Everyone loves him."

The gushing and overattentiveness the child receives from outsiders eventually evoke negative reactions from some parents, since they view it as overcompensation for being a black, and it is impossible to avert the special treatment the child receives from strangers. (See Chapter 11.) This singling out can in some cases be disruptive to the family's internal settling down, as it often necessitates intervention by a parent or sibling. Eventually, however, the attentiveness the child receives from the family is normalized and he or she settles down to being an ordinary member of the family, to the extent possible. Dywasuk states, ". . . gradually this excitement and fascination will die down. In its place will develop a much deeper, more meaningful relationship. Brothers and sisters interact, compete, and grow together in the same way whether they are adopted or biological. They learn to love and respect each other as persons. They come to be so much a part of each other's life that they don't think or care about the fact that they are not related by blood."[8] (See Chapter 10.)

After the child has become somewhat routinized in the family, the parents not only bestow affection on this child, but they also begin to impart discipline, including spankings, just as they do to their other children. As one mother said, "You soon get used to any child, including your black adopted one. Bobby is no different from Alvin and Sherry, except he is a lot younger. I treat them all the same." A mother in Maryland expressed a similar attitude when she said, "I'm not going to isolate any one child in our family for special treatment because she's different. I think you have to stress certain values in all your children. . . . You can't isolate them."

The parents say they have the same expectations of their adopted and their biological children. Although some are aware of racial myths that might have an effect upon their child's achievement in school ("blacks' intellectual development is slower than whites'," etc.), they maintain that they do not share any of these stereotypes, and expect each child to develop at his or her *individual* pace. One mother said, "I don't think we ever had any expectations of our black child one way or another. You just take him in and love him like you would your biological children. It's just another dimension." Many parents agreed that they have approached the adoption with a minimum of preconceived ideals, goals, and expectations. "You really can't help *any* child to develop his maximum potential if you are all hung up on your own expectations," allowed one father. One father eloquently voiced his feelings: "I expect nothing more or less from Phillip than I do from the other children in our family. . . . I don't want Phillip to be a doctor, I don't want him to be a carpenter, I don't want him to pitch for the Pittsburgh Pirates, and they are my favorite baseball team. I want him to be a healthy human being . . . who is fully concerned about his brothers and sisters. I don't really expect anything, but at the same time I want a lot from him." As stable middle-class, educated parents, they highly value achievement through education. Thus one of the prevalent themes they express is their desire to provide an education for their black children. The vast majority of these adopted children will be exposed to and experience all the privileges of a middle-class lifestyle. The majority will have the economical means to go to college. Because their parents value achievement, they will, necessarily, transmit this value to all their children. Some parents said the primary, and sometimes only requirement they made on their application to the agency was that the child have high intellectual potential. They wanted to know that the child they were to adopt had high-achieving biological parents. "We were not concerned about complexion, sex, or anything else one might ordinarily want in a child," said a father. "The two requests we had, by the way, which were irrevocable as far as we were concerned, were that the child be a potential high achiever and be in good health—in that order." This father, who is an accomplished scholar, and his wife adopted a bright, outgoing child who blends well into the family and shares the intellectual interests of the other family members.

The parents say they feel that what you put into a child is what you will eventually get out. Emphasizing that they are teaching positive values and attitudes to *all* their children, they hope this element of their socialization will provide positive returns. One father said, "My responsibility to my black son and my white daughters is to live the most quality life around them and hope it rubs off. I don't make a distinction in the values I want to impart to any of them. They are all children who need the best parental guidance they can get." There are, however, a number of variations. For example, one couple told me they felt they had to try to be "black parents to our black child and white parents to our two white kids." A mother said, "Our black child might not be able to go as far in the world as our other children because he is different, so we try to keep that in mind as she is growing up." There are also a few parents who seem to be set on proving that their black child can develop intellectually at the same level as their white children. The black child takes on the appearance of being part of an experiment in which the parents are more anxious to prove the child's capabilities than in treating him or her as a normal child. One wonders if the parents are fighting some subconscious racist feelings they have about black inferiority.

In the end result the great majority of parents say they made the right decision when they adopted across racial boundaries, yet there are a few who are ambivalent about having done so. After having been criticized by family and attacked by hostile strangers, one couple said, "We never would have adopted a black baby if we had known there would be so much trouble, especially with our families." Another said, "We aren't sure we did the right thing by adopting, but it's too late to change that now." This kind of ambivalence and, for some, acknowledgment that an error had been committed is sure to have disastrous effects on the child and his or her relationship to all the members of their family. Certainly the parents' subtle attitudes can be conveyed to the black child, who may eventually feel that he or she is not wanted.

Although transracial adoptions can be rife with problems, most of them are created by forces outside the nuclear family. As a rule, the patterns of interaction and interpersonal relationships within the immediate family are generally good. Since the children are still very young, one cannot predict with certainty if this pattern will remain the same as they grow into adolescence and adulthood. Being young children, they are still totally dependent on their families for nurturance. Overt conflicts, due to their young ages, have not yet arisen.

THE MOTIVATION TO ADOPT

Given the status of race relations in the United States, why would any middle-class, privileged white person voluntarily adopt a black child, a child who comes from one of the most racially oppressed groups in this society, and a child who will continue to bear the stigma and lower caste and class status that being a black will have for years to come? The most perplexing and controversial aspect of transracial adoption is parental motivation. Members of all groups in the society, whether hostile or sympathetic observers, are equally anxious to know from these parents, "Why did you adopt *this* kind of child?"

Contrary to popular opinion, people adopt across racial lines for many of the same reasons they adopt a child of their own race. The overriding factor in most adoptions, regardless of parental background, is the desire to have a child. Of course, there are intermingling and secondary reasons that make this basic motivation more complex.

The most often cited reasons these parents give for having adopted a black child are the desire to have a family; they want to provide a home for a child least likely to be adopted; concern about the population explosion; a lack of interest in reproducing oneself; infertility; and a desire to solve social problems, including problems of race relations. According to Billingsley and Giovanonni, interracial adoption follows a "continuum based on skin color," and a continuum reflecting community attitude toward a particular racial minority.[1] Lighter-skinned children are far easier to place than the dark-skinned. Studies show that it is easier to place black children in Canada, where there are few blacks in the population, but more difficult to place Indian children in those areas of Canada where the Indian population is large. The same has been the case for those areas of the United States where there are many Indians. In the great majority of cases, transracial adoption involves children of *mixed* parentage. Gallay found that over a twelve-year period, of the 115 nonwhite children adopted by whites in Canada, 107 or 92 per cent were part white.[2] A majority of the children in this study had one white parent.

A review of the literature on transracial adoption reveals the complexity of analyzing motivations for adopting. The majority of studies, primarily doctoral dissertations and journal articles, show that most parents are motivated to some degree by their concern for the plight of the hard-to-place child. Studies conducted by Falk; Nutt and Snyder; and Zastrow and Simon found that a frequently cited reason for adopting transracially was "compassion for children without homes."[3] In a study in which the motivations of parents who adopted transracially were compared to those who adopted in-race, Falk found that "the transracial couples more frequently referred to the child's needs, while the in-race couples more frequently indicated that they desired a child or more children, or had some special feelings about or for the child.[4] Nutt and Snyder note that their nationwide survey indicates that "nearly all (86.9 per cent) made specific requests for transracial adoptions.[5] On the other hand, other studies have shown that a higher percentage of black children were adopted by white parents because of infertility. In a study conducted by Pepper in California, he notes that while roughly 25 per cent of these parents expressed the desire "to help a child," the couples who adopted mixed-race children did not differ significantly in their motivations from those couples who adopted children like themselves, but he reclassified them as "neotraditionalists" because they saw a need to help these children.[6]

It has been suggested that there is a difference between those couples who adopt at the suggestion of the agency and those who express transracial adoption as their *own* preference. In one study, half of the couples had the idea of adopting transracially initiated by the agency. "Of the self-initiated couples, 83 per cent of the reasons were in the social-consciousness category (concern about overpopulation or nonadoption of children), compared to 25 per cent of the reasons of agency-initiated couples."[7] Priddy and Kirgan also found that couples who expressed transracial adoption as their own preference were more likely to live in integrated neighborhoods than those whose transracial adoption was agency-initiated. Interestingly, "the authors believe . . . that the majority of the agency-initiated couples came to the agency because of their own inability to reproduce, but were flexible about the type of child they would adopt."[8]

These motives may appear contradictory. However, it is possible that many couples who are unable to reproduce want a child so much that they are willing to accept whatever child is available. This could conceivably occur without preferences. Therefore, while some couples might ideally hope to adopt a Caucasian child, they might accept a mixed-race child or a child of another race because of the limited alternatives. This may also be one way of explaining why many of these couples state that they had no preferences, while in fact they did, but quickly eliminated such preferences for a Caucasian infant when they realized that none were available. Interpreted in this light, no doubt the data would be reflected somewhat differently.

Motivations to adopt across racial boundaries are related to some of the social issues and concerns many Americans had during the sixties and early seventies. It is difficult to imagine that a large number of whites would have considered, or even thought of, adopting a black child had they not been confronted with the white infant shortage, the zero population growth movement, and the heightened consciousness toward homeless black children. The overriding factor one must consider is that these social issues made it possible for these adoptions to occur. To validate this point, one has only to look at the period of the fifties and early sixties to see how few interracial adoptions occurred. In effect, there was a coming together of the social issues and the people, without which this unusual phenomenon could not have occurred.

How adoptive parents describe their motives is wholly different from the motives that are imputed to them. They are aware of the various negative motives observers assign them, and feel they have been misunderstood. As one mother said, "It both angers and hurts me that people think I adopted my black son to fulfill some sort of racial fantasy. But what can I do? Certainly I can't go around telling everyone who gives me that suspicious look that I adopted Charlie because I simply wanted a baby." Another mother was very candid about why they adopted a black child:

INTERVIEWER: What were your primary reasons for adopting a black child?

RESPONDENT: We simply wanted a child.

INTERVIEWER: Did you apply to the agency for any specific type of child?

RESPONDENT: I guess you could say we did at first. We told them we wanted a boy because we'd already had a girl. Our daughter was four and I hadn't gotten pregnant again.

INTERVIEWER: What about race? Did you make a specific request in that area?

RESPONDENT: On our first visit [to the agency] we told them we wanted a white infant, but when they told us how slim our chances were, we got very discouraged. Our worker told us they had been placing a few biracial babies and we told her we would go home and think about it.

INTERVIEWER: How long did it take you to decide?

RESPONDENT: Not long. A few days, I guess. We couldn't see any obstacles. In fact, we started looking at it in a good way because it would mean giving a home to one of the children who are hard to place. One child is as good as another.

INTERVIEWER: How has the adoption worked out?

RESPONDENT: We have no complaints. Of course, we get tired of the stares, but I guess that's to be expected. Neal is a great kid. He's very independent and friendly. We've never had any second thoughts about our decision to adopt.

This couple lived in a predominantly white middle-class suburban community. Neal goes to an integrated nursery school and appears to be an average, adjusted child. Perhaps this couple is representative of those individuals who approach the agency with one type of child in mind as their preference, but after deciding to adopt a child who is waiting, are pleased with having made such a decision, primarily because they made a strong commitment to their act and have encountered no major problems that would cause them to have second guesses as to whether they made the wisest decision. Of course, all of the adoptions involving these dynamics do not work out so well.

There is an interplay among a variety of forces in assessing motivation, the dynamics of which are not that easy to sort out. Yet, in the minds of most parents are a fairly clear-cut set of reasons they can articulate. It may well be that given the atypical nature of transracial adoption, many of these parents are more certain as to why they made this decision than they would have been and/or are about a number of other important decisions they have had to make. I cannot honestly say that I neither entirely believed nor disbelieved many of the reasons some of them said they adopted black children.

Trying to understand and have the parents articulate their motives was challenging. Initially, most parents had a rote answer for the question they had so often been asked by family, friends, adoption workers, and strangers alike. When I queried them on why they chose to adopt a black child instead of waiting for a white one, all too often they wanted to convince me that they did it not only because they wanted a child, but also for altruistic reasons. A few were willing, however, to confront themselves, as they discussed and probed some of the factors they had rarely dealt with or thought about, such as their own upbringing and how their values were markedly different from their own parents'.

The overwhelming majority of parents in this study stated that they adopted because they wanted a child. This finding is validated by all other studies that have been conducted on interracial adoption. Although this was the primary reason, it has already been stated that many adopted transracially only after being told by the agency that no white children were available. So strong was their desire to have a child that color became a less important consideration. Eighty per cent of the parents in this study already had biological children and did not look forward to years of waiting for the healthy white infant, since adoption agencies usually give priority to childless couples. For the majority of these parents, a biracial child (usually a white mother and black father) became the alternative. For a smaller number, a child with two black parents was acceptable.

Enlarging one's family was the motivation for many of these couples, and they had decided that they would rather adopt additional children because of financial, health, and social reasons. For example, several individuals experienced infertility after their first children were born, and were thus unable to have additional ones. Some mothers could not afford to drop out of the labor force for an extended period of time to have a baby. As already mentioned, others did not want to risk having another child of the same sex, as indicated in the remarks made by a young St. Louis mother:

> Our single most important reason was our desire to have another child. We had two boys, and we were ready for a girl. [They subsequently adopted two girls.]

This couple also had strong secondary motivations:

> We talked with our social worker about the types of children who needed homes, and we decided that the need was greatest among racially mixed—black and white—children.

Finally, an important underlying influence was the following:

> My husband and his sister were adopted. That's why we even thought of adopting. He was grateful to have been given a home like he had and he felt that he would like very much to give another child the same kind of home.

In many other cases, eventually adopting a child had been decided very early in the couple's marriage. A few said they had seriously discussed it while engaged to be married. Adopting was not a sudden venture, a sentiment voiced by Jane Peters, a housewife, whose husband is a lawyer:

> We had always planned on adopting regardless of whether or not we had our own biological children because my husband feels that it is socially irresponsible to have more than two kids, and I'd like to have a larger family. Within that structure, we had always talked about adopting either older children or transracially.

It didn't make any difference to us. It was the need for children to have homes, so that when we started [applied to agency], we were specifically looking to adopt transracially.

A few of these parents became concerned quite early in life about the problems of orphaned children. They had grown up in families where this was a prevalent concern. Their parents had expressed compassion for hard-to-place children, and some of *them* were adopted, or had relatives who had adopted. Thus there was a long-standing tradition that placed great value on the welfare of children, and, more specifically, on adopting.

As the above-mentioned parents proceeded toward adulthood and eventually had families of their own, they too embraced this long-standing family tradition. Their values regarding child welfare and the sanctity of the family had been nurtured long before they adopted. This lifetime commitment, which eventually culminated in adopting interracially, is illustrated in the life of Marie Donald, a young mother on the East Coast, who explained: "My mother is a retired social worker, and I was reared with the idea of knowing the social problems that children without homes encounter. I always thought, even before marriage, that it would be nice to give birth to some children, to have a large family, and then to adopt the rest of the children. And I knew that I could love children that I didn't give birth to." After twelve years of marriage and two children, she and her husband, Kevin, decided to adopt. "My earliest specific recollection of wanting to adopt interracially came from having been introduced by my mother to Pearl Buck's books. My parents are radical, and I just grew up that way." Kevin said, "Marie was speaking her convictions about homeless children even before we got married." As to why they adopted across racial lines, Marie explained, "It was because these were the children who were waiting. The primary decision was to adopt a child who was not getting adopted, and in this society that would be older white children or very medically handicapped children or a minority child."

Adopting is most often a deliberate plan that was nurtured and executed for very personal reasons. Often this is the case with individuals who were themselves adopted. It is to be expected that they would not only grow up with a feeling that adop-

tion is a normal way to have a family, but also that it has social value. In the case mentioned in Chapter 1, Vicky Katz who,
with her husband, adopted four "hard to place" children (one racially mixed, one black, and two white medically handicapped) is
such a person. Vicky was herself adopted when she was a year old.
Adopted into a strong Catholic extended family in which there was
a large number of children, she said, "Early in life we learned
that children are very important people who are to be taken
seriously. My parents didn't view kids as little creatures roaming
around. They *listened* to what kids had to say. I cannot remember a
time when there were not a lot of kids—cousins and neighbors—
in our home. A cousin or aunt was always having a baby, and they
always left their other children with us when they went to the hos-
pital. So I was literally surrounded by lots of children. And my
parents felt this was the normal thing to do."

When asked why she and her Jewish husband decided to adopt
several "hard to place" children and not have any of their own,
she replied, "It was something I *always* knew I would do. Fortunately, I married a man who also had strong feelings about the
needs of kids and their belonging in permanent homes."

The Katzes are not in any way representative of the majority of adoptive parents. The welfare of all children is a serious
concern for them. It matters far less that the children they
adopted are black or white, but that these children would have
found it extremely difficult to be adopted by most individuals
seeking to adopt. In other words, they adopted the hardest of the
"hard to place."

There are other parents who early in life had a *desire* to eventually adopt but without the willfulness of those described above.
One father put it succinctly: "Somewhere in the back of my mind
I always wanted to adopt a child because I knew there were many
homeless kids out there. I also knew I wanted to perpetuate myself. So it was only after we had our two children that we decided
it was time to adopt." Others said they could not recall precisely
when they first began thinking about adopting. As a mother remarked, "We knew that at some point we would include a child
in our family who might not have had a home otherwise."

In this study it was found that these types far outnumbered the
parents who approached the adoption with great zeal.

Adopting a *black* child is usually *not* decided on early in the deliberations. In a sense, one can separate the abstract "intention to adopt a needy child one day" from the reality of adopting a black one. It was only after they either learned that the children who most needed homes were black or that there were no available healthy white babies in need of parents, or both, that the subject of a black child was raised. A young couple explained how they happened to adopt a black child:

HUSBAND: These were the children who needed homes and we could not have children of our own. The white child was not in need of adoption and we were interested in being part of the answer to some needs of children. The ones available were racially mixed so the first child we adopted was Korean and the second child was black. We hadn't completely considered all the implications of adopting a child who was black and white [mixed].

WIFE: We were told that there was a little boy available for adoption and were asked if we were interested. We had two girls and we had talked about whether to adopt another one. I just sort of made the decision then to adopt. It was later that they told me his background was black and white. We didn't care about his race. Only that he needed parents.

Prior to going to the adoption agency to apply for a baby, some parents were already aware of the difficulty of finding homes for black children. Through newspapers, magazines, and television programs in which the subject was discussed, and by talking to other whites who had adopted, they were well informed. As a rule they are sophisticated on social issues, although most would not be considered activists.

Yet there were others who were not informed, and were not very concerned about the child's background. They went to the adoption agency initially without any specific choices as to race, sex, or religious background. They were willing to accept whatever the agency describes as the "hard to place" child, within certain limits. Such parents are frequently more concerned about such a child's age and health than these other factors. The Bradleys are representative of such parents:

WIFE: I think at the time we wanted to adopt where there was the greatest need for homes. We believed the greatest need to be among black and biracial children. Our agency felt the same. We did not care what sex the child was.

HUSBAND: We did specify that the baby should be under two years old. We also wanted to be of the greatest service, and at the same time, we wanted another child.

Some parents must be made aware of the predicament of "hard to place" children before they seek to adopt them. They occasionally have friends, neighbors, and family who adopt minority children, and are influenced enough to do the same. They might attend a persuasive lecture on the subject, or hear a sermon by their minister. It may also grow out of their deeply felt commitment to human welfare—a belief that all individuals deserve the opportunity to develop to their maximum potential. They translate this to mean that children have the right to grow up in permanent, secure homes with parents. From this philosophical belief, they proceed to put into practice their ideals. Adopting is only one of many ways in which such parents can carry out their commitments. For example, some of these individuals also become foster parents. Occasionally these foster parents eventually adopt the child in their care.

On the negative side, too many parents drift into transracial adoption. They initially have no intention of adopting a black child. It is only after they learn that they will not be able to get a healthy white infant that they settle for a black baby as second best. Most often this is a mixed-race child. Those who already have had biological children learned that agencies were giving priority to childless couples. Even those persons who were infertile were finding the wait for a baby stretching over the years. Many agencies were no longer taking applications from anyone, childless or not, while other agencies reported that they had a five-year waiting list. The older white child and the white child with medical handicaps held no appeal to them. As an alternative to the possibility of never getting a child, or at the very least, of waiting several years, many turned to the healthy biracial baby. A mother echoed their sentiments:

A white child wasn't practical anyway because it was impossible to get one. Our agency didn't have any white children available.

There were numerous cases in this study in which the parents would have adopted a white child rather than a black one, had a white child been available. Mary Smith, whose husband, Charles, is a physician, admitted that they applied for a white child but said, "We felt foolish to stand in line waiting for Caucasian children when there were so few available." Another parent who had initially applied for a white child told the interviewer, "We didn't want to wait for a child that we didn't feel was any better than those who were waiting for us. Finally, a father put it this way: "Sure I would have taken a white baby if they had had one to offer us as a first choice. But since that wasn't possible, you might say we settled for second best, but we are happy about the choice we made. We have no regrets."

Such parents as the above-mentioned prefer that the child be fair-skinned or brown, thus avoiding what they consider the unnecessary problems a dark-skinned child might cause for them. Thus a mother remarked, "I didn't mind adopting a racially mixed child, but I was not willing to accept a very dark child because I wanted to minimize the stares and the questions I was sure to get. There was no reason to invite problems that could be avoided."

These parents make one most suspicious of their motives for adopting. If they considered the racially mixed child second best, then were they likely to reveal this in subtle ways to the child? Some of these parents were rearing the child as though he or she were white. One mother who had two very fair-skinned children, but who were identifiably black, became indignant when the interviewer asked her if she intended to teach them an appreciation of their black cultural heritage. "What black cultural heritage?" she asked. "No, I don't plan to teach them any of that stuff. They aren't black! They are half white!" The inevitable question this mother must eventually come to grips with is that of resolving for these children and herself an identity crisis that they are almost certain to experience.

A very small number of parents said they adopted a racially

mixed child because they felt it was time for whites to start assuming responsibility for these children instead of allowing the burden
of responsibility for their care to continue to fall upon the black
community. They reasoned that these children were at least half
Caucasian, and should be cared for by whites as well as blacks.
They also seemed more able to identify with the racially mixed
children, who, in some sense, represented part of them, than those
children with both black parents. They were careful to point out
what the child's white parent's nationality and ethnic background
were and what kind of physical characteristics the parent had. In
fact, they seemed to have a preoccupation with nationality. It was
emphasized in the majority of the interviews, oftentimes over the
child's racial background.

A persistent theme among these parents is their need to "help,"
to be "of the most service," and "to do some good." Some express
strong feelings about the need to adopt not just any child, but
only where there is the greatest need, and where they, in turn, can
make their most worthy contribution. A father explained it this
way: "We thought that if we were going to do any good, it
wouldn't be done by adopting a child with blue eyes and blond
hair or the so-called 'blue-ribbon' baby." Others described it as
being "more socially useful" to adopt. A father stated:

> I knew there was a premium on white kids and that there was an
> excess of black children. I knew that I could provide a home for
> a kid who otherwise would not have one. We made the decision
> to do something that was more socially useful.

When the researcher asked one parent if he worried that critics of
transracial adoption would accuse him of having a missionary attitude because of his emphasis on the adoption being a service to the
child, he replied sharply:

> That's up to them [critics] to feel any way they want to. Maybe I
> do have a missionary attitude. But you must remember that a lot
> of good has been done by "missionaries." I also happen to love
> and respect my son. I happen to be proud to be his father, and I
> hope he is never for any reason ashamed to be my son. As for the
> critics, why didn't they adopt Mike?

For some parents, adopting a black child was motivated or influenced by clear-cut social issues. The adoption is a way of expressing their commitment to solving some of the world's social problems. This is very clearly the case for those who adopted a black child because of their adherence to the zero population growth and equal rights movements. It is in the same context, although on an international level, that some of these same parents adopted Vietnamese-American children. Because of their abhorrence of the Vietnam war, and the effects it had upon that country's children, they felt a responsibility for their welfare.

A philosophy of racial equality and a commitment to better race relations influence a few people to adopt across racial boundaries. The decade of the 1960s brought with it an unprecedented desire by liberal whites to make amends in American race relations. Their concern was expressed in many ways. While some became active in various social programs such as tutoring black inner-city children, advocacy of welfare rights, protests against deteriorated housing, and advocacy of better employment opportunities and equal educational opportunities, still a much larger group were passive sympathizers who never actively participated in any of these civil rights programs. Their support was financial or ideological. Interracial adoption was a by-product of this movement in that it reflected the philosophy of integration and racial brotherhood to which some of these parents adhered. One father said that adopting a black child gives him a feeling of universal brotherhood. With great fervor, another father said, "I walked civil rights picket lines, I collected food and clothing for poor blacks in Alabama, and eventually we adopted a black child. That is a reflection of the level of my commitment." When the researcher asked him how he responded to critics who say that one should not adopt for this reason, he replied, "I love Danny as if he were from my own genes. I tell the critics that it's one thing to pity the race, but quite another to walk the floor at 2:00 A.M. with a teething or colicky baby."

The population explosion also influenced a small number of these people to adopt. Most parents who mentioned the population explosion as a motive adhere to its aims, for the most part, without participating in any related organization. As a rule they have already borne children and have subsequently become converts to the zero population growth philosophy. Although they themselves have engaged in the process of reproduction, some are now convinced that if they had to do it over, they would place less emphasis on biological parenthood, and would probably have fewer, if any, children of their own. As a group they are impressively nonego involved, and attach a stronger value to social than to biological parenthood. They emphasize that they are not "hung up" on reproducing themselves, and one mother said that in addition to the adoption helping to curb population growth, "It is also a way of enlarging the gene pool of my grandchildren." A father said, "You have to be secure with your manhood in order to be able to take the position that reproducing yourself is not terribly important." They attached great importance to the satisfaction the child brings because parenthood was viewed as a deliberate and voluntary act—a matter of choice void of the pressures to reproduce a child in one's likeness. In fact, to choose to adopt a black child as a first choice can be interpreted as the parents' lack of concern with the traditional "matching" concept in adoption. As a father stated, "Our adopting *black* children means that we didn't give a damn about having children. You can put together a family any way you want to. Who is to say that giving birth is the only way to have a family?" His wife added, "Some of the women in the neighborhood have asked me if I wasn't sorry that I couldn't have children. When I tell them that I can but don't want to contribute to the overpopulation, they can't understand me. They have one of two reactions: They either pity me because they don't believe me, or they think we're crazy." Her husband noted, "You can't win. Most people are so conditioned to think one way. They just can't believe that I don't measure my manhood by making Jenny pregnant, and they treat Jenny like she's only part woman, since we choose to adopt instead of having children."

These socially conscious parents also have a greater activist orientation than the other parents in the study, although they could by no means be considered *strong* activists. They are especially aware of international and national social issues that relate to population problems. A small number worked with famine relief programs for Biafra and Bangladesh. Several couples had lived and taught in developing countries, including African countries, prior to adopting. One couple's biological children were born in Africa. This experience was a strong motivating factor in adopting a black child.

In spite of this adherence to population control, few parents decided to forego biological parenthood entirely because of their commitment. Although a lot of the parents were strongly interested in population problems, *very* few said it was their primary reason for adopting interracially. Rather, most cited it as a strong, but secondary factor. Again, their desire to have a family was their foremost motivation.

The same small number of parents who felt strongly about racial equality and curbing population growth also opposed the Vietnam war. They had an international perspective, and their commitment to orphaned Vietnamese babies was as strong as it was to black American children. A father, who said he and his wife had been reared in highly prejudiced homes, said: "Having family from various racial and nationality backgrounds was one of the best ways we could go about rearing our children different than we were brought up." Both of these parents are social workers.

The American involvement in the Vietnam war had an influence on two couples to adopt both interracially *and* internationally. A father who is a psychiatrist and who adopted a black American and a black Vietnamese child told why he did so:

> The decision was really made when I was in Vietnam, and was based on my experiences there. As a medical doctor, I was visiting a number of orphanages and there were a large number of children of American and Vietnamese heritage who had been abandoned there, particularly the black kids. So that's what prompted the idea of adopting one of these children. . . . It also kind of tied up with my feelings about the whole American effort in Vietnam anyway, and that these kids were symbols of that.

Notably, other influences on this couple's decision included the unavailability of white infants, a desire to have a diverse family, having friends who had adopted, and a relative who worked in interracial adoptive placements for many years.

While many of the parents are regular churchgoers and express a belief in a Supreme Being, only one couple listed their religious faith as the major motivation for adopting—they were members of the Bahai faith, which stresses international and interracial brotherhood. "This was one way of demonstrating our belief in integration," said this father.

In spite of all the speculation observers have on the motives of whites who adopt across racial boundaries, the evidence shows that the majority simply want a child, or another child. Some are not without racial prejudice because, while they would accept a mixed-race child, they would not be willing to accept a child with two black parents, or a very dark child. The findings from this study are consistent with other studies that show that the majority of these parents did not have as their primary reason for adopting that of showing an expression of their commitment to an integrated society. Such parents are in a minority.

White parents who adopt black children must contend with the curiosity, suspicion, compliments, hostility, and other expressions from a public who react intensely to the adoption. Motives are, as stated, complex and multifaceted. A fairly large number of these parents probably never questioned seriously their motives prior to adopting. Others may have done so, but only superficially. Still others might have been dishonest in stating their reasons to others, even when they themselves were well aware of why they adopted. One factor that gives rise to this dissembling is the need to appear as near-perfect parents, with a minimum of problems. It is especially important that these parents put forth the image that the adoption has not caused problems, because they ventured into an area where others cautioned them not to enter. After taking such a defiant stand, to admit failure, weakness, or vulnerability would be catastrophic.

In summary, the motivations of parents who adopt across racial boundaries cover a vast range. Some simply wanted a specific-sex child; others only slightly masked their racial stereotypes and contempt for blacks other than their adopted child; some had taken up the banner to secure "homes for black children" because they erroneously believed that "blacks don't adopt"; others talked incessantly about the picture of the "cute little boy" they had seen in a publication and knew immediately that they had to adopt him; and there were a lot of parents who simply love children and wanted to expand their families. More often than not, these families are far from exotic. There is a strong quality of "ordinariness" about them that defies many of the images presented by their foes.

While one can view these adoptions of "hard to place" children as meeting the needs of the child, they are also equally meeting the needs of the parents, and in this sense alone are no different from any other type of adoption.

4

BLACK/WHITE ADOPTION IN HISTORICAL CONTEXT

"Adoption involves becoming a parent through a legal and social process rather than through a biological process. . . . Adoption provides permanent substitute care for the child when his natural parents are unable, or unwilling to care for him, and have been legally freed of any ties to the child."[1] Adoptions fall into two categories: related and nonrelated. The majority of nonrelated adoptions are handled by adoption agencies, whereas most related adoptions are handled independently and involve the child being adopted by grandparents, aunts, uncles, or cousins. Traditionally, black adoptions have been formal (legal) or informal (nonlegal), with the vast majority being informal.[2] Adoption did not become established as a major element in child-welfare services until well into the twentieth century. Billingsley and Giovanonni state, "But its intent to benefit the adoptive parents rather than the child has been a persistent character of adoption as a child welfare service."[3]

The American adoption movement was conceived to meet the needs of infertile white middle-class couples, and only secondarily to meet the needs of the orphaned children.[4] Since the primary focus was on parental needs, the adoption policies and practices were formulated and functioned in behalf of this small clientele.

Up until the last decade, little consideration was given to what was in the best interests of the child, since it was felt that the child's needs were being served by virtue of the fact that he or she was being provided a permanent home with adoptive instead of

foster parents. Adoption agencies, particularly voluntary ones, adhered to the philosophy that the ideal pairing of parents with children existed when the two were matched on physical, intellectual,
social, and other characteristics and potential. Thus a blond Catholic couple was quite likely to receive a child whose biological parents were Catholic and were possibly blond.

The agencies, also, designed rigid policies and procedures these
couples had to meet if they expected to qualify to adopt. Often
they had to own their homes, be able to provide a separate bed-
room for the child, have a modest bank account, be financially
able to provide a decent education for the child, prove infertility,
show proof of having been married several years, and declare religious affiliation. Agencies wielded strong power, and parents often
found themselves at the mercy of a single eccentric social worker
who had the authority to grant or withhold a desperately wanted
child. Applicants rarely protested these policies, because of the
fear of being rejected. Their conformity reinforced the prevailing
norms. This limited agency focus also produced a virulent form of
discrimination against all other types of children and prospective
parents who did not conform to the agencies' clientele and criteria. Those excluded were the poor, racial minorities, single persons, the middle-aged, and those who had an unorthodox lifestyle.

Religion, social class, and race are three variables that have
been used to exclude children and prospective parents from the
adoptive process. Since many voluntary agencies were organized
by religious denominations, the agencies had as their primary goal
that of serving their church members. Religious guidelines were
rigidly enforced in child placements and incorporated into state
statutes. According to Kadushin, "The 'child saving' activity of one
group is perceived as a 'child snatching' activity by another group.
One of the most vehement controversies in the history of child
welfare took place in late nineteenth-century America, when
Catholic organizations charged that placement agencies such as
the Children's Aid Society were maintained for the purpose of
bribing poor destitute Catholics to abandon their faith. Placing
Catholic children in Protestant homes was not charity, it was
claimed, but sectarian zeal designed to destroy a child's faith in
the religion of his parents."[5] Even today, sectarian agencies, particularly the Catholic and Jewish, are reluctant to place a child of

their faith with parents of a different faith. While agencies may permit birth parents to sign religious waivers so the child can be adopted by parents outside their denomination, religion remains an important factor to be contended with in the adoptive process in many states. For example, the New York State statutes require that adoptive parents pledge to rear the child in a given (unspecified) religious faith, although birth parents may exercise the option of signing a religious waiver. New York statutes also permit the agencies to use their final discretion in determining whether the religious requirements made by the birth parents can or should be reasonably adhered to. Indeed, as late as July 1975, an agency on the West Coast refused to place a Vietnamese refugee child with the applicant family who had been the child's physician. They refused to make the placement solely because the applicant did not share the religion of the agency. The child's religion was not known or even in question.[6]

Social class is another significant determinant for adoptive placement, although it appears to be less a factor today with the infant shortage than in the years when there was a larger supply of children. In conforming with the "matching" concept, the philosophy was that children and adoptive parents should, if possible, come from similar economic backgrounds. Achievement and motivation were important areas on which children were matched with parents. Therefore a child born to middle-class, high-achieving parents would, if possible, be placed with a couple of similar background. It was reasoned that a child whose mother was an underachiever would, ultimately, be a poor choice for a highly intelligent, high-achieving couple, and vice versa.

Race was the criterion that was most rigidly adhered to under the "matching" philosophy. In the attempt to give an infertile couple the child they had proven incapable of having, it was axiomatic that the adopted child and parents would be of the same race, allowing the child to blend into this couple's life and to give the appearance that this was their biological offspring. If there were exceptions, black applicants were far less likely to be permitted to adopt a white child than whites were to adopt a black child, since the tradition of black racial subordination made such a prospect untenable. Today there are very few documented cases in which white children were legally adopted by black parents in the United States. Several southern states forbade the legal adoption of a child across racial lines until 1972, when a federal court struck down a Louisiana statute that prohibited adopting across racial boundaries. The court opinion stated, "It is obvious that the Louisiana statute making race a decisive factor in adoption subordinates a child's best interest in some circumstances to the racial discrimination." The judges said, "To justify the classifications in the statute, the defendants must convince the court that under all circumstances it is against the child's best interest to have racially different parents."[7] Although it is now illegal for a state to prohibit adoption across racial lines, very few occur in the Deep South, and in other states that have small black populations.

Adopting across racial lines appears to have started almost accidentally. Throughout the United States there is a scattering of black adults who grew up in white homes. A small number were legally adopted, while others were foster children, or were reared as the couple's child without the benefit of legal adoption. Perhaps more children would have been legally adopted had the laws permitted. Some of those children who were adopted, it has been reported, were originally thought to be of white parentage.[8] As the children grew older it became obvious to the parents that the child was of mixed parentage. No one knows how many of these children were returned to the agencies or disposed of in other ways, but some were kept by their adoptive parents despite the mixup in their racial backgrounds. Another category of blacks who grew up in white homes were the sons and daughters of household servants who deliberately sought employment among wealthy whites so their children could be exposed to white upper-class culture. Many of these white employers sent their servants' children to college, thus enabling them to achieve social mobility.[9]

The earliest record of a transracial placement documented in this investigation occurred in Minneapolis, Minnesota, in 1948. This placement was made by Laura Gaskin, a black social worker, who is now director of the Hennepin County Department of Adoptions. Mrs. Gaskin, a native of Louisville, Kentucky, recalled this experience in an interview: "I remember a black infant boy was brought to my attention as being in need of a permanent home. After the child had been in many foster homes in a few

months," she said, "I refused to place this baby in yet another foster home. At the time the black population in Minneapolis-St.
Paul was very small. Black parents were hard to recruit because of
the small number living in the area. When no black home could
be located for him, and when a white family wanted very much to
adopt him, I decided to place him in this permanent home. They
were fully aware of his race, and it made no difference to them."
Although she refused to reveal his identity she reported that he is
now a well-adjusted college student.[10]

In the late 1940s and early 1950s there were no official policies in
adoption agencies that permitted whites to adopt black children.
Those children who were placed with white families were the objects of highly individualized circumstances, as in the Minneapolis
case cited above. Black children, for the most part, remained outside the scope of adoption services. In an analysis of the history of
black children and their relationship to American child welfare institutions, Billingsley and Giovanonni assert that it was immediately following World War II that adoption agencies began trying
to include black children in their programs. "When these agencies were unable to place black children as fast as white children,
the agencies began to define the children and the families as
'problems,'" these authors assert. "The fact that the agencies had
long excluded black children and families, and were thus inexperienced in serving them, was quickly forgotten. The children were
'hard to place'; the families were 'hard to reach.'"[11]

The first organized attempt by white agencies to find homes for
black children was initiated in 1955 by the Minority Adoption
Recruitment of Children's Homes (MARCH), a federation of
public and private agencies in the San Francisco Bay area.
MARCH recruited homes for children of Mexican-American,
black, native American, and to a lesser degree, children of European minority descent. Although their objective was to find parents of these children's racial and ethnic backgrounds, a small
number of the black children were adopted by whites.[12]

Parents to Adopt Minority Youngsters (PAMY) was organized
in Minnesota in 1957 to publicize the need for adoptive homes for
minority race children and to act as a referral center for people interested in adopting native American, Chicano, or black children.
The project was sponsored by all the adoption agencies in the

state as well as by a number of other interested welfare organizations, and was administered by the Minnesota Department of Public Welfare. PAMY's original goal was to find black homes for black children, but requests about these children also came from white families during PAMY's two-year existence. The progressively larger numbers of transracial adoptions occurring in subsequent years in Minnesota are attributed to the initial impetus by PAMY.[13]

Another influence on the transracial adoption movement in the United States came from Canada where, in 1959, the first chapter of the Open Door Society in North America was organized in Montreal. Three white couples who adopted mixed-race children came together because of their concern for the large number of black and mixed-race children in need of permanent homes. The Montreal Open Door Society worked closely with the Adoption Department of the Children's Service Centre of Montreal to assist them in finding adoptive parents for these waiting children. Only four years after the Open Door Society was formed, their success was evidenced by a 1963 published progress report, which states:

> As a result of the combined efforts of this voluntary organization, the Open Door Society, and the professional adoption agency, 201 children of mixed and minority racial background, mostly Negro and part Negro, have been placed with adoptive families during the last six years. Ninety-five percent of these families are of a different racial background from their adopted children; this has meant the creation, by adoption, of inter-racial families.[14]

This parents' organization served as a model for the formation of similar ones throughout North America and Europe. There is also one affiliate in Australia, which deals with the welfare problems of aborigine children. Throughout the 1960s chapters of the Open Door Society, and a sister organization, the Council on Adoptable Children (COAC), sprang up throughout the United States and Canada. Similar groups bearing different names but motivated by similar concerns now exist throughout North America. As adoptive parents have migrated to other cities, they took their interest and message with them, where they formed new chapters of these organizations. Since 1969, the Open Door Society, Council on Adoptable Children, and local affiliates have held three North American conferences.

Thus the transracial adoption movement came into existence as it sought to proselytize other individuals to adopt, and to influence agencies to take the radical step from making in-racial placements to transracial ones. However, in the pioneering years of the transracial adoption movement, parents appeared to have been motivated primarily out of their concern for homeless minority children. As the infant shortage increased, parents became motivated by the desire to adopt whatever child the agencies had available. The racially mixed child was an acceptable alternative to many.

It is important to observe that since their founding, the objectives of the Open Door Society and the Council on Adoptable Children's chapters have been modified with the changing social concerns. While most of the groups began with the objective of finding homes for black and other minority children, and usually limited their recruitment to white homes, they now advocate the adoption of the older white and older black child and the handicapped child, as well as legislative reforms in child welfare.

Much of the early impetus to make transracial placements did not come from the agencies but from interested white applicants. Usually it was after these young couples went to the agencies and requested that they be allowed to adopt a black child that there was a reformulation of agency policy that permitted the practice to occur. However, it has also been documented that, on occasion, social workers suggested to applicants that they might want to adopt a waiting "hard to place" (that is, black) child.[15] Unfortunately, few agencies spent an adequate amount of time, nor did they conduct the necessary research and other pertinent investigations before making these early placements. Vernon Wiehe, the director of the St. Louis Lutheran Family and Children's Services Adoptions Department, said, "I think most of us working in adoptions talked about it among ourselves but we failed to bring in consultants and other authorities to brainstorm this with us *before* we got deeply involved in it. By the time we decided we needed to consider this more carefully, a lot of children had already been placed." As a result of what his agency considered a lack of careful planning and some poor placements, they placed a moratorium on making further transracial placements until they were more certain that these placements were in the best interests of the children. The St. Louis Open Door Society was angered by the agency's decision, and in a face-to-face confrontation accused the agency personnel of retarding progress in race relations and of impeding the process of finding homes for the "hard to place" children.

In this study, many parents said they approached the agency with the request to adopt a black child. Some agencies they applied to had never before made such a placement. This strange request was discussed in staff meetings and with the agency's boards of directors. Invariably adoption workers were curious as to why a white middle-class couple would want to deviate from traditional adoption practice. While some agencies considered these requests so bizarre that they turned down the applicants immediately and refused to enter the arena of transracial adoption altogether, other agencies turned down particular applicants but did make occasional placements. Still, the curiosity remained a strong factor among the adoption workers. For example, a Washington, D.C., adoption supervisor described her reaction to the first such couple she screened: "Although they were very intelligent and sincere, they seemed a bit odd. I couldn't quite figure out their motives at first. I had been trained to regard an adopted child as an extension of oneself. To want a black child was contradictory to traditional adoption practice."

Some agencies earned the reputation for being inclined to allow whites to adopt black children with minimum screening and short waiting periods, while others were known by the parents to be opposed to or skeptical about such arrangements. A number of agencies allowed the placements to be made only by those workers who felt comfortable in doing so. Many of the older workers refused to alter their traditional attitudes and philosophies to conform to the agencies' new policies. An adoption supervisor in a sectarian agency in Washington, D.C., explained what happened in her agency when they began making transracial placements: "We have two or three older workers who do not agree with the agency policy of placing black children in white families. We decided that they should not be compelled to handle these cases, feeling the way they do. Attitudes are very hard to change and they are old, so the other workers do the transracial placements and the older workers continue to make the same kind of placements they always did." On the other hand, I was told of numerous young workers in various agencies who were opposed to transracial placements because they did not consider them to be in the best interests of the child, and created heated debates in staff meetings as to the advisability of such placements.

Some of the sectarian agencies that received financial support from their church denominations and assumed primary responsibility for placing children in the homes of individuals associated with their religious group continued to adhere to the orthodoxy of the past. Transracial adoption would not be considered any more readily than would the practice of transreligious placement. A director of adoptions in a Catholic agency, who had worked in the same agency for over twenty-five years, told the researcher, "We have not been affected by this new kind of adoption that a lot of agencies are making. Of course we have had a number of couples to come in and ask us to place a black child with them. But we believe that a child should be with his own kind. A good Catholic home is not enough. The child should also be able to identify with his parents. So we place light-complexioned Negro children with light-complexioned parents, and so forth. I don't think we are going to change this policy, because it works for our clients."

Black adoption has, historically, been a matter of what Hill calls "informal" adoption, whereby a child is taken into a home and reared as one's own child, except that it is never legalized in the courts.[16] Because this practice was without legal sanction, and thus was never entered as an adoption statistic, the myth arose in this society that blacks do not adopt. The fact is that although blacks adopted in large numbers, the practice of legal adoption is still a relatively new phenomenon for many blacks, especially the working class.

There is a historical precedent for blacks adopting and caring for the homeless children within their midsts. During slavery, countless children were separated from their parents by slave-owners whose major concern was that of maximizing their profits instead of maintaining intact families. These children were cared for by surrogate parents. Writing in 1909, DuBois said:

"Among the slaves the charitable work was chiefly in the line of adopting children and caring for the sick. The habit of adopting is still widespread and beneficent."[17] Informal adoption required that homeless and parentless children were taken in and became bona fide members of the families of relatives, neighbors, or total strangers. Elderly women especially served as surrogate mothers.

The tradition of informal adoption continued after slavery. Johnson noted that it was prevalent among poor blacks in the South in the early part of the twentieth century: "The breaking-up of families, through desertion or migration, results in the turning over of children to relatives or friends, and since little distinction of treatment enters, they soon are indistinguishable from the natural children. . . . children orphaned by any circumstances are spontaneously taken into childless families."[18]

There was a strong value attached to children. Oftentimes informally adopted children were granted a special place in their new families, perhaps as a way of compensating for their birth parents' absence. Such children were "pitied" in a manner that evoked tender feelings from others, since a prevailing religious value among these southern rural people was that orphaned children were to be regarded as "special," and adults were duty-bound to provide for them. Again, Johnson notes that "the sentiment is sometimes carried to the point of surrounding the child with an importance which many children in normal families lack."[19] Powdermaker makes a similar observation of black families' attitudes toward adoption in Mississippi in the 1930s: "Adoption is practically never made legal, and is referred to as 'giving' the children away. . . . Because of the strong desire most people have for children, there is always someone ready to take them in."[20] Ordinarily it is not considered a misfortune to be a "gift child," a name that was applied to such children.[21]

The "adopted" child was expected to grow up with the knowledge of who his or her biological parents were and what happened to them. The circumstances surrounding the child's separation from their parents were generally revealed to the child. The practice of agencies today that emphasizes that the child should not know the answers to these questions would have been inconceivable to the majority of these blacks. The prevailing attitude was that every child is entitled to know his or her roots—

biologically and socially. And as far as this practice was extended, the children appear to have adapted very well. This practice was aided by the insular nature of the extended family, into which many of the children were adopted. Members of the small communities of the South where informal adoption was and still is most prevalent, were expected to protect the child from the insults and assaults that the child's adoptive and oftentimes out-of-wedlock status might occasionally evoke. The child, it was reasoned, should not suffer because of the transgressions of his parents. He was to be spared the labels of "child of sin," or "bastard." This is not to imply that they were always spared, for on occasion they suffered psychological damage because of insulting treatment they received. But, in the main, people adhered to this strong value placed in children regardless of their birth status. Parents who informally adopted these children were usually of the same lower economic status as their neighbors. Their benevolence influenced them to want to share whatever resources, meager though they were, with such a child. Today in small southern communities older blacks continue to display a kind of tenderness toward these children that is unlike that which is expressed toward children with parents. Persons who adhere to these traditional values feel pity toward these children—pity that evokes memories of the Negro spiritual titled "Sometimes I Feel Like a Motherless Child."

Frequently it was regarded as shameful for parents to give a child to a complete stranger. Lewis suggests that regardless of how difficult the family conditions may have been, one was expected to "stick to your own, take care of your own, and never turn them away."[22] This maxim applied to one's daughter having a child outside wedlock, one's son getting into trouble with the law, or whatever. Ordinarily, parents did not disown their children because they got into "trouble." There were, of course, some exceptions whereby daughters were banished from the household by embarrassed, angered fathers; or daughters were sent away to have the child and give it up for adoption. "Shotgun" marriage was another option resorted to.

It would be misleading to assume that all black children were informally adopted or taken care of by their extended families, or wider communities. Some children became wards of the courts, which entrusted them to the care of public agencies. They were either legally adopted, or placed in foster homes or in institutions. It was well into the twentieth century that organized social welfare institutions, including adoption services, moved from total exclusion to partial inclusion of black children. Billingsley and Giovanonni cite three reasons for this shift. First, the increasing population shift of blacks from the rural South to the urban North necessitated more agency involvement. Second, child welfare services traditionally have been utilized by poor people. As the white population has increasingly achieved economic security while the black and other minority groups have been slower in doing so, the bulk of the welfare services clientele has followed these racial and ethnic patterns. This is especially the status of public agencies. Finally, the present "integrationist" ideology opposes exclusionary practices, and child welfare institutions have made some attempts to comply.[23]

Public adoption agencies assume more responsibility for the welfare of black children than private agencies, since the public agencies have little choice but to comply, even if in a partial way, because they have been entrusted with the care of these children, who are wards of the courts. Private agencies have traditionally been allowed the opportunity to practice exclusion, since they were often founded by special-interest groups to service a specified clientele. Of course, many private agencies were founded for the explicit purpose of caring for black children. Black orphanages organized around the turn of the century were founded by black churches, fraternal societies, women's clubs, through donations, and a few were endowed by black philanthropists.[24] Thus faced with the historically unsympathetic, insensitive, and occasionally hostile social welfare institutions, it is little wonder that many blacks continued to follow the old custom of "informally" adopting the child or that the unwed mother and her family decided to keep the child rather than turn it over to such an impersonal, unsympathetic, and unknown white agency. Only the truly destitute even turned to the black agencies.

A prevailing myth held by many Americans is that, because of the tradition of "informal" adoption, blacks do not practice *legal* adoption. A large number of white parents in this investigation said they were influenced to adopt a black child, in part, because blacks do not *believe* in adopting. There are also some older adoption agency personnel who adhere to the same ideas and philosophies, although this is not as prevalent as in the past. Because they have never geared their programs toward this segment of the population, and have had few blacks to apply to their agencies, they use this experience to document their belief that legal adoption is a white middle-class phenomenon. Unfortunately, the notion that blacks do not adopt in any significant numbers is also held by people in government who formulate child welfare legislation and policies.

In spite of these myths, blacks do adopt, formally and informally. In a study conducted by the National Urban League, Hill found that informal adoption is still quite prevalent among blacks, especially in the South. He writes, "Each year black families demonstrate their ability to 'adopt' children with a placement rate more than ten times that of formal adoption agencies."[25] Other studies indicate that when social class is controlled, black families *formally* adopt children at a greater rate than white families of comparable means. Although it is not known precisely how many of these legal adoptions are independent (not carried out through an agency), many undoubtedly are. Hill found that for the year 1968, for all the black children adopted, some 90 per cent were adopted by the informal method (the comparable number for whites was 7 per cent).[26] This lends support to the conclusion that the informal adoption tradition still persists. The fact that adoption agencies do not carry out a brisk business in placing children in black homes should not be used as documentation for the myth that blacks do not adopt. It is probably more reasonable to examine the effectiveness of agencies in locating and recruiting black adoptive parents.

It was not until the late 1960s that significant numbers of whites adopted black children. The full impact of the white infant shortage was realized, and this new, abundant market of babies was looked to as a new source to replace the scarce commodity. The social concerns of many white Americans turned to the child welfare of blacks. By 1970 transracial adoptions had occurred in every state except Alabama, Arkansas, Louisiana, Mississippi, and South Carolina. According to one estimate, transracial adoptions tripled between 1968 and 1971. In 1971, of all the black children placed, 35 per cent were adopted by whites.[27] Transracial adoptions suffered a downward trend from 1972 to 1975. The 1976 opportunity survey indicates that transracial adoptions are now on the increase.

Transracial adoption is, to a great extent, a product of the civil rights era of the 1960s, when the social welfare needs of black Americans were highlighted. One of the most critical areas of social welfare that received attention was the needs of black children. Government and voluntary groups initiated policies and programs aimed at improving the life chances of black children, in the inner cities and small towns equally. The emphasis on black child welfare, coupled with a declining white adoptable baby market, created the proper climate for transracial adoption to flourish. Thus many Americans turned their attention to the orphaned black children in their midst. They reasoned that an investment in the welfare of these children eventually would yield great benefits not only for them and the children, but also for society at large. The rallying cry became that of finding "homes for black children." Notably, a black adoption agency in Detroit bears the name Homes for Black Children.

Simultaneously, another startling phenomenon was taking place. The white birth rate was declining sharply as more permissive sexual attitudes encouraged contraception and abortion. Also, a growing number of middle-class white females began to choose to keep their out-of-wedlock children rather than place them for adoption. According to the United States Bureau of the Census, in 1974 more than two hundred thousand teen-agers gave birth to out-of-wedlock children, accounting for over half the total number of such births. Some eighty-five thousand of these were white. However, there has been a startling increase in white teen-age births since 1971. Between 1971 and 1974, out-of-wedlock births for white girls aged fifteen to nineteen increased by 12 per cent, while the increase for black girls of the same age group was only 5 per cent. The increase for white females under fifteen was even more startling. The out-of-wedlock births increased by 32 per cent, with a corresponding 3 per cent increase for blacks. Westoff reports that, whereas "in 1966 an estimated 65 per cent of white illegitimate babies were given away for adoption," researchers estimate that only 18 per cent were given away for adoption in 1971.[28]

The statistics indicate a dramatic reversal in out-of-wedlock births and their disposition. Whereas white females traditionally gave their babies up for adoption, and blacks usually kept theirs, today, increasingly, white women choose to rear their children themselves. On the other hand, black women are turning increasingly to contraceptives, abortion, and in some cases foster care and legal adoption.

Historically, the babies born to young white women made up the largest source of adoptable infants to agencies. Suddenly adoption agencies found themselves with few young children to place. This is borne out by a study by the Child Welfare League of America, which has conducted a semiannual survey of forty-nine voluntary and eighteen public agencies since 1969. According to this report recruitment of nonwhite homes has a long way to go to match or exceed the number of white children accepted.[29]

To meet this crisis in the baby market, agencies chose one of the several options open to them. So acute was the infant shortage that some agencies closed down their adoption programs altogether. Others continued to place a small number of children but expanded their foster care units to make up for the losses they suffered in the adoption market. A few agencies made a concerted effort to attract black middle-class applicants, since black infants could still be found for adoption. Agencies also began specializing in placing children with special needs, the "hard to place" children. This included the older child, the handicapped, the minority child, and sibling groups. Many agencies that remained in the adoption business began to look to new sources of supply to supplement or replace the scarce commodity their traditional, white middle-class clientele desperately wanted—the healthy white infant. Overseas adoptions, primarily Korean and Vietnamese, increased sharply, although Korean children had been adopted by American families since the 1950s. Since the end of the Vietnam war, agencies have turned increasingly to South America. Agencies also tapped an important source within their midst—native American, Chicano, Puerto Rican, and black children.

Faced with the scarcity of adoptable white infants, white middle-income couples turned to one of the few alternatives available to them. Some held on to the slim chance that they would be able to adopt a "blue-ribbon" baby and placed their names on waiting lists. Sometimes years passed before they received a child. Others were not so lucky, and out of desperation turned to adoption brokers who operated out of the flourishing "black" and "gray" market. These couples paid thousands of dollars to brokers, who arranged independent adoptions, often through devious and illegal methods. Increasing numbers of adoptive applicants turned to the older white child. There was a time when the "older child" was considered to be two or three years old. Today the lack of babies on the market has driven the age up by several years in every major city in the country. The quieter the market, the more willing adoptive applicants are to take a child who, in a flourishing market, would not have been considered. Other prospective parents were willing to settle for a white infant with a mild correctable physical handicap. And still others turned to the healthy black and, more often, biracial infant.

5

VALUES IN CONFLICT: I
Black Autonomy

In no other area has the conflict in values in transracial adoption been more apparent than in the position taken by the black social workers, who emerged as the chief opponents of this practice. From 1965 to 1971, the relatively small number of transracial placements occurred without being widely noticed. It was not until there was a rapid increase in such placements—coupled with the emergence of a cultural pluralism perspective in child welfare, advocated by black social workers—that transracial adoption was defined as a problem of the social structure. By 1971, transracial adoption commanded widespread attention and was perceived by its opponents to be a challenge to existing institutional arrangements.

According to Fuller and Myers, central to all social problems are "conflicts in the value system of the culture."[1] In this context, social problems result when different groups in the society struggle to achieve their own vested interests. Rubington and Weinberg note that "the value-conflict perspective deals with what the world is and should be. When groups have confronted one another about these conflicting interpretations, the conditions for the development of a social problem have emerged.[2] It has been suggested further that "only after the interested parties continually focus attention on the values in conflict, set forth an alternative, mobilize a social base, and seek to achieve what they see as a solution, [that] the social problem becomes most apparent."[3]

However, such a process is usually accompanied by an effort by each group to inform the wider public of that group's values and to convince the public of their superiority.

Transracial adoption became a social problem when, on the one hand, adoptive parents and adoption agencies and, on the other, black social workers and black nationalists enunciated two fundamentally different sets of values. The values in conflict are racial integration, espoused by the adoptive families, and black autonomy, a preliminary step to the development of cultural pluralism, advocated by black social workers and their allies. Cultural pluralism is not alien to American society, since most ethnic groups in the United States have at various times organized themselves into power blocs in an effort to improve their status.[4] Newman notes: "Even as groups attempt to assimilate into the social, political and economic mainstream of a society, they must organize and develop a sense of their group distinctiveness in order to enter the social process."[5] Actually, blacks were late in arriving at the position where they perceived of themselves as a potential ethnic power bloc that would be able to achieve certain collective goals.

The transracial adoption controversy arose at a key historical point in America. In the late 1960s many blacks abandoned the civil rights movement for the more militant "black power" movement, which was, perhaps, the first major thrust in the black community toward developing cultural pluralism. The failure of blacks to achieve equality as rapidly as they had expected caused many to turn to autonomy, since they saw it as a more viable ideology and strategy.

According to Carmichael and Hamilton, *"before a group can enter the open society, it must first close ranks* . . . group solidarity is necessary before a group can operate effectively from a bargaining position of strength in a pluralistic society."[6] As a result of the growing social consciousness of blacks, autonomy became a highly politicized concept and was defined in terms of the political clout, the achievement of economic parity and self-sufficiency, and community control of schools. Ultimately, this thrust, which many labeled the "black power" movement, acted as a catalyst for the emergence of white ethnics, a major feature of American intergroup relations.[7]

As a preliminary step toward developing cultural pluralism, blacks viewed autonomy as the ability to exercise control on behalf of the welfare and interests of the group. One author notes, "While differences of opinion exist as to the extent to which autonomy from the larger society is necessary [ranging from local community control to the formation of a separate state], there is general agreement that, given the nature of American society, some degree of autonomy is necessary for self-determination."[8] Thus autonomy became the fundamental concept around which the militant black movement was organized. Autonomy became an all-encompassing ideology that eventually pervaded many areas of black life. Black autonomy also had a temporal quality, with some nationalists maintaining "temporary autonomy is sufficient, while others advocated permanent separation from the United States."[9]

As a newly emergent value, autonomy was, for some of its advocates, antithetical to the philosophy of integration into the mainstream of American society. They proclaimed that the assimilationist model that blacks had traditionally embraced should be rejected. Autonomy for this group represented racial separatism, and it was the separatist-influenced black social workers who were the most vocal in denouncing transracial adoption and in enunciating a value system counter to it. Others saw black autonomy as a temporary and transitional stage to the development of cultural pluralism which, in its ideal state, would function for blacks in much the same way it has functioned for European immigrants in the United States. This second group reasoned that once blacks had achieved a strong degree of group solidarity and distinctiveness, they would be ready to enter the mainstream as a unified force, from a position of power instead of weakness.

Black autonomy entered the realm of child welfare when the National Association of Black Social Workers declared transracial adoption to be a "lethal incursion on the black family [that] must be stopped."[10] In enunciating their philosophy of autonomy, the social workers argued: "Black children belong physically, psychologically and culturally in Black families in order that they receive the total sense of themselves . . ."[11] They rejected the notion that transracial adoption as seen by its advocates was the antithesis of racial segregation and would foster interracial co-operation.

As adherents to the black autonomy philosophy, the National Association of Black Social Workers moved transracial adoption from the realm of political neutrality and forced all those involved in any central or tangential way to confront what they thought to be the broad negative implications of this adoption practice. Adoption agencies could no longer make these placements without a major assessment and review of the social, political, and cultural factors involved. White adoptive parents and those who were considering adopting a black child were made to consider the issues being raised by the black social workers, and by doing so, to engage in a personal assessment of their own values and motivations, and the long-range implications of rearing a child of a different race.

At its third annual meeting in 1972, the National Association of Black Social Workers passed a resolution against transracial adoption. An excerpt from this resolution states:

. . . Black children should be placed only with Black families whether in foster care or for adoption. Black children belong physically, psychologically and culturally in Black families in order that they receive the total sense of themselves and develop a sound projection of their future. Human beings are products of their environment and develop their sense of values, attitudes and self concept within their family structures. Black children in white homes are cut off from the healthy development of themselves as Black people."[12]

This resolution touched off a nationwide, heated controversy, and its impact was soon observed in the practices of adoption agencies and among the parents who had adopted black children. The black social workers' position paper is credited by some with having brought about a decline in the numbers of children placed transracially by adoption agencies. Of course, the factors are more complicated, and a more detailed examination of such diverse variables will be examined below. Reporting on the black social workers' controversial resolution, the New York *Times* wrote:

Adoptions of black children by white families . . . were termed "a diabolical trick" by Audrey Russell of Philadelphia. She said, "Black children belong with black folk. This is a lethal incursion on the black family, just weakening us. It needs to be stopped."[13]

Other newspapers and magazines throughout the nation also picked up the story. It was not until the "issue" became public and moved from the completely private thoughts and sacred values of individuals that most Americans, perhaps, became aware of transracial adoption for the first time, since prior to then the small numbers had allowed these adoptions to go virtually unnoticed.

Transracial adoption, after being defined as a social problem, was debated by a sizable sector of blacks and was the subject of inquiry in major black publications.[14] The most outspoken opposition continues to come from the National Association of Black Social Workers, since their professional duties placed many of them in sustained close contact with black child welfare concerns as well as those welfare needs and priorities of the largely low-income black populace. As social workers, they are the one group of blacks who have probably had more firsthand contact with transracial adoption than any other, and perhaps it is for this reason that they emerged as the strongest opponents of this adoptive practice.

The black social workers' attack on transracial placements evoked sharp reactions from all quarters. White parents were understandably upset and they reacted to the attacks, some with equal force and others with quiet resignation. Many took the criticism personally, by accusing the social workers of forming hasty judgments about their inability to be good parents without personally knowing them. Others went on the offensive by attacking the "reverse racism," vowing that the black social workers would never be successful in accomplishing their alleged aim—that of taking their children from them. Still others confided that they would not have adopted had they known this controversy was going to erupt.

From black supporters of the social workers' position came the expected responses, ranging from viewing transracial placements as a reflection of the lack of concern the agencies have in finding black homes, to a "genocidal plot" designed to destroy the black race.

The most critical issue raised by the black social workers was that white parents were unable to transmit a black identity to the child. A corollary principle, the social workers stated, is the matter of survival in a "hostile, racist society." In their position paper, they state:

> The socialization process of every child begins at birth. Included in the socialization process is the child's cultural heritage which is an important segment of the total process. This must begin at the earliest moment, otherwise our children will not have the background and knowledge which is necessary to survive in a racist society. This is impossible if the child is placed with white parents in a white environment.[15]

Two weeks after this resolution was passed, Audrey Russell, a member of the Transracial Adoption Task Force, appeared before a meeting of the North American Conference on Adoptable Children in St. Louis. Russell, then a Philadelphia social worker, told this parents' group: "A child achieves his identity from his own family—it is the primary teaching facility. You can take care of a black child, give him shelter and feed him, but you cannot give him a black identity because you don't have it yourself to give."[16] At that same meeting, some black social workers disagreed with the NABSW's position. The New York *Times* reports that an unnamed social worker applauded white families for stepping forward when her "own brothers and sisters ran from the responsibility."[17] Other black social workers, particularly those working in adoption, supported her. Many blacks, while sympathizing with the black social workers' position paper, feel that many black children would remain in foster and institutional care if they were not adopted into white families. Hence, a common sentiment is "a white home is better than no home." This sentiment was expressed by a black educator, who wrote in *Encore* magazine:

> I respect the concept and practice of the Black family for Black children, but I strongly believe that Black children should not remain in foster homes or institutions if a white family is able to

adopt them. I base my position on the principle that every child should be given the opportunity of a home and family, since it is the love and affection of the family for the child that is paramount.[18]

Amid the controversy, several major issues, themes, and problems predominate.

The most recurrent theme expressed against transracial adoption involves black identity. The black social workers argue that the need for the child to understand his or her racial and ethnic identity is of primary importance. Moreover, they do not feel that white parents are able to transmit black identity to the child simply because they are white and, by definition, have not experienced what it means to be black. The NABSW's position paper speaks to this point:

> Identity grows on the three levels of all human development, the physical, psychological and cultural and the nurturing of the self identity is a prime function of the family. The incongruence of a white family performing this function for a black child is easily recognized. The physical factor stands to maintain that child's difference from his family.[19]

In describing the socialization process of transracially adopted children, they state:

> He [black child] assumes . . . their posture and frame of reference, different from and often antithetical to that of his ethnics which can only result in conflict and confusion when he does become aware of the social system in which he lives.[20]

The concern with identity grows out of the black "autonomy" philosophy, which considers it imperative that positive self-concepts be developed before the individual can have the security, confidence, and sense of adequacy necessary for exercising control over his or her welfare and that of their group. They are intensely interested in the development of black identity in children whose tradition, they maintain, has long been that of negative self-concepts and feelings of powerlessness.

In speaking of the identity problem, Cenie Williams, past president of the NABSW, alludes that even black parents have difficulty transmitting positive identity to their children:

> We believe that white parents have difficulty in helping Black kids develop a positive self-image, something they need in order to be healthy and effective in this society. It takes the average Black male more than 21 years to really develop a feeling of manhood and a positive self-image because so many obstacles intervene in its development. In a white family with Black children, the problem is even more difficult.[21]

Opponents of transracial adoptions say there is such uniqueness to being black, that it embodies such an esoteric quality, that one has to *be* black in order to understand and transmit its meanings. Further, they believe that the black identity derives from one having been a *victim* of racism and poverty. As one remarked in *Essence* magazine, "Never in a billion years will any white really know what it's like to be a Black! So how in the world could white parents give a Black child that deep-down knowledge and feeling of Blackness?"[22] In the same magazine article a young mother of three said: "The Black child can only be brought up within his own environment because of a history which is engraved on our Blackness. Our race shows a story of slavery, segregation, roaches and rats, but it is also a story of human strength and weaknesses."[23]

An equally important corollary to black identity is the black survival skill, which the opponents of transracial adoption feel a child must have in order to cope with the discrimination practices of a racist society. In other contexts, various writers have taken up the preoccupation that one finds in black communities with the concern for survival.[24] According to Blauner, "When black people talk about surviving, they are even more pointedly referring to the problem of maintaining life, dignity, and sanity in a racist society."[25] There is a strong notion among blacks that the larger society, which has traditionally blocked social and economic opportunities for blacks, is to be regarded with caution. Hence, children should be socialized at an early age to acquire various adaptive techniques for *surviving* when presented with problems emanating from racism and poverty. In their position paper the black social workers place survival skills within the context of socialization. "Black children are taught . . . highly sophisticated coping techniques to deal with racist practices perpetrated by individuals and institutions. These coping techniques become successfully integrated into ego functions and can be incorporated only through the process of developing positive identification with significant Black others. Only a Black family can transmit the emotional and sensitive subtleties of perception and reaction essential for a Black child's survival in a racist society."[26] Black survival techniques are thought to comprise a broad repertoire of psychological attitudes and behavioral acts on the overt and covert level. They include gestures, sentiments, feelings, languages, and physical manipulations.

Strategies of survival are viewed on the *external* and *internal* levels—that is, certain blacks often refer to the ability to adapt and defend themselves in the mainstream society (external) as well as within the black society (internal). Rainwater discusses the "survival strategies" of the black who interacts with his peers within the ghetto.[27]

There has been an increased concern with "survival techniques" in recent years of black politicization. Many black politicians speak frequently of *survival*, and view such problems as police brutality, imprisonment of blacks, and birth control campaigns aimed at welfare clients as *threats* to black survival. Blauner states that the preoccupation with "making it" grows out of the victimized status of poverty and racism.[28]

According to the proponents of black survival skills, they are the creation of blacks, and need only be used by blacks; their transmission is, therefore, limited to those who have lived the black experience. Thus survival skills go hand in hand with one's identity. Writing in *Encore* magazine, one young black man put it this way: "What do white people know about anything that Black parents do to instill in our young the Black pride in our color and heritage that it takes to ready them for the innumerable assaults on their minds that are sure to come from the world outside the home? . . . By virtue of being white, white people cannot possibly provide the insight required to explain the complexities and subtleties of three-hundred years of genocide."[29] In a perceptive article titled "Dilemmas of Biracial Adoptions," Leon Chestang, a black social work professor, poses a series of questions that the black child and his white parents will be faced with:

> Coping in this society requires the development of adaptive modes that provide protection from the destructive effects of society. What hazards to the development of these modes lie in estrangement from the black community during the formative years? Can white parents equip a black child for the inevitable assaults on his personality from a society that considers his color to be enough reason to reject him? Can they learn to do this without having internalized the duality of character so necessary for survival? How can the black child learn the necessary maneuvering, seduction, self-enhancement, through redefinition, and many other tactics taught by black parents, by word and deed, directly and indirectly?[30]

The transracially adopted child has been regarded as the victim of improper socialization. Critics caution that the child will become marginal to both the black and the white worlds, because he or she will not have been adequately prepared to function in either. The social workers say that these children will not know how to function as a black because their white parents will not have known how to give them a black identity and survival skills; and although they will have a white identity, whites will refuse to accept them because of their color. Chestang suggests that this "bicultural" child will probably be regarded as a "freak" by blacks and whites and will be harshly subjected to a series of lifelong identity crises. Thus the children will never be comfortable with their identity because they will not be granted the opportunity by blacks or whites to adapt in their worlds.[31]

One author notes that the greatest test the transracially adopted child must meet involves "being raised by persons who [can] not teach her where or when to expect the knives of racial injustice to appear or to cut. To have these people as family means having no place to withdraw except within oneself. And to miss mingling and being nourished by people, who because they look like you, have had the same experiences."[32]

The black social worker critics argue that these parents who adopt because of their compassion for the "hard to place" children have good intentions, are undoubtedly child-centered families, and have a genuine interest in doing what they think is in the best interests of the child, such as teaching them black history and attending seminars and discussion groups. However, they criticize these parents' child-rearing practices as having an artificial aura more akin to experimentation rather than a more natural, instinctive, and spontaneous process. Such practices, they argue, are unnatural and are, thus, destined to have negative effects on the growing child. Almost brutally they attack these practices:

> White parents . . . seek out special help with their parenting; help with acquiring the normal and usually instinctual parental behaviors inherent in the cultural and psychological development of children. It is tantamount to having to be taught to do what comes naturally.[33]

In referring to the "deliberate" nature of this phenomenon, the National Association of Black Social Workers' position paper states:

> Special programming in learning to handle Black children's hair, learning Black culture, "trying to become Black," puts normal family activities in the form of special family projects to accommodate the odd member of the family.[34]

To be the "odd family member" means that the child will suffer from the feeling that he or she is abnormal. All of the special treatment they are accorded may heighten their awareness of themselves as different.

To summarize, one critic put it this way: "What is a child going to think if you make such a big issue and teaching experiment out of everything involving him, from combing his kinky hair to reading him a bedtime story on black history?"

Some critics have cynically labeled this so-called special programming as the "pet mentality," or the "cute kid" syndrome.

They argue that some of these whites view the black adopted child in the same way as they regard their animals. Wendell Rivers, a St. Louis clinical psychologist who was interviewed for this study, explained how the "pet" syndrome works: "Dogs, cats, and birds become members of families and they are taken care of quite well. But there are boundaries that are placed upon these animals that assign them to a nonhuman role. The same kind of mentality operates with some whites adopting black children."[35] Although he conceded that these children receive good physical care, he argues that there are emotional and intellectual boundaries, in many cases, that the child is not allowed to cross. One of the most significant boundaries, it is thought, will come during adolescence when dating and intimate relationships are formed, and the parents must carefully examine their deeper feelings toward such questions as interracial marriage.

The "cute kid" also becomes the object of "special programming" in bringing up these children. Those who feel that these adoptions are undesirable say that too many whites adopt because they become attached to a particular child whom they may first be introduced to by a photograph in the newspaper or on television, or by some other chance occurrence. Some black social workers have accused the white parents of viewing this particular child as an exception to other blacks. Parents who become attracted to the "cute kid" must someday live with the fact that the "kid" has become an adolescent, and later, an adult. The question becomes: Can the initial attraction turn into the positive and necessary qualities that must exist between parent and child so as to enhance the healthy emotional development and functioning of the child within his or her adoptive family?

There is a great amount of antagonism toward those whites whom black social workers feel are motivated by their desire to remedy the alleged pathology in the black community. Such individuals, the social workers maintain, are operating under racist assumptions and will be detrimental to the child. A black male social worker told me in an interview that parents feel they are "rescuing" the child from a life of misery that the child would be subjected to if they did not adopt him or her. It is assumed by the critics that parents who have this "rescue fantasy" are far less concerned about the welfare of the *individual* child than about the cause they have embraced—taking in a homeless, impoverished black child whom blacks themselves did not want to adopt. Such a child is labeled "hard to place," which by definition places him or her in the lower stratum of adoptable children.

These parents, the critics argue, are anxious to do something that would "uplift" the black community and to "pull it out of its alleged disorganization and decay." A black male social worker who has worked in an adoption agency in Detroit said, "I think it is very significant that these white couples come into the agency and say 'I want to adopt a black child because of the deficiencies in the black community.'"

These parents are said to be naïve and guilty of eventually causing more harm to the child than good. One social worker put it this way:

Many of the white adopting couples operate under the racist assumption that they can do a better job in raising Black children than we can; many are solely motivated by some distorted rescue fantasy; and many view it as a status symbol.

From the interviews conducted with psychiatrists and psychologists for this study, one of the portraits they introduced of the parents who adopt transracially is that they are operating with a "rescue mission" that is driven by their collective guilt. It is felt that some adoptive parents have this guilt because they feel responsible for the racial injustice whites have inflicted upon blacks. They become the carriers of guilt and seek to do something that can relieve them of it. According to Alvin Poussaint, author of *Black Child Care*, "transracial adoption becomes a historical response for the sins of their forefathers and provides them with commitment to a cause, which can be a catharsis for their culpability."[36] Comer, a Yale child psychiatrist, suggested that it can provide a "denial of racism which they can prove publicly by adopting." It is as though the parents are saying, "Look at us. We are not like the other whites because we even adopted a black child."[37] Robert Williams, past president of the National Associ-

ation of Black Psychologists and a clinical psychologist, elaborates
on the collective guilt syndrome:

> There is a lot of collective guilt involved in some of these cases
> either by commission or omission. These parents say, "I haven't
> been doing enough and here is a problem." They have this kind
> of social work and missionary zeal. "I've got to do something,
> and I just heard on the radio that there are a lot of little black
> kids who don't have homes, so let's adopt one." That is by omis-
> sion. And the other is one of commission where they have been
> engaged in some racist practices in the past, or their parents are
> still racist and they've got to do something in order to undo these
> racial feelings. They get involved in that way. Another type is
> people who want to become experts in the black experience and
> think they will adopt a black child and this will provide them
> with an entree into the black community. They say "See, here I
> am." I know of such a couple. . . .[38]

Many of the opponents of transracial adoption willingly concede that there are whites who care about the welfare of black
children. But, they ask, does this require that they adopt them?
Aren't there other, more satisfactory ways to express their caring?
Andrew Billingsley, author of the book on black child welfare, *Children of the Storm*, suggests that they "provide the financial support
which would enable a black family to adopt."[39] Others have pro-
posed that they lobby for progressive child welfare legislation, including subsidies, and to act as advocates for black child welfare by
working to eliminate the restrictive adoption agency guidelines that
eliminate the many black applicants, including low-income,
middle-aged, and single persons. Still others urge concerned whites
to try to change the racially biased attitudes of other whites toward
school desegregation and to work for the abolition of housing and
employment discrimination—thereby strengthening the ability of
black parents to adequately provide for their own children. In view
of these kinds of contributions they could make, the critics say the
white parents are "copping out" by adopting the child. It is, they
argue, the far easier road to take, since it does not involve the alteration of racially discriminatory practices in the social structure.

Many blacks readily admit that whites who adopt transracially
probably have great love and affection for their children. But they

caution that "love is not enough," and as a woman put it, "a home and love are not enough to pay for loss of identity." A member of the National Association of Black Social Workers' transracial adoption task force put it succinctly when she stated:

> We don't always feel that love is enough. Our concern is not that white people can't love black children. They can. [But what is more important] is a sense of security, and of being a part of a historical ethnic family base. These are essential to developing a black identity, and these children are denied that.[40]

The same attitude holds for white parents being able to provide a comfortable home with adequate food, clothing, shelter, and the opportunity for a middle-class education. So strong is the feeling that black identity and survival skills are critical to the child's socialization, that Cenie Williams, past president of the National Association of Black Social Workers, stated that he would prefer that black children remain in institutions, foster homes, or be placed with black welfare families than to be placed in white middle-class homes.[41] In response to this writer's question regarding whether *any* whites could teach black culture and provide the child with a black identity, a black social worker put it this way: "You can't teach what you don't know."[42] This seems to get to the essence of the views expressed by the opponents of transracial adoptions.

What happens to the children as they grow up? Are the adoptive parents as likely to remain enthusiastic and committed to them as they were when they were lovable babies? Are they cognizant of the long-range problems and consequences of their acts? Those who denounce these adoptions are especially concerned about the adolescence of these youngsters. What of the parents' expectations of the child's physical, emotional, and intellectual development and achievement? Are the parents concerned, at the time of adoption, about the child being able to meet such critical future expectations? Will the parents be able to continue to identify and empathize with this child as though he or she is indistinguishable from their biological child? And if not, what will be the consequences if the child falls short of their expectations? None of these issues are considered at the time the decision is being made to adopt, the opponents argue. They further contend that if they were considered, fewer would adopt. Rather, the parents are only concerned with the here and now. Louise Beasley, a social work professor, cautioned:

> When [whites] adopt a very young black child, they are concerned with the here and now. But a little black boy is going to grow up and be a big black man. These kids don't stay babies all the time. They are going to have to deal with these kids as they grow up and try and find themselves in a society that is oppressive to blacks. These families are not equipped to handle that in the way that black families are able to develop and transmit a highly sophisticated mechanism of survival in a white racist society. As long as these kids are little and cute then they are non-threatening to everyone. But they don't remain babies.[43]

That they do not remain babies is a foregone conclusion.

The political and social issues raised by the hard-core denouncers insist that they are a threat to the survival of the black family, and for some, can cause a "dilution" of the Negroid race. While most opponents, if pressed, will admit that these placements involve such a small number of black children that no serious threat is imposed, a highly vocal minority insist that actual numbers are irrelevant, and that they should be viewed symbolically.

The fear of what has been called "cultural genocide," which some may perceive as a serious threat to black autonomy, stems from the recent era of black ethnic pride. Militant blacks have, over the past decade, waged a cultural movement aimed at reclaiming the African heritage and affirming the black American culture. Transracial adoptions, like interracial marriages, are viewed as threatening the further development of this identification process. These adoptions are also viewed as a menace to the right and ability of blacks to keep, rear, and maintain control over children of their racial group. That these children have been adopted by whites is tantamount to them having been taken against the wishes of their elders. Taking it for granted that the child will be socialized in a white world instead of a black world, the black social workers are worried that the child may eventually wish to be white, and that he or she will never have any identification within the black community. Commenting on this potential problem, a young black man told this writer, "It is our duty to spare these children from becoming 'freaks.' If they are adopted by white people they will have black faces with white minds. They won't know who they are, where they came from, or where they are going. I will truly feel sorry for them."

It is in this context that the harshest opponents of transracial adoption have accused the white parents of having deliberately organized and waged a conspiracy to commit "cultural genocide" against Afro-Americans.

While only several hundred black children were adopted by whites annually, some perceived it as a major threat to the black family.[44] They feel that whites are deliberately interfering with and retarding the goal of achieving positive self-concepts that are being realized by many blacks for the first time. This is the first generation of young black parents in American history who are deeply absorbed in socializing their offspring to have strong positive racial self-concepts. At no other time has there been such an absorption with destroying racial stereotypes. For these blacks, the adoption of black children by whites is a carefully planned and executed plot to destroy the black race. A young black states it this way:

> Transracial adoption is one of the many conspiracies being waged against Black people. It is one of the white man's latest moves to wipe out the last vestiges of our culture if not us. He made progress in brainwashing us and our young with his churches, his schools, and birth control. And now he wishes to use his latest trick of mental genocide.[45]

A newspaper even termed it a genocidal plot designed to decrease the strength of the black race, and imputed strange if not preposterous motives to whites who adopt transracially. In the newspaper *Muhammad Speaks*, Chester Sheard wrote:

> It is only natural that the white male, being unable to produce a child of color, would be less inclined to foster any idea of adopting a Black child and possibly would resent the move. It is con-

ceivable that the male's racist inclinations would be carried over after the adoption of the Black child, especially the Black male child. . . . Being unable or unwilling to openly make the effort to deal outright with Black men, many Caucasian women have used the Black baby to partially gratify their needs.[46]

The alleged plot is also thought to involve preferential adoption of male children for the expressed purpose of brainwashing a future generation of black men.[47] There is no evidence that whites prefer adopting males rather than females. In fact, some adoption agencies report that applicants frequently express a preference for girls. It is highly doubtful that whites who adopt black children have deliberately done so in order to contribute to the destruction of the black family.

The "genocidal" plot revolves around the potential threat to the development of black political, educational, economic, and religious institutions, with the black family being the basic institution around which these revolve. As a "social" institution, the black family, with its value system and socialization patterns, is viewed as being severely threatened by transracial adoptions, since these adoptions theoretically remove black children from the care and control of the black community. In this context, they were viewed as a threat to the development of black autonomy, and for others such as Audrey Russell, they posed an even more serious threat:

"The issues of nation building and identity present the crucial base for our concern about the abominable program of transracial adoption of our children. We must all arise in vigorous, vehement and voracious opposition to this practice and exert all efforts to stemming the tide."[48] The central issue is one of black autonomy. It involves the opportunity of blacks to rear their offspring from birth to adulthood. As Cenie Williams, past president of the National Association of Black Social Workers, stated, "Black people, like any other race, have the responsibility to take care of their own. It is a natural instinct for any race of people to attempt to affirm themselves."[49]

As a social and political argument, the "cultural genocide" theory is flawed with inaccurate information and a kind of hysterical reaction to what I consider a relatively nonthreatening phenomenon. Far too few black children have been adopted by whites for a threat to have been posed to any significant segment of the black population. An estimated fifteen thousand transracial placements in the United States certainly will not reverse the tide of ethnic pride, nor will they inflict any significant damage to the black family institution.

It is generally felt that the protest of the black social workers and their allies has had an effect on curtailing transracial placements. However, they eventually came under criticism by those who argued that if they felt so strongly that black children should not be adopted by whites, then they must create viable alternatives for these children's welfare. This meant finding homes. It was at this point that they began to organize programs geared toward finding black parents for the waiting children. (This point will be discussed more fully in Chapter 12.)

6

VALUES IN CONFLICT: II
Racial Integration

Ever since the black social workers and other foes of transracial adoptions launched their attack, white parents have been forced to defend, rationalize, and even reconsider having adopted across racial lines. When they adopted most did not know they would be plunged into the midst of a heated controversy and have their motives become suspect. One mother said, "If we had known our adoption was going to cause us so much trouble, we never would have gone through with it." The fact that they were surprised and even shocked that they would be criticized for adopting a black child is an indication of how unprepared they were to consider the long-range implications of the social and political issues raised by blacks. Although many of the parents have tried to shun the controversy by retreating further into their white suburban enclaves, others have agreed with many of the issues raised, and still others have responded by issuing countercharges.

Outspoken defenders of transracial placements are well informed of the arguments of their critics. Having read the black social workers' resolution and other literature, they have also heard them deliver their antitransracial adoption speeches. A few have had face-to-face confrontations with their adversaries, while others have engaged in constructive dialogue with the hope of eliminating some of the prevailing hostilities. But for the most part, the black social workers, adoptive parents, child welfare workers (including those in adoption), clinicians, and those allied with each remain far apart on many of the basic issues, as will be discussed below.

Transracial adoptions symbolize, for many parents, their belief in racial integration. It sets the living example that people can love each other and live together in harmony, without regard for racial differences. They acknowledge that, although transracial adoption will have but a small impact on creating their idealized integrated society, it is, nevertheless, an expression of their commitment to the philosophy of the "brotherhood of man."

Herein one notes the sharpest conflict in values between the parents and other supporters of transracial adoption, and their critics—especially those who embrace the ideology of "black autonomy" in child welfare. Those parents who view transracial adoption as building a multiracial society are expressing a value that poses a strong and irreconcilable conflict with the black social workers and others who are committed to black autonomy.

Although parents who adopt transracially come from a vast range of backgrounds, have had widely different experiences, and had different motivations for adopting, as a group they by and large adhere to the goal of achieving a racially integrated society, and they are also strongly committed to improving the welfare of needy children. In a national survey of transracially adoptive parents conducted by Nutt and Snyder, "family formation is an intentional valuative act. Whether or not its ramifications are fully understood or consciously intended, a transracial adoption is a personal statement of what the society ought to be. The broader involvement of transracially adoptive parents, whether individually or as a group, in effecting changes in child welfare practices is probably the most immediate example of a wider commitment to the welfare of a community."[1]

Many of these parents have a commitment to the goals of an integrated society whereby individuals are judged on their own merit instead of being evaluated on their racial group membership. Their commitment is also to justice, equality, understanding, and acceptance of all people, without regard for their racial, cultural, religious, or other background. In this sense, their lives are generally guided by a strong sense of purpose, and by living out their commitments, many of them are also idealistic, independent of the views of other family members and very family centered. Transracial adoptive parents have a strong commitment to a value that is no longer held strongly by a fairly significant segment of the black population. Their emphasis upon universal brotherhood and acceptance of individual differences comes at a time in the social, political, and cultural arena of this society when many blacks are adhering to a black autonomy ideology. There is a tendency for these blacks to view individual whites as part of a collectivity and to assign them the label of "racist." For one to have adopted a black child is insignificant to such blacks, since they frequently impute a variety of sinister motives to these parents. The parents are accused of having adopted with the intention of destroying black culture, of seeking to weaken the black family, of projecting their psychological needs and fantasies onto black children, especially male children, and of "taking" black children away from the black community to brainwash them. Such blacks usually have rendered their verdict long before meeting a white parent who has adopted a black child. If face-to-face contact does occur, the opponents do not ordinarily alter their attitudes.

Because the two groups are operating at different levels of awareness, commitment, and ideological and philosophical persuasion, there has been little ground for consensus. Whereas black social workers emphasize group solidarity, political *control*, and a developing social consciousness among blacks *as black people*, the white parents emphasize the value of the nuclear family unit and the necessity for it to be allowed to develop and function to its fullest capacity in the manner in which the parents decide. Various studies have concluded that these parents are more child-centered and maintain that the welfare of the child should be placed above all else. They reject the idea that politics has a place in child welfare concerns. Child socialization, they maintain, is to be divorced from the broader social and political issues of the society. Nutt and Snyder found that transracially adoptive parents view "the world as a place to be made humane. They have grown up in a world [of] power and control, and found lacking their application through the conventional institutions of society. [They] are refocusing on the family as the locus for creating a new definition of the world, one of humanity, trust and mature love."[2] Of course, it is considerably easier to reject power and control if one has been exposed to these factors or has been socialized in a culture where one had access to these. It is vastly different, however, if this access has been denied.

Understandably, the adoptive parents and agency personnel who feel that these placements are in the best interest of the child are disturbed by the criticisms, criticisms often made by persons who are complete strangers to them. Thus some parents have countercharged that the social workers are irresponsible in their attacks—that they are too abstract and theoretical about these important issues affecting *tangible* children. The majority of parents interviewed in this study are in agreement that child welfare, including adoption, is first and foremost a personal and individual matter affecting the child and his family, and only secondarily should the sociopolitical and cultural factors be considered. Therefore, they argue, it should not be placed in the framework of and debated on the broader societal level.

Some parents who expressed confusion over the issues raised by the social workers were perplexed as to how the social workers and other advocates of black autonomy could so authoritatively discuss their inability to rear healthy black children without knowing them as individuals. A father in St. Louis who adopted a black girl put it this way: "If you heard them talking you'd think they knew us intimately. The sad truth is I doubt they ever had a face-to-face discussion with any white who has adopted a black kid." A Washington, D.C., mother said: "I'll bet none of them have kids. They sound like they don't know what parenthood is all about. They're too busy making a political issue out of these little babies' welfare."

Many parents felt that the black social workers were too politicized. The parents were appalled that adoption was cast into the arena of political controversy. So strong was their disagreement with their foes on this issue that they accused them of using the children to try to achieve broader political goals. They called the black social workers' position paper nothing more than a "protest" statement. They felt that the black social workers' objective was only to stop transracial placements and not to find homes for the children. A mother in Missouri asked: "Why are they spending all of their time attacking us with their rhetoric instead of canvassing the black community to find homes for these kids?" The parents strongly believed that the test of the social workers' sincerity about the welfare of black children would be their ability to find black parents for them. "Anything less," according to a father who described himself as an "angry attacker" of the black social workers' statement, "is pure unadulterated rhetoric." A mother felt the same way, as indicated by her comment: "I think they should be more concerned with these little black babies rather than with their theories."

There are some parents who object to the possessiveness the black social workers display toward the black children who have been adopted by whites. They argued that no group in the society has the right to imply ownership of its offspring. A father who is a medical doctor in Maryland said, "The black social workers' statement constantly referred to them as 'our children,' as if somehow they had acquired ownership of these children by virtue of the fact that they were black. That bothered me a great deal because I don't think children get owned by people because of their skin color or even by giving birth. To talk about large groups of children as 'our children' somehow seems to mean the children are controlled by somebody. I don't find that very sensible."

While the charges and countercharges are often rather general in content, some of the positions the parents have taken are as carefully conceived as the black social workers' resolution.

Transracially adoptive parents believe strongly that their act of commitment and conscience to a more humane system of child welfare has been beneficial to them as well as to the child. Indeed, many parents maintain that it has perhaps done more for them as a family than for their adopted child. They cite such things as an expansion of their knowledge about black life and culture, and enhancing their ability to provide love and affection to an individual who is assumed by the society to be "different" from themselves. One parent remarked, "The gain of loving another person is loving yourself more. . . . just by sharing my love with my black child has enhanced my view of myself and my behavior around other people." Other parents cite a change in their racial attitudes as well. This includes a deeper sensitivity to the problems of all blacks. As one of these parents stated,

> . . . You don't just grow up in a racist country like America and be white and not be racist. It is not possible. I think my black child has helped me.

The most moving expression heard by the researcher during the course of this study came from a parent in Minnesota who said that adopting a black child had made him identify with other blacks so much that whenever he saw police brutality against blacks on television, he wanted to strike out against whites and come to the defense of "my son's people." Perhaps the most important value attached to these adoptions is that these parents perceive a strong positive influence on the lives of their biological children. They feel that the goals they project, and this philosophical commitment, will be achieved much more by their children, who will have learned to accept and love people of different backgrounds through their having had a black sibling. They expect their biological children to have a strong sense of racial justice, equality, and to abhor racial discrimination. They value this outcome highly, because their children will, in the process, also develop a stronger sense of security and well-being for themselves as individuals. A few parents feel that the occasional insults their children experience will also make them tougher and more independent. Of course, no parent ideally looks forward to his or her child having to experience racial slurs and other insults. But these parents view this experience as a painful lesson that their children will learn about the unpleasant aspects of their society.

One of the accusations made against the social workers and other foes of transracial adoption is that they are black racists. Advocates of these adoptions feel the black foes are antiwhite, much too abstract and theoretical about racial matters, and instead of focusing on the needs of individual children, they resorted to making a "political" protest statement. Some parents are embittered over the controversy black social workers have aroused because it places them in the midst of it and forces them to defend their actions. They had considered their adoption to be a personal statement of their commitment to better child welfare services, equality, and an integrated society. When the social workers challenged their right to parent black children, and when their motives for having adopted were attacked by individuals who accused them of being racists—individuals with whom they had never had personal or other contact—some parents began to retreat, while others fought back. Had not their very behavior been sufficient proof that they were not racist, but that they believed in equality and a fair opportunity for blacks? Indeed, they reasoned that the act of making a lifetime commitment to care for, protect, and love a child who is unrelated to them by birth, and who happens also to be a member of an entirely different race, should have been more than enough proof that they are committed and worthy of respect and trust from blacks.

Parents also argued that the problem these adoptions might cause for the child are greatly exaggerated by the black social workers. The parents feel that the level and breadth of the controversy is disproportionate to the actual numbers of children being adopted. The majority of the parents interviewed did not feel that the adoptions pose any significant threat to the black family and black culture because of the very small numbers of children involved. As one parent remarked, "I just can't see these adoptions as having any great cultural significance. . . . I just see it as human interaction between a relatively limited number of people. And it sure doesn't pose a threat." In addition to the question of numbers, there is also the concern that the black social workers are arguing on a theoretical level, and that their position is based on political assumptions and concerns. For these parents, the real problem is the individual child whose needs should be met by a set of parents, regardless of their racial background. They feel that it is an easy way out for black social workers to raise the political questions without following them up with the necessary programs to insure more black adoptions.

Black social workers have also been accused of being too ego involved and of having rendered an absurd position. A couple in a large midwestern city told the researcher:

MRS. JACOBS: They [black social workers] stated that the adoptions are a form of genocide which I can't even deal with. I don't think that because fifteen thousand children have white parents, a threat is being posed to anyone. We feel that we are raising our daughter to be able to plug into the black community at any level and at any time she wants to. It's just a political statement.

MR. JACOBS: It's an absurd statement [the black social workers' position paper]. It may only serve as an ego trip for the people who wrote it. I don't think it represents a significant segment of the black population. It's really an insult to the black family because the black family isn't going to fall apart because some whites have black children. It's also a statement that shows a crude insensitivity to the needs of children who don't have homes, whether they are black homes or white homes or in-between homes. I think it shows up in foster homes or institutions. It doesn't deal with the issues at hand, which is child and human development.

It appalls me that social workers know so little about human development that they would prefer that children grow up in institutions and in foster care. Further along in the statement there is a mention of the black association of social workers' New York chapter having a membership of one thousand who could apply for children. It doesn't say anything about social workers as parents. It just says that they are black and therefore they are qualified. This is somewhat upsetting because it is poor social work practice and they should know better.

There is the persistent theme expressed among the parents that black critics are not very concerned about the individual child. One parent remarked, "I think they should be more concerned with these little black babies rather than with their theories."

In a different context, white parents have often counterattacked the black social workers and other critics by asserting that if the critics had adopted homeless black children, there would not have been a need for whites to do so. "Why should they criticize us for doing something they weren't willing to do themselves?" asked a St. Louis mother.

In defending why they adopted, a mother in Maryland said, "When we adopted Betsy no one was adopting these black infants. Statistics show that there are between forty thousand and sixty thousand minority race children available. If they had all been placed in black homes, we wouldn't have adopted. But they weren't, and these black social workers weren't adopting them either. Maybe in five years there won't be the need. But five years may be too late; they need a home now."

Therefore, the most provocative countercharge the parents have made is that if the social workers really care about the welfare of black children, why don't they adopt? It is a challenging criticism that cannot be ignored, and a charge that is difficult for the foes of transracial placements to answer. Before this problem is resolved it demands personal or group commitment to the cause. Countless parents asked, "If the black social workers believe so strongly that these children should be in black homes, then why don't *they* provide some of the homes instead of leaving it up to the 'black community' to do so?" A black who advocated transracial adoption wrote in *Encore* magazine, "I don't see many of these black social workers adopting black children. . . . By the way, is Cenie Williams [former head of the National Association of Black Social Workers] adopting any children?"[3] in response to Williams' outspoken criticism.

There have always been a lot of misinformation and myths surrounding the transracial adoption phenomenon. A myth that has had some far-reaching consequences is the one discussed earlier and held by many white parents that maintains that blacks do not adopt. As some of the parents in this study indicated, they adopted black children because blacks have no tradition for doing so, and the children would not have been adopted. It is difficult to ascertain how and where the myth originated. It may be that adoption agencies contributed to it by not actively recruiting black applicants. Thus when few children were legally adopted by blacks, this was used as evidence that they do not adopt. The end result is that some parents adopted clearly for the wrong reasons.

The placements were made in the beginning with a minimum of planning. Inadequate screening of the parents, very few and oftentimes no supportive services (counseling, etc.), and almost no follow-up beyond the required were characteristic of most of the early adoptions. It was only recently that adoption agencies began to evaluate seriously the long-range consequences of transracial placements and to become more concerned with the characteristics and motivations of applicants. The agencies' policies did more to contribute to the misconceptions regarding blacks and adoption than to inform. Therefore it is not surprising that a great many of these white parents were motivated by the need to provide homes to children whom they felt would be the least likely to be adopted. It is also likely that some of the transracially adoptive parents approached the adoption with a "rescue fantasy."

Parents take pride in having adopted for some of the same reasons for which they are criticized. While the black social workers have attacked them for adopting for "social" reasons, the parents say that it should be regarded as a social contribution to adopt a "hard to place" child. One father asked, "What is wrong with saying you want to adopt a child who might not otherwise be adopted. Why do the black social workers say we have a 'rescue fantasy' for doing this?" Thus the parents insist that it is not socially or personally useful to "stand in line and wait for one of the 'blue-ribbon' babies," as several parents put it. Such a child is in great demand and is, therefore, assured of a permanent home. As one mother said, "Why adopt a child who is no different from the three kids we already had? We had no desire for another white child. We never went to the agency with that kind of request." They maintain that it is quite acceptable to view the adoption as a social contribution so long as this is not the primary motivating force. One must, first of all, have a desire for family, as well as love and value the individual child. And although one may have been guided by social consciousness to adopt, the child should *never* be treated as a social cause. In accordance with the values of these parents, providing a home to the child means that the parents want to share with the child their material resources, provide him or her with love and security, and assume financial responsibility for their education, medical care, and other parental responsibilities. Very importantly, the parents argue that unlike rearing a foster child, adoptive parents are assuming a lifelong obligation to the child that cannot be revoked. It involves changing the structure, content, and interaction of the nuclear and extended families. Transracial adoptions are representative of the departure from the monolithic, traditional family forms. They redefine the family's kinship unit, and the adoptions also affect the family legally, socially, biologically, and racially. According to one father, "It expands the gene pool of our offspring." "It would have been very easy for us to have settled down with our two biological children and lived happily ever after," said a father in the Midwest. "But that would not have been fulfilling. What would happen to all the homeless children if everyone were so selfish?" To be able to see a child that one has adopted grow and develop, they say, is the greatest sense of fulfillment one could have. And if this kind of social contribution is inappropriate, then so be it.

7

RACIAL IDENTITY

Racial identity has been the most controversial issue and has presented the most serious challenge to the adoptive parents. Many can easily dismiss the criticisms regarding their motives for adopting; few dismiss the questions that have been raised regarding white parents' ability to socialize the child to have a black identity and survival skills.

Erik Erikson, the pioneer of the concept of identity, defines it as "the creation of a sense of sameness, a unity of personality now felt by the individual and recognized by others as having consistency in time—of being, as it were, an irreversible historical fact."[1] Erikson emphasizes the importance of *individual* and *communal* identities if one is to form a mature, healthy personality.

For no other group in American society has the quest for self-identity been more complex than for blacks. The dominant theme in much of the scholarly literature written on black identity prior to the 1960s fit one of society's stereotypes and portrayed blacks as possessing negative self-image, low self-esteem, and generalized feelings of inadequacy and worthlessness. Several studies maintained that the development of a positive identity in black children would be hampered by the abundance of negative role models and the effects of racial oppression. These studies examined black children growing up in the homes of black parents.[2] A classic work from this school of thought is Kardiner's and Ovesey's *The Mark of Oppression*,[3] which examines the serious personality disorders they felt blacks experienced. They argued that the self-esteem of blacks suffers because of their perceptions of the negative images and behavior others express toward them. The body of literature is replete with this kind of evidence on black personality formation. It was in the 1960s that the scholarly literature began to reflect the changing conceptions of the black personality. Black identity came into prominence in the 1960s, when blacks sought to achieve pride and awareness of themselves as a previously rejected group, which carried the stigma of racial inferiority. Increasing emphasis was placed upon the psychological needs blacks had to rid themselves of this historical burden of racial inferiority.

The black movement of the 1960s and early 1970s emphasized black "consciousness" and "pride." This movement had a strong impact on transforming the negative self-perceptions of blacks from that of occupying a racially subjugated status to being empowered to abolish the discriminatory patterns to which they have been subjected.[4] Young blacks became more assertive, often denouncing any and all things Caucasian. Concerted and deliberate efforts were made to discard negative self-images and labels and substitute for them positive, powerful black models. Some advocated black separatism in the belief that black identity could only be achieved if blacks cut themselves off from all contact with whites. They argued that it was the only way to avoid the traditional patterns of *dependence. Independence*, socially and psychologically, was equated with being separate and apart from whites. Nationalism flourished as an ideology and as a way of life.[5] Black social workers, as late as 1971, spoke of the need to halt transracial adoptions because they were said to be interfering with "nation-building," which was defined as a parallel black society.

Little importance was placed on the development of *individual* identity during this era. The overwhelming emphasis was placed upon the development of a healthy *racial* and *ethnic* identity. I see it, retrospectively, as having been an absolutely necessary *process* for many blacks in order to counteract the overwhelming sense of immersion into white American society, their feelings of powerlessness, and the quest for psychological independence. Blacks would swing to the opposite end of the pendulum as they opposed, challenged, and rejected. As the pendulum swings back to its proper balance, individuals recognize that they must make room in their psyches for healthy black and individual identities. A healthy integrated personality involves one's having a stable concept of self as an *individual* as well as a *group* (black) identity.

Some psychiatrists who have studied the development of black identity, in the tradition of Erikson, insist that every child, regardless of racial background, has a primary or core identity early in life. "With the proper nurturance," says black child psychiatrist James Comer, "a child develops a positive sense of self." According to Comer and Poussaint, "All children develop a positive self-image mainly from the consistent love and care of their parents and other significant adults in their environment. This is especially true for the children of minority groups, since parental nurturing must offset the effects of an antagonistic society." As the child's psychosocial development proceeds, he or she begins to take on other identities. "The child begins to separate from the parents and develop intellectually and gradually begins to identify with outside persons, values, and concepts. Finally, Comer says, "he identifies with groups—class, race, nation. . . . This is thought to be the final and last stage of his budding self-concept.[6]

Black identity, then, becomes an extension of the child's core identity. It is a consciousness of self as belonging to a specific group that is different from other groups by physical and other characteristics. Authorities assert that most children begin to recognize racial differences between three and five years old. It is the early stages of identity formation that the critics of transracial adoption are most concerned about. They contend that this "critical period" of the child's development is the time that all of his or her role models are white, when they should, according to the critics, be black.

Few studies have been conducted on the attitudes white parents have regarding the racial identification of their black children. In 1965, Suzuki and Horn report that in a study of fifteen families who adopted transracially in the Los Angeles area in the early 1960s, "seven families stated frankly that they would tell their children about their backgrounds [and] . . . six families indicated that they did not know to what extent they would share the information about the children's racial backgrounds. . . . The majority of these families had Caucasian-appearing children." Some parents had requested a child who, although transracial, was not visibly Negro.[7] Simon, in a study conducted in 1972 with 204 parents in Michigan, Missouri, Wisconsin, and Minnesota who had adopted transracially, found that "while only 5 per cent of the parents who adopted Negro children and 11 per cent of those who adopted Indian or Korean children currently perceive those children as White; 27 and 39 per cents, respectively, expect that those same children eventually will identify themselves as White." However, Simon found that 50 per cent said that, as a result of the adoption, their families are now "mixed"; 30 per cent said they consider their family white, and the remaining 20 per cent said that their family identified with the 'human' race; a few said with no race."[8]

Falk published findings from a study in 1968 in which he used a matched sample of 170 Caucasian parents who adopted Caucasian children, and 186 parents who adopted transracially in ten upper midwestern states. He found that the transracially adopting parents anticipate there will be some difficulty related to racial identity. "About 35 per cent anticipate difficulties in school such as teasing, heckling, and being called derogatory names. Some of these anticipations seem reasonable in that 42 per cent of the 52 transracial parents whose children are in school have experienced these kinds of difficulties, though insults made directly to parents have been relatively few. Ten per cent of the transracial couples had been bothered by nasty phone calls and remarks about their adoptions."[9]

In a longitudinal study of 97 families residing in 15 states who adopted native American children, Fanshel found that "the Indian child was not always viewed in the same manner as children of other minority groups. . . . Many adoptive parents indicated they could not have taken Negro children."[10] Native American children did not symbolize the same negatively perceived racial traits as black children. Fanshel, who conducted his study from 1958 to 1967, cautions that this be viewed as only one form of transracial adoptions. On the matter of identity, he states:

> While most of the parents did not specifically seek out an Indian child for adoption—only one in five reported doing so—the overall impression is that they not only became quite comfortable with

the Indian characteristics of their children, but for most of the parents this took on a quite positive quality. . . . Many of the families began to take on a strong, positive interest in the Indian background of their children and planned to encourage their children's interest in their own backgrounds. . . . However, because of the young age of the children, it is still too early to determine how the children have integrated the information that they are of a different racial background from their parents. . . . There was little evidence that the children felt uncomfortable about being physically different, at least as perceived, by their adoptive parents.[11]

An exploratory study was conducted in 1963 with eighteen members of the Montreal Open Door Society, who related their experiences in interracial adoption. In response to the question, "What troubles, if any, did you expect to encounter on the child's entrance to school . . . when he/she begins to date . . . and to seek employment?" four families expected some trouble when their children entered school; ten families expected that their children might encounter difficulties when seeking employment, and all eighteen families expected to encounter some dilemmas when their children reached the dating age. . . . Most families . . . admitted that they thought that race differences might exaggerate the difficulties."[12] In a more recent exploratory study (1972), Edgar interviewed six of the black children in Montreal who had reached adolescence and young adulthood. One had been adopted in infancy, and the others were adopted as small children. She also studied a group of five foster children, four of whom were in white homes. The foster children had particularly acute problems related to race, according to Edgar. The adopted children had more ego strength and were, in general, more secure in dealing with racial problems than the foster children. She attributed this to the more secure home environment of the adopted children. All of the children, however, had experienced discrimination, especially in dating. Edgar stated that when whites initially began adopting transracially in Montreal, "we were thinking only in terms of bringing up a child, children we cherished and loved. . . . And it wasn't until they were in school that we realized that they had problems . . . problems for which we had not been prepared . . . of which we had no knowledge and with which we could not deal.

By 1965 our children were beginning to enter school, and by 1967 we knew they were in trouble. Most of the children who were in school at the time . . . our bright children who had done very well at home, suddenly began to do not quite so well at school. They had problems with friends, some of them didn't seem to be quite so clever in the teachers' estimation as we had taught them; and we began to realize that there were some problems we were facing with them and that they were facing that had to be coped with. That is when we began to look at our responsibilities as parents. . . .[13]

She said this was the turning point for the Montreal ODS, the point when they decided they must develop a liaison with the black community "and to learn to be black."[14]

There is an even greater scarcity of studies conducted with the children themselves. Simon's work examines color preference in adopted children (1972). In a replication of the Clark and Clark doll study when children are presented with dolls of different races and asked their preferences, with 199 adopted white, black, native American, and Asian American children, and 167 biological children, Simon found that:

. . . Negro children who are reared in the special setting of multi-racial families do not acquire the ambivalence toward their own race that has been reported among all other groups of young Negro children. Our results also show that White children do not prefer "White" to other groups, and that there are no significant differences in the racial attitudes of any of the categories of children.[15]

On the matter of racial identity, Simon found "no evidence that White children made more accurate designations than did Negro children."[16] The Indian and Asian children had lower scores, but Simon attributes this to poor equipment and faulty design rather than to accurate measures of their sense of identity. The only area "in which the Negro children showed a lower sense of awareness or perhaps ambivalence about their identity than did the White children . . . was on the matter of selecting puzzle figures that matched the skin shades of their own parents."[17] All of the minority group children erred more frequently on this test than did the white children. This seems to indicate that these children had a clearer concept of their own racial identity than they did of their parents'. Of course, neither the Edgar nor the Simon study provides the definitive answers that are being sought by the critics and the advocates.

Other studies have focused on the overall outcome of children who were transracially adopted. Raynor studied fifty-one nonwhite children (of African, Asian, and West Indian ancestry) who had been placed in white families in Britain. A majority (83 per cent) of the parents who were interviewed from one to four years after the child's placement termed the success of the adoption as "very good."[18] In a comparative study of in-race and transracial adoptive parents in Wisconsin who were interviewed from one to six years after placement, Zastrow found that both groups expressed equally high satisfaction with the adoptions. Some 88 per cent of the parents of the forty-four black children described the adoptions as "extremely satisfying."[19]

Fanshel's study of the outcome of ninety-seven Indian children who were adopted into white families in the United States is one of the most comprehensive. He conducted annual interviews with these parents over a period of five years after placement, and concluded that the children had adjusted remarkably well as a group.

> In the realm of personality and behavior patterns, there are more incipient signs of difficulties than in other areas, but this is true of only 30 per cent of the children and most of these are seen to have moderate rather than serious problems. The children appear to be well imbedded within their adoptive families and the relationships appear to be as close and devoted as one would find in other kinds of adoptive families or in biological family units.[20]

However, Fanshel issues a note of caution: "My study has followed the children while they are still relatively young and just about to embark upon their school careers. . . . It is to be expected that as our Indian adoptees get older, the prevalence of problems will increase."[21] The most comprehensive study of transracial adoption of black children in the United States was recently conducted by the Child Welfare League of America. In a study of 125 adoptions throughout the United States, they interviewed the parents at the point of selection and again a year later. In addition, the children were given a psychological test, and their teachers rated their classroom performance. Grow and Shapiro note, at the end of the first and second interviews, the research interviewers rated various aspects of the family's and child's adjustment, as well as the parents' ability to handle the racial aspects of the adoption.[22] They conclude, "The apparent success of the large majority (77 per cent) of adoptions in this study suggests that we should not reject the alternative of adoption of black children by white parents."[23]

It must be observed again, however, that the great majority of children in each of the studies cited were relatively young. No future outcomes can be predicted, based on the present findings.

Some of the advocates of transracial adoption feel that the most important facet of the child's psychological development is his or her ability to view themselves as a strong, secure, and confident *human being,* and is secondary to an awareness of themselves as a *black* (or whatever the racial background) person. There are, of course, exceptions. A small number of parents whom I interviewed felt that *black identity* is more important than any considerations of the universal assumption that "all people are the same." There are some parents who do not even concede that they have adopted a "black" child, but emphasize that he or she is "part white," "biracial," or a "*human being.*" Since they did not adopt for social reasons but because they wanted a child and could not get any other, social and political concerns are unimportant. Therefore, they are dismayed that the black social workers would dare confuse child welfare with politics. One mother said: "What does adoption have to do with Negroes' politics? I fail to see the connection. I think they are making a big mistake with this whole thing." Many of the parents felt that issues had been created and distorted. "People have no right to make children the object of social issues," said one parent.

Parents who felt the identity issue was unimportant usually lived in all-white communities and were rearing their mixed-race children as Caucasians, for the most part. Their children will not be taught black art, literature, and history because the parents emphasized their whiteness over their blackness. A black social worker who organized a chapter of the Open Door Society in his city said, "Some parents who are members of our Open Door Society insist that . . . my child is a child and I don't want to bring him up as a black child or a white child." Emphasizing that the society has different expectations of black children than it does for white children, he said, "Families living in a totally white area, with no black friends and associates for the child . . . cannot give the child a black identity." Such parents did not perceive the possibility that the child might eventually have identity problems when confronted with racism in the society. As one mother said, "Davey is not going to have any identity problems because we will teach him to be a secure individual. If he develops self-confidence, he can fortify himself against anything. Racial identity is not important at all."

Adoption workers recall countless experiences they have had with such families. A worker in the Midwest told me about a family with whom she placed a black infant boy. When the placement was made, the family was living in an integrated neighborhood in the city. Soon thereafter they moved to an all-white suburb, because the mother said "we wanted to get away from all the problems in the city." By the time the child reached two years old, he cried whenever a dark-skinned person approached him. When the social worker inquired into the problem, the mother replied, "Oh, he does that because he doesn't ever see any of those kind of people out here." She tried to reassure the social worker by saying, "You don't have to worry about it because I doubt he'll ever live near black people. I know he won't as long as he is growing up." The child himself was dark brown-skinned. When I asked one mother in Washington, D.C., if their four-year-old black son had asked questions about his color, she replied: "I think he has begun to recognize the difference between blacks and whites because he asked me, "Mommy, do black women know how to drive cars?" This family lived in an all-white suburb, had no black friends, and the child only saw blacks when he was on an outing with his parents. In a study conducted with 204 parents who had adopted transracially in 5 midwestern states, Simon found that 27 per cent expected that their children eventually will identify themselves as white.[24] This is quite likely an indication of how their parents perceive and treat them.

Those who adhere to the notion that the child should have a

stable and secure human identity stress individuality and a belief that everyone should be able to develop his or her potential to the fullest, without regard for their racial, ethnic, religious, national, or social class group membership. Thus they maintain that they have adopted nonracial "human beings" instead of "black" children, and adapt their childrearing accordingly. Their blind insensitivity to the aforementioned differences in people—differences based on their group membership—is sometimes extreme. For example, a mother told me, "I don't believe in identifying people by which race they belong to. God said we are all members of the human race, and that is what I am teaching Susie [six years old]. We don't discuss black or white in our home." It may be that these parents do not consider color to be important, but such a blind attitude toward the role of group differences in the society is unwise. It is possible for the parents to convey to their children that they, themselves, do not judge and relate to people on the basis of their skin color, but they should also tell the child that many people in the society do. Failure to do this will obviously leave the child unprepared to understand and deal with the first time he or she is called "nigger" or some other racial slur.

Many of the premises of the "human" identity concept were formulated by a Minnesota social worker, Clayton Hagen, an advocate of transracial adoptions in the 1960s. As a national spokesman he so completely minimized the importance of racial identity that even some of the adoptive parents felt his position was unrealistic. Hagen states: "Interracial adoption is a matter of people removing the walls [and] . . . artificial lines which separate people from each other. . . . It is a matter of seeing people first as individuals . . . in their own unique individuality. . . ."[25] Ignoring the racial attitudes of the society, he wrote, "We cannot wait until society is prepared." This futuristic philosophy emphasizes how parents feel the society should be, instead of how it is. Transracially adoptive couples are ". . . viewing the world as a place to be made humane. . . . [They] are refocusing on the family as the locus for creating a new definition of the world, one of humanity, trust and mature love."[26]

These parents say that emphasizing racial differences is detrimental in childrearing because the major problems and concerns that parents must face transcend color boundaries. The most important problems they anticipate, if there are any at all, will come when the child seeks to resolve his or her "genealogical bewilderment," or search for identity as an adopted person. They, like other adoptive parents, express concern as to how they will eventually deal with identity problems arising from being adopted. As a Minnesota mother said, "If I can get it over to our son that we love him in spite of his questions about who his real mother and father were, and why they gave him up for adoption, I am sure I can get past the hurdle of race."

It has been argued that the transracially adopted child might find it easier to resolve his or her "genealogical bewilderment" and racial identity crisis than it would be for a child who has been matched to have similar characteristics with his or her adoptive parents. Because of the obvious racial differences, the child is not deluded into thinking that he or she is the same as or a part of the biological family. "It may be that a child who is raised with parents of another race may be better prepared to see himself as an individual," says Hagen, . . . "than can the child who is raised by parents of his own race." One father, who is a psychology professor, told the writer that he and his wife intentionally adopted black-skinned children so as to eliminate any delusions their children might have about their genealogy. Had they adopted white or very fair-skinned children, the children may have had an identity crisis over the adoption. He said, "As it stands now they will automatically know that we adopted them because we wanted them for what they are and not for what we wanted them to be. They will never have to wonder if we settled for second choice." The value of emphasizing differences, it is felt, makes for a more open and honest relationship between parent and child. In an interview with Charles Olds, director of Pierce-Warwick Adoption Agency in Washington, D.C., and a pioneer in international and transracial adoption, he said,

In a way it is easier for the adopted child who is black in a white family to resolve his identity, than it would be for the child who is in the family where he appears to be physically the same as his parents, and they have deluded him to think he is a part of the family when biologically he isn't. . . . In adoption we try to help people face the fact of difference about being in the family through the role of being adopted rather than being born into it. With the child who is obviously of different biological heritage, there is no pretense. Once having arrived into the family he takes on everything that pertains to the family. As far as helping him to recognize his heritage, they then talk about the heritage that he brings with him. . . . [He] brings with him something that is special and valuable.[27]

The major emphases authorities of transracial placements have made is that only those parents who are able to accept and live with differences should be allowed to adopt. Any parent who engages in denial—involving the child's color, hair texture, biological parentage, or any other overt or latent characteristic—is laying the groundwork for fostering in the child an unhealthy emotional attitude and self-image. Speaking about Montreal adolescents who were adopted early in life, Scyner notes, "Almost every child at some period . . . has denied that he was black, has found himself hating or being afraid of black people. . . . If the question of identification is not worked through, then this uncertainty shows up in denial . . . or in the child's . . . lack of self-esteem. . . . Parents . . . have to show their acceptance [of] the child without denying the realities . . . and without dismissing the effects of society on the child."[28]

There is much denial inherent in the conception of "human" identity. No one can argue that a stable, secure self-concept is most important. But it does not negate the individual's need also to develop secondary identities, including the racial and ethnic. One wonders what these parents fear in racial identity. Why do they stress its lack of importance? Is "human" identity merely a smoke screen for antipathies they may have toward parenting a black child? Indeed, it has been suggested that it is their method of denying the child is black. As one critic said, "If you conveniently make everyone a faceless human being, you don't have to deal with your prejudices. You can keep them hidden."

The adherents to the "human" identity concept prevailed before the escalation of the black social worker controversy, when it was easier to treat the adoption almost as if it were of the traditional type. Quite a number of parents evolved from the "human" identity concept to a combination of "human" and "black" identity philosophy, largely as a result of becoming aware of the issues raised by blacks. The evolution in their philosophy also involves personal growth for many of them. For example, one often hears them describe themselves "having been a white family that included a black child," but now they are an "integrated family." One father said, "As soon as you bring a black child into your family your family stops being a white family. You become sensitive to a lot of issues you weren't aware of before. I think Johnny has really opened up our lives in an important way." The parents in this study who have decided that it is important for their child to have a black identity are the more educated, socially conscious, and generally enlightened about societal issues. Many tend to have an intellectual outlook on life. Thus it is only in keeping with their expectations of themselves that they would remain informed and in the forefront of current trends and obligations.

Invariably parents who are members of the Open Door Society, the Council on Adoptable Children, and similar groups acknowledge the importance of black identity. And to varying degrees they are sympathetic to the black social workers' protest statement. Through their parents' groups they have organized "black culture" enrichment programs for their children and themselves. They frequently enlist the aid of black professionals to give them a seminar or to lead an intensive encounter-type discussion group —geared toward sensitizing them to black culture and to any racial biases they may have. Their black and white children are taught black literature and history, they see films on blacks, eat black "soul" foods, and are generally well informed for their ages. One father said, "Our children probably know more about what has been written on black culture than most black kids their ages," which is probably true for many. The children's knowledge must, however, be viewed as a function of their parents' social class background. Their parents' high educational attainment means that they would educate their children—regardless of color —about anything they deem important.

These parents have been criticized for treating black culture— and black identity—as abstractions. The black social workers argue that learning black history and literature is no substitute for knowing and interacting with blacks on a regular basis, in a rela-

tionship based on equality. John Banks, a college professor, acknowledged that there are some deficiencies in his approach to
developing a black identity in his four-year-old son. "Reading
black nursery rhymes to him is not going to get him a black identity. But it will at least help. He won't be as deprived of his heritage as a lot of the kids who don't even learn that much from their
parents. As he gets older his exposure to blacks will increase."

Most of the parents who have evolved in their awareness to the
stage where they now accept the black identity concept say they
have, as a result, developed more social consciousness. Admitting
that they initially adopted with much naïveté about racial issues,
they no longer believe that love is sufficient to sustain them
through any problems they might have with the adoption. It was
only after they got the child, took him or her on outings where
they met the glaring stares and insulting comments of strangers,
to the homes of apprehensive and hostile family and friends, that
they changed their attitudes. The cuddly little infant became a
target for the generalized hostility some people have toward
blacks. Not only did the family have to contend with the hostility,
but also with what one mother called the "reverse hostility"—the
gushing, overfriendly attitude displayed by a large number of people. This drew them into the spotlight more often than the hostility. The more they experienced, the more their awareness of racial
issues increased. "Suddenly we realized that our child was not
biracial to the strangers we met," said a mother in the Midwest.
"She was black!"

Through these continuous experiences, some of these families
would find it difficult *not* to come to grips with the problems of
identity. Those who live in diversified urban areas find it inescap-
able. It is easier to isolate one's family in a segregated and homogeneous suburban community and simply ignore the criticisms.

Their awareness, of course, is carried out on different levels and
to different degrees. Some parents continue to approach the identity formation problem on an intellectual and abstract basis. It is
largely a secondary process through which *information about*
black culture is transmitted to the child and the parents, as opposed to altering their lifestyles in such a manner as to make the
black identity formation process one that is deeply ingrained in
their day-to-day socialization. Although some parents make it a

point to cultivate a few black friends, their overall lifestyles are rarely altered very much. Whatever efforts they make in the child's behalf are in addition to that which they have been doing in the past. The majority continue to live in predominantly white neighborhoods, but do make an effort to know the few blacks who live nearby. As middle-class people, most say they have found it difficult to find a more racially mixed neighborhood with quality schools. Thus the alternative they follow is to remain where they are and to expend more efforts cultivating friendships with blacks, participating in their black culture programs, and engaging in activities outside their neighborhoods. Having settled on this approach, the parents feel they can equip their child with the necessary black identity. A father in a Virginia suburb said that although their neighborhood does not have as many black families as they would like, "Our son is being taught to be proud of his racial heritage and also to understand that the hostility or overfriendliness he meets is directed to him not as an *individual* but because of his color." Similarly, a mother said, "We are not willing to move into an all-black neighborhood with inferior schools, but we do consider it our duty to do anything else we possibly can to make Gracie proud of her heritage."

Some methods parents used to develop a black identity had already begun to show in the children's self-perceptions. These parents felt that their black children knew, to varying degrees, that they were something other than white. For example, some older children said such things as "I'm black and I'm proud," or "I'm black and my sisters and brothers are white." A five-year-old girl I met, who had several adopted sisters and brothers of different races and nationalities, asked her mother if she could get an Afro hairstyle, whereupon her mother agreed. "From that point on, her hair became her greatest source of pride," said her mother. Many of these children are familiar with black heroic figures such as Martin Luther King, Jr., Frederick Douglass, Malcolm X, and others. A few children have been named for these black heroic personalities.

One cannot predict what long-range effects these parents' child-rearing methods will have, or what they will produce. The parents are quick to enumerate the many positive effects it has already had for the entire family. "Having a child of another race has broadened the horizons of all our children and ourselves," one parent remarked. "We never would have had as many different experiences, and we would not have met so many other people had we not adopted." The adoptive experience has also made them more sensitive to the problems of blacks. They say they are, for the first time in their lives, aware of what blacks feel when they are insulted with racial slurs, since it also has happened to them. A St. Louis mother commented, "As the day-to-day insults increased and intensified because of our adopted child, I became filled with a 'black rage' as sweet as any known to Nat Turner."[29]

On the matter of black survival skills, few of the parents would argue that they are capable of teaching them. Unlike black identity, which can probably be transmitted somewhat easier, survival skills entail a more direct defensive posture enacted against specific hostile acts. Some parents argue, however, that it is not as necessary that their children know these, since their middle-class status will not expose them to acts of hostility as often as the poor child. Therefore they feel comfortable in avoiding the nuances, symbolisms, language, gestures, defensive postures, and other manifestations of black survival skills. As one father said, "If Danny needs to know them later on, I'm sure he will pick them up on his own. We don't know how to give them to him." Also there are others who do not place a lot of value on survival skills, as indicated by this father's comments: "We can give Justin what is important, and that is a good sense of self. I'm not convinced that a lot of black families are dealing with the self-image any better than we are. If I had to take my choice in learning some survival skills and having to view myself as a beautiful and solid person, I would take the latter. Hopefully we can give him that and from that he can learn whatever he needs to know to make it."

While these parents accept the legitimacy of black identity, they still feel that the development of a secure individual identity forms the core of the child's personality. They stress the importance of the child belonging to a stable family unit, in which he or she will have permanence. "Black" identity then becomes an ancillary component of the basic or core identity.

During the course of this investigation, the writer interviewed several (twelve) white parents who decided they must "become a part of the black community" if they were serious about parenting a black child. In accordance with this philosophy, their lifestyles were changed so that they physically lived in black neighborhoods (as the only white family), and in practically every aspect of their lives they were totally immersed in black experiences. It was almost as though they had denounced their whiteness. All of these families had had children before adopting transracially. The men worked in middle-level professional positions (social work and education). Although they have adopted black children, they are in total agreement with the black social workers' protest statement, and are some of the chief advocates of "black homes for black children." All developed this consciousness after they adopted. Now, they argue, they would not adopt another black child because they should have black parents, unless, of course, no black parents could be found for a waiting child.

Since they live in black communities (in Atlanta and Washington, D.C.), most of their friends are black, all of their children attend predominantly black schools, and their childrearing practices do not appear to be contrived in the way it is with the parents described above. Thus they do not have to organize special seminars for themselves and black culture schools for their children. As one mother said, "We don't teach it from the books. We live it." The fact is that they do not dwell on black culture and identity. In a very different way, the children are influenced by it as much as any black child with black parents, in the school, with playmates, and with other blacks in their neighborhoods. Since the children are saturated with black role models (teachers, neighbors, their parents' friends, et al.), the parents feel secure that their children will have few problems learning survival skills and in forming secure black identities. A white father in Atlanta said, "If my two-year-old son has a solid image and awareness of himself as a black human being, no amount of outside abuse can really get him off the ground." This father, who is a social worker with black youth, said their son might have another kind of problem: racism. He said, "Our son's biggest barrier to developing a solid image of himself may be us, as white people."

These parents utilize more flexibility in their childrearing. Whatever is eventually required to enhance their children's development, they are willing to try. They do not attach value to material possessions, since their homes are very sparsely furnished, and they exhibit no outward signs of conspicuous consumption patterns. In fact, one family lives in a commune. A couple who had adopted a black and Korean child, and had some of their own, said that they would do whatever was necessary to develop their son's black identity. "We will do whatever is possible for white people to do. If it means our son going to Africa and living for a few years, then he will be in Africa for a few years. So how do you prepare a child for racism? I'd say you should prepare him on the inside. . . . If a man is in love with himself, he will survive. If he doesn't, I don't think there is anything I can do."

The parents described above have little in common with the majority of those who adopt across racial boundaries. They are more straightforward and honest in expressing their feelings. They do not hesitate in discussing their real motives for adopting. In fact, they are all too willing to allow the interviewer to probe and raise tough questions, and as one mother said, "to lay it on the line." Instead of retreating from the transracial adoption controversy, their lifestyles are geared toward confrontation. A father said he is just as suspicious of those whites who insist they have adopted a "human being" as he is of avowed white racists. If pressed, they will also criticize black nationalists who attack all whites, simply because they are white. They do not shun controversy.

On a rare occasion a group of Open Door Society members engaged in an intense discussion that focused on the total range of identity perceptions and problems. A transcript of the dialogue follows:

An adoptive parents group was talking about black identity. Near the end of the meeting a soft-spoken young mother, who had two biological children and one black adopted child, rose to speak.

"I have sat here and listened to everyone express their feelings for the last three hours. Some of you seem to be saying that your black child is a *human*. Some of you seem to want to be 'supermilitants,' so you're convinced that you are going to give the child a black identity, and that you can do it as well as any black parent. Some of you think he is a *human* and a *black*. And quite frankly, some of you don't seem to know how to regard your child. You seem confused, and I'm not sure you know why you adopted, or if you did the right thing. All evening I sat here wondering how all of this is going to turn out, say, fifteen years from now. God help our children and ourselves.

"I am angry. I am angry because this preoccupation with race and identity, legitimate though it may be, has diverted most of our creative energies away from the total personalities of our children, and from ourselves. Will we ever solve this riddle of our children's identity? If they're black, aren't they also human, and vice versa? Does one preclude the other? Why do we have to separate them?"

A man rose to answer: "We see them as either *black* or *human* because we hide behind the definitions. As long as we can hide behind the security of definitions, we don't have to deal with the problems. That's a beautiful place for whites to hide. . . . Rather than discuss an issue like color, we fight over definitions and therefore we don't have to discuss the *issue*. It's a constant technique that allows us to evade the real issue."

A woman added: "I get the feeling that people who say that a person is neither black nor white but human feel that one or the other category isn't human. I think it's unreal. Families may see their children in this way, but the world in which they *really* live identifies that strong ancestral part of them." The mother of several children—adopted and her own—told the group, "Not to be facetious or anything, I don't see how I can lose any more sleep worrying over the problems of my young black children than I did when my teen-agers were going through their adolescent rebellion. There were nights when I didn't sleep at all. The thing that frightens me most now is that we will have several children to reach adolescence at one point. I am not frightened that they are adopted or that they are minority children. I just worry about adolescence."

Did any of the parents have a stronger instinct to protect their black children than their white ones? someone asked. A black woman who had come to the meeting out of curiosity with one of her white friends, said: "Your children should know that no parent, including his own, can offer him 100 per cent protection from those hostile forces out there. If you teach the child that those are some of the things he can expect from life, then he might be prepared for it. Your children should be told that they will come into contact with lots of people, and these people represent at least two worlds, a black one and a white one. Because of their peculiar position, these kids are going to be expected to function and make it in both. All of you parents should be concerned that your children be given the benefit of knowing something about black culture so that when they interact with blacks they will also be able to deal with black kids and black people. . . . Whether you like it or not, demands are going to be made on the child to interact in both cultures." "I agree with what you're saying," a father said, "but my feeling is that teaching a child to cope is a very complex thing. It can work both ways. If you take a lot of black kids out of all-black environments they wouldn't know how to cope in a white middle-class world. The child might be strong in some ways and weak in others. If any child hasn't dealt with something before he might have some difficulty coping with it."

One woman asked if anyone in the group had thought about the more subtle patterns of discrimination one often finds in "integrated" communities. She said, "I don't know if any integrated community prepares a transracially adopted child for better functioning in the larger society than a segregated community. I think the identity problem is more a crisis in a community like ours than it might be in others where the racial boundaries are more clearly drawn. It's been our experience that the subtle patterns of discrimination confuse our black children. There are a lot of attitudes here that suggest that they are *human*, and not black or white. They learn later on that there are some things that happen to them and that go on in their world that they aren't quite sure of. They don't have a clear-cut definition of what these things are, but they do know they identify, as a rule, with those children they get a visual image of. And so they get confused with their own identity." A father turned to her and said, "I agree with you. We've had arguments with friends of ours—very close friends who say to us, 'Shirley is a human being.' And we constantly tell them, 'Grant that, but the fact that she is black is our foremost thought. Our major concern is to be able to get this across to her so she can have some survival skills in an integrated area and in the real world on the outside."

A father said, "I think all of this discussion is beneficial. But no one has come up with the answer to my riddle: How do *we* as white people go about doing all this? I want some *methods*, some *techniques*." All eyes were upon the black woman, as though she had the magic answers they wanted. Sensing this, she told the group, "A social worker friend of mine who has worked in adoptions told me that the best thing white parents can do is begin to identify with your black children. What she meant was that instead of continuing to see yourselves as whites who have adopted across racial lines, you can begin to view yourselves as being related to your black children's ancestors. If that identity link is forged, then you will begin to lobby in behalf of the interests and needs of black people." A father spoke up by saying, "Because theirs are also our interests. *All* of those interests are our interests. Margie [his wife] and I find ourselves going into the schools and raising hell about the textbooks and this sort of thing. If we were just a typical white family we might not, because we would not have the personal involvement that transracial adoption requires. You see, our kids come home with these books and they have two Indian children in them and they are portrayed as savage and everything else negative. You just have to be concerned about that because you don't want your kids to have that kind of image of themselves. Your black children are taught from the same kinds of racist books. You just have to be very personally involved. You can't avoid it." Realizing that the time had come for the meeting to end, a man asked the chairperson if he could make a final remark. The man said, "All of us are familiar with the anti-transracial adoption resolution of the black social workers, but let me say that Betty [his wife] and I don't feel defensive about that resolution. We feel that transracial adoption is a good thing, and if we are ever going to move ahead in society, people are going to have to live together. And to us, we just don't feel defensive. We don't have to defend ourselves to any group—black, white, interracial. We did it, and we're happy we did it. It's a good thing. It's been good for us. We feel that it's good for our family. We just don't feel defensive about it."

The psychiatrists interviewed for this study feel it is possible for some white parents to rear emotionally healthy black children. According to black child psychiatrist, James Comer, "If a child is

adopted into a family that provides a warm, secure, and honest home life, his opportunity for developing the racial [black] identity will be all the easier."[30] To assume that no white parent can help a child to develop a black identity means also that any parent of one race cannot transmit a healthy identity to a child of another race. One could simply reverse the process and ask the question, Can any black person transmit a healthy identity to a white child? As one black put it, "Black nannies have done it with white children for centuries, and they have done it well." Black psychiatrist James L. Curtis, who has worked for decades as a psychiatric consultant to adoption agencies, asserts, "It has been demonstrated endlessly that a similar racial-group membership alone cannot serve as a reliable guarantee of a successful marriage, family, or home."[31]

Child development experts have argued that the most important thing the young child needs is the feeling of belonging. Translated, this means that he or she should have a secure home and family. No child can get this if he or she is institutionalized or shuttled from one foster home to another. Mae Neely, the black director of Adoption Services for New York City Department of Social Services, says, "If a child feels he belongs to someone, I don't think ethnic differences is a major problem."[32] Kenneth Clark, author of *Prejudice and Your Child*, a study of the formation of racial attitudes in black children, said, "Race is not a predominant factor in determining the quality of parenthood. The problem, if there is a problem, is related to specific qualities in the parents. A child can make a very successful adjustment in an interracial home if he gets love, sympathy, and understanding."[33] When asked in an interview why he felt white parents adopt black children, he replied, "Maybe, it is because the white family wants to escape the prison of whiteness. Have you thought of that possibility? I once said that whites are as much prisoners of American racism as I am."

On the question of motives, Charles Prudhomme, a black psychoanalyst, said, "I don't know if you can generalize on why white families adopt black children. I think it's possible that a white family might adopt a black child out of pure altruistic, well-meaning motives, and then others might do it to experiment, to see what they can do in the rearing of the child." But he goes

on to point out that "parents who have [biological] children may want to see if *they* can rear a healthy, successful child." He feels that the motives of all adoptive parents might bear some similarities. He raises the question:

> Why does a white family adopt a black child? The reason they give is that no one wants to adopt the child. . . . But that is not a good reason. . . . The adopted child is just like your natural child. You don't know what is going to happen, you don't know how the child is going to turn out. You hope you can give them the material things. You convey to the child that you want him, that you love him. . . . [In that sense] whites have just as good a chance of rearing a healthy black child as a black family. There is certainly a chance that the white family might be in a better position materially, economically, but we don't know. I don't know if I can say, or would want to say that a white family cannot successfully rear a black child.

He also addresses the complexity that the dimension of race brings to the adoption:

> The problems become increasingly more difficult today because there is such a big controversy made about black and white [race]. But these adoptions have gone on for years in Minnesota and Canada. And these children are not reared as "blackies" but as bona-fide, genuine members of families. At least that's the impression I get. . . . I think the white family has as much chance of rearing a healthy black child as the *environment* will allow, as the *society* will allow [his emphases].

He notes that during puberty, the black child's black peer group members can place strong pressures on him to identify with them. This might cause the child to "want to identify with the blacks so strongly that they will reject their white benefactor [parents]." Yet Prudhomme feels that the child should go through this rebellious period, and will probably survive it.[34]

Yet the authorities on black child welfare do not give blanket endorsement to transracial adoption. Most seem to feel that a quality black home is preferable because it eliminates many problems created by the society over which white parents have no con-

trol. If white parents are permitted to adopt black children, the parents should be mature; able to accept racial and other differences; be sensitive to and aware of their own prejudices and racism; and should certainly have a lifestyle that will permit their family to have sustained contacts with other blacks on an equal basis.

8

WHO THEY ARE
Case Studies

Each white couple who adopted across racial boundaries has its own unique way of perceiving their black child's identity needs and unique method for transmitting the particular kind of identity they feel their child needs most, whether it is "human," "black," "biracial," or a combination of these. Because each couple's motivations for adopting and subsequent experiences have also been different, one readily observes an almost infinite number of episodes that occur in their lives on a frequent basis. Thus, on closer examination, the uniformity that appears to be a characteristic of these families disappears. Their diversity, shaped by their individual biographies, emerges instead. In the following section, the reader can interpret the obviously different perceptions and approaches they take to racial identity as it relates to their black child.

THE REALISTIC FAMILY

Mary and Joe Langley were sitting on their lawn playing Scrabble when I arrived to interview them. Their rambling, white frame house, with its peeling paint, sits across the street from a large park on the fringes of the inner city. Their neighbors on one side are black and on the opposite are white. In their neighborhood there are two interracial couples. There is an abundance of young children throughout the neighborhood. I had previously met Joe at a lecture when he was introduced to me by a mutual friend as "a white man who has a black daughter." When I told Joe about my study of transracial adoptions, he invited me to his home to meet his wife and children, and consented to be interviewed. After introducing me to Mary, he went into the house to get his children and mother and father-in-law, Mr. and Mrs. Robertson, who were visiting from another state. In the meantime, Mary told me that she is active in the Open Door Society and that they adopted a nine-month-old son, Robert, who is now a year and a half. Both of Robert's parents are black. The Langleys also have two other children, Thomas, who is in first grade, and Carrie, a four-year-old.

A few minutes later, Joe reappeared with everyone. After introducing me to the children, they said their niceties and were quickly off to resume their game of hide-and-seek. Little Robert, a very dark-skinned toddler, was led away by the hand by Carrie. Mr. and Mrs. Robertson explained to me that this was their second visit since Robert was adopted. They came for his baptism when he had been with the family only two months. "I would have been here the day he arrived if we didn't live so far away," the white-haired woman said. "I was with Mary when both the children were born. Of course, that's easy for me to do now that I am retired from teaching." Mary explained that they had only five days' notice that Robert would be arriving when he did. "If we had had more lead time mother would have been here giving me advice and orders as usual." Mr. Robertson, a tall, portly man with mixed gray hair, said he announced to his church that he had a new grandson. "Our minister and the congregation were delighted. They thought it was such a wonderful thing to do." Mr. Robertson is a retired engineer.

After the Robertsons' departure for a concert, I continued my discussion with Joe and Mary. Their adoption of Robert grew out of their involvement with tutoring black children, a concern for curbing population growth, and a love for children. Mary and Joe had always lived in integrated neighborhoods, sent their children to school with blacks, and had almost as many black friends as white. "Before we made the final decision to adopt a black child, we went through a lot of intrafamily therapy. We examined our attitudes and motivations," said Joe. "We wanted to make sure that we weren't going into this for some self-sacrificing reason. It just grew out of our other involvement." Neither could remember when they first learned of the need for adoptive homes for black children. Mary commented, "I guess we always knew about this kind of thing because we were involved. It was not a sudden discovery at all. I read books by Pearl Buck as far back as I can remember. I was a social worker until the children were born, so I had some inside knowledge about the problem. Joe's work in population research on his job and when he was in graduate school has given him a lot of insight. He also tutored before he got so busy with his work." Mary is thin with blond hair, and very casual in appearance. Joe reminds one of a slightly disheveled professor. Their appearance reflects their casual, easygoing lifestyle. In exploring their ideas on transracial adoption, both were very thoughtful and deliberate as they talked about their feelings on the controversial aspects. "I try to be logical in my approach to what the black social workers are saying," Joe said in his soft-spoken but forceful manner. "I am not alarmed that they are protesting. I am just a bit surprised that they are making such blanket pronouncements by saying that 'no white family can do this or do that with black children.' They have some training in human development and psychology. They should know that there are individual human differences, just as there are similarities. I am insulted that they are willing to lump me in the category with all other white people—racists and radical leftists—simply because I am white. I know that all whites in this society are influenced by white racism. But don't some of us handle it better than others? Are all of us 'white cultural imperialists'? I think they should be more sophisticated than they are. How would they like it if I put them in the same category with the 'Uncle Toms' and the black bourgeoisie? Wouldn't they protest, as I am doing?"

As Mary described some of the insulting remarks she had overheard people make about her children, she said, "I oftentimes wonder if any of these people stop and ask themselves, 'Why am I saying these things about this woman whose name I don't even know?'" Joe asked her, "Would it make a difference if they knew your name? I doubt it would, because they don't care about who you are. They don't even want to know who you are, because their minds are already made up. You are just bad news to them. If they allowed themselves to wonder what your name is, where you grew up, what you do, then they'd have to consider all kinds of options. They are secure when they can keep you neatly typed in a little box in their minds. They can't afford to let you get out of it because you might destroy some of their cherished myths. The old white ladies you meet in the supermarket can't deal with the possibility that you might be like their own daughters. And the blacks can't afford to think that you might believe in some of the same things they value, and have a lot else in common with them. If they did, it might crack away at some of their stereotypes about white people." Mary replied, "You know, you might be right. I never thought of it in that way before. I just felt it emotionally as I tried to explain to Thomas and Carrie why the people we met were sometimes mean."

Joe feels that many people who criticize them for adopting Robert are afraid that they are unaware of the need to give him a black identity. This particularly disturbs him, since his lifestyle would automatically make the child sensitive to his blackness. "But we would be presumptuous to assume that we can give him an exclusively black identity. By definition his world is dual—it is white and black. I don't agree with people who say the child has to live in an all-black or predominantly black world or white world, for that matter, in order to have a well-formed identity. That's the same as saying that a white child has to live in an all-white world in order to have a white identity. Look at all the children who grow up traveling around the world with their parents. Children of career military people. Foreign service officers. International businessmen. Missionaries. Teachers. These children's identities are not diluted. Robbie is a very dark-skinned child. He already knows he is different from us, just by looking at the differences. We fully expect him to ask us all the questions any normal child will ask. We don't intend to keep anything from him or any of the other children. We know we can't rear him in precisely the same way a black family would, so I refuse to debate that point. But I do know that I can give him a lot of understanding, security, love, companionship, guidance, and all of the other things that people who love and respect children pass on to them. Since I am aware of the need for every individual to know his roots and to be able to relate to them, I can definitely make him aware of them." "But this shouldn't mean giving him lectures on blackness, should it, Joe?" asked Mary. "I don't agree with what I see a lot of white parents doing with their black children. It seems that they feel compelled to point out every black person they see to the child. They are constantly 'teaching' them instead of letting them learn it more naturally. I'm sure that as these kids get older they're going to wonder why all the lectures, why all the emphasizing and the special treatment. Sure they need to know it, but not in the way these parents are going about it."

Mary said, "We know this couple, the Starks, who read a story about a black hero to their black daughter every night and they read a regular fairy-tale bedtime story to their white kids. The wife said she is trying to instill blackness into their three-year-old. It's almost ludicrous because you can see that they aren't comfortable with having adopted her. They don't really know what to do with her. Why should they deprive her of a fairy tale just because she is black? And why deprive their two white children of a story about a black hero because they are white?" Joe said, "They do it because they are confused and probably never should have been allowed to adopt in the first place. They are trying to be black parents to their black child and white parents to their white children. In the end they probably won't be good parents to either. All of those kids are eventually going to have doubts about who and what they are." "You know, you're right," said Mary. "Because the wife asked a group of us at the Open Door meeting last week if any of our white kids ever said they wanted to be black. When nobody in the group said that had happened to us, she said her five-year-old daughter told her she wanted to be black so she could have an Afro and have a lot of books like her little sister. She also told her mother that she wanted to be 'black and beautiful' too. We tried to explain to her that her white child felt neglected because she had showed a difference between her and her black sister. The child was emotionally hurt. One man said they had had a similar problem with their kids until they learned that they had to be more subtle about black identity. When they saw that their children were feeling neglected with all the attention being paid to the black child by the rest of the family and by friends and people they meet, they found themselves constantly telling *all* their children how much they loved them. He said, 'It can be an awful burden on the other children if you aren't aware of it.'" When I asked Mary if the woman profited from this discussion, she said, "It's really hard to tell. She might have and she might not have. She and her husband are very intellectually involved with black identity, but they don't seem to understand themselves and their children. They are following every trend they hear about. A couple in our group who knew them from another city said the Starks adopted that little girl because some of their friends were adopting and it was the 'chic' thing to do. When they heard that the black social workers were opposed to it, they jumped on another bandwagon. This time people were saying that whites shouldn't adopt black kids because they can't give them a black identity. So they set out to show everyone that they could be among the few whites who could give a child a black identity." "What they're really doing," said Joe, "is ramming it down the child's throat. It's too bad that transracial adoption is making some parents forget the *overall* needs of all their kids. Some of them are so defensive and so anxious to do the right thing by their black child that they are neglecting to see that child, or any of their children, as total individuals. That child is certainly going to know he is 'black and beautiful!' Most of these kids will probably know more about black history than the average black kid with black parents. But I am concerned about trying to meet Robbie's total needs as any parent does with a growing youngster. Unfortunately, only part of that need will be identified with his color."

The Mini-"United Nations" Family

Some whites who adopt black children also adopt children of other racial and nationality backgrounds. They are frequently called little "United Nations" families. In such a family, the important question is not only that of how to enable a black child to develop his racial identity, but also the Korean, the Vietnamese, the South American, the native American, and Caucasian children. If the parents take their task seriously, they find themselves trying to convey to each, but yet *all* of their children, who they are, where they came from, and the like. Most important, they must also find the common thread that holds them all together as a very diverse family unit.

Carla and Desmond Hall have one biological child and four adopted children. When they were married they always thought it would be a nice idea to adopt a child after they had two of their own. After the birth of their first child, several years passed, and Carla didn't get pregnant. They went to the doctor to have fertility tests, which proved positive. Still nothing happened. As Dottie was approaching school age, they decided to go ahead and adopt, with the hope that they would eventually have the biological son they wanted. With this decision in mind, they applied for and eventually were able to adopt a girl of racially mixed parentage. Her father was black and her mother was white. Desmond, a businessman, said, "I always loved kids since I grew up in a large family myself. But I *never* had any dream of having this many." On the other hand, Carla described herself as "not being able to say 'No'" to any child in need of a home. "As a kid, I always picked up the stray puppies and brought them home with me. When I was a teen-ager I was the 'play Mommy' to all the young children in our neighborhood. I always wanted to be involved with kids in some way." After they adopted Caroline, they became active in a parents' group that promoted transracial placements. Actually, they had adopted a mixed-race child because they heard that they were "hard to place." "Neither Desmond nor I had ever had many black friends," said Carla, "since we grew up and went to college in small towns where there weren't that many blacks. Still, we were humanists. We didn't believe in racial discrimination. But we weren't activists either. We were what some people might call 'good white liberals' with a belief in racial brotherhood." They were never active in social causes. They lived fairly quiet lives in a small town, with a strong family orientation. "We always did things together as a family," said Desmond. Two years after the adoption of Caroline, Carla brought up the subject of adopting a little Indian boy who had come to her attention through their adoption agency. Carla still hadn't gotten pregnant and everything was, according to her, "in a state of limbo as far as getting pregnant was concerned. I wanted to *have* another baby, but Desmond and I were getting resigned to the fact that that might not ever happen." Over a period of several months Carla finally convinced Desmond that they should adopt a boy, since she may not conceive again. When he agreed, their social worker made the placement within a few months. "She had hoped all along that we would adopt Wade," said Carla.

With three children of different racial backgrounds, Desmond and Carla found themselves confronted with constant questions from strangers about why they adopted "those" children. Couldn't they find some 'nice' white babies to adopt? And most important, how are you going to raise all those different children? The latter question, confessed Desmond, not only intrigued him but also made him extremely conscious of what they had done. "We had sort of gone into it in a simpleminded way. We loved children and wanted more of them. We hadn't at all seriously considered the racial and ethnic ramifications of what we had done." "You're right," Carla said. "Sure I knew we had adopted a child who was part Negro and another one who was full-blooded Indian. But I hadn't asked myself any of the hard-nosed questions about identity. I thought a dabble of black history and a bit of Indian history would be sufficient while they were young. My attitude was that the future would take care of itself, so I hadn't given any thought to what would it be like as they got older."

As more publicity was given the Hall family, people started calling them for advice about adopting a minority child and requesting that they give speeches before civic groups. Soon they found the need to start a parents' group for adoptive families. "Our personal time became so much in demand that we thought these problems and requests people were presenting us with would be handled much better if we had a group," said Carla. "That would also be a good vehicle to encourage more people to adopt minority kids." The more involved they became with adoption agencies, the more they saw the need to find parents for the waiting children. "Each time Carla came and told me about some lovely little kid she had seen who needed a home, I knew in her subtle way she was suggesting that we adopt another," Desmond said. "One day she came home and told me about this little Indian boy who had been in foster care for a long time with no prospective adoptive family in sight. Before she finished telling me about him, she was in tears. I said to her, 'All right, Carla, you can bring him home.' She was overwhelmed with joy. Within a couple of months Joey, our second Indian child, joined our family." In the meantime Desmond and Carla had agreed that there would be no further adoptions. They continued to counsel other families, and they worked diligently with agencies in locating potential adoptive parents. Their lives were relatively free of a great amount of hostility from outsiders, who tended to be more curious than hostile. They had always enjoyed the acceptance of their children from their own parents and family members. None had expressed objections. They frequently visited their relatives and, on occasion, the children stayed over with their grandparents.

As the dissension over the Vietnam war increased, "we found ourselves morally outraged over the atrocities that were happening with the children," said Desmond. "As we watched napalmed villages over the television news, we began to discuss the possibility of helping to get some of the orphans out of Vietnam. We knew there was a lot of red tape involved, but we started spreading the word, and we encouraged a few of these adoptions. One night after one of our meetings ended here at our home, Carla turned to me and said, 'I know you have been thinking about our adopting a Vietnamese child.' After living with me all these years, I should have known that she could tell what I was thinking." They put in their application, and some eighteen months later received a four-year-old Vietnamese orphan. The other children were so overjoyed that they stayed home from school and went to the airport to meet their new sister. With children of Caucasian, Indian, black, and Vietnamese backgrounds, the Halls refer to their family as the "little UN." They feel that they must instill within all their children a strong *human* identity and a sensitivity to and appreciation of their racial and cultural heritages. "We recognize how difficult it is to spend a great deal of time with each individual child on this question, so we try to combine a lot of it," Desmond explained. "All of the children are involved in his sister's or brother's learning experiences. If we decide to see a black film, all of the kids go. If there is an exhibit of Indian crafts, everyone goes, and each child is made to feel that it has some importance to him or her, even though it is our Indian child who knows that it comes from his people. This is the only way we can do it, and it is the way it should be done," said Desmond. "Yet we recognize that we live in a society that harshly condemns black people. We would be evading our responsibility if we didn't try to, in some very direct way, let Caroline know that she will face hostility solely because she is black," Desmond said. "But don't you also feel that she has learned a hell of a lot about how awful people can be—that they can wage wars against their fellowman, and how bad the Indians have it on their reservations?" Carla asked Desmond. "Each of our children, including our biological daughter, learns from the other's group experiences. We don't put a value judgment on either by saying that one will be good and the other will be bad. We also prepare them not only for the terrible things they might face, but for the joys of life. I want them to be able to accept both."

The "Ethnic" Family

Some parents do not emphasize *black* nor *human* identity with their adopted child. Barbara and Richard Kaplan, who live in the Midwest, are imparting a Jewish identity to Nathan, their three-year-old black son. That he is of Negroid ancestry (both his parents were black) is of little concern to them since they are totally immersed in Jewish ethnic and religious culture. Nathan is enrolled in a nursery operated by their synagogue. Richard, thirty-one, is a medical researcher, while Barbara is now a housewife. She taught grade school prior to the birth of their six-year-old daughter, Sarah. After several miscarriages, they decided to adopt a son.

They learned of the white infant shortage after inquiring of several agencies, and were told that it might take years before they could be considered, since they already had a child. "Several agencies weren't even taking applications," said the outgoing Barbara. When they called one agency, the social worker told them that they had biracial and black children available if they were interested. "We really didn't care if the child had one black parent or two," Richard explained, "just so long as he wasn't too dark in color. We wanted him to be able to blend into our family." It is of some concern to them that Nathan's complexion has darkened a lot since they adopted him.

Barbara and Richard grew up on the East Coast of Orthodox Jewish parents. Both of their fathers were successful businessmen, and they described their mothers as "traditional and typical Jewish mothers." All four grandparents were opposed to the adoption, and one set of grandparents have indicated that they would rather not see the child or his parents again. They were subsequently disinherited.

The Kaplans spent a great deal of time discussing racial and ethnic identity before they decided to adopt Nathan. "We never once considered that we would rear him to be anything but Jewish," said Richard. "We are totally aware of all the conflicting arguments about the need for black children to have black identities. I have probably read everything that was ever published about it. But we have strong Jewish identity, and that is what we want our children to have." Barbara echoed the sentiments of her husband when she said, "I don't see any reason for us confusing Nathan about who he is. I think he'd be very mixed up if we hammered into his head this black identity stuff, along with his Jewish identity. I don't think he would be able to put the two together, so I'd rather give him one strong identity, and that is the Jewish." Richard, however, said he actually *prefers* that his son be brought up in the Jewish culture, to the exclusion of all others, including the black. "I don't worry about confusing him. It's just that I don't want to bring him up a black. I want him to be what we are. We aren't black. We're Jewish." He later conceded that his views might change when Nathan grows older.

The Kaplans are insensitive to the criticism of black social workers and some of their fellow transracially adoptive parents. They do not belong to one of the adoptive parents' groups, and have no intention of joining. "We don't have the need for that kind of backup support that a lot of these people have," Richard emphasized. "We don't have that much in common with them. The fact that all of us may have adopted black children is not sufficient reason for me to make friends with them."

When asked if they wanted Nathan to marry a black or a white, Barbara replied, "We would hope he will marry someone Jewish." Richard agreed.

THE "BIRACIAL" FAMILY

The notion that a child is legally and socially designated black because he or she has one black parent deeply perplexes some adoptive parents. They wonder if this is justified, given the fact that many mixed-race children are more Caucasian than Negroid in appearance. Nelson and Margaret Webb have a five-year-old biological daughter, Betsy, and an eighteen-month-old adopted son, Johnny, whose father was black and whose mother was white. Nelson, a businessman, and Margaret, a housewife, adopted Johnny after their own son died of multiple complications in early infancy. Acknowledging that it would have been difficult to adopt a child with two black parents, Nelson is unwilling to concede that Johnny is or should be considered *black*. "While I don't have any objections to calling Johnny *black*, I don't think he is any more black than he is white," said Nelson. Margaret takes a different view, since she is more willing to acknowledge and accept the social and legal definition of her son's race. "I have been impressed by the statement made by the black social workers that Johnny will be accepted by society as black," she said. "He will be discriminated against as a black." Margaret also realizes that, "Living in a white family, Johnny will not, no matter what, be able to learn the defenses that are taught to kids in black families." Nelson agreed with his wife on this point: "You're right," he said. "I don't think that, in any way, we can equip him as a black family could. Johnny will be going to a predominantly black school when he is old enough. It is the one that Betsy goes to now. He will learn a lot of the defenses he needs to know in the school from the black kids instead of from us. He will learn the language of the ghetto and the lifestyles of the white middle class."

Connie and Russ Parker adopted a mixed-race daughter, Tara, who is now two. Connie considers the societal designation of these children as black to be a social problem. "As far as I am concerned, the fact that society has decreed that anybody with black blood is black," said Connie, "is a social problem, since I don't believe there is any biological evidence to support this assumption." She continued, "Since I assume that Tara is just as much white as black, in spite of all these so-called legal definitions of her race, then the question is, Would it not be better for her to be adopted by a white family who will accept her for what she is than to be placed in a foster home or an institution?" Russ disagreed. "Whether we like it or not," he said to Connie, "our daughter is going to be *treated* as a black. I guess I too would like to see her as a white child too. But we have to deal with the reality of the situation because, unfortunately, it is not left up to us alone to define her. Pretty soon she'll be entering grade school. Then on to high school, and before we know it she'll be entering college. Somewhere along the way, we will have fallen by the wayside in terms of being major influences on her and our two boys. Children don't remain in the cocoon of their parents' protection. They are breaking out sooner and sooner each day. So where does that leave us?" With great emphasis, he said, "It means we have to *accept* the legal definition of her as a *black* person and teach her how to take care of herself and what to expect." Connie was not swayed by her husband's argument. "I wish I could agree with you," she said. "Maybe it is my own ego that's involved. As a white woman, who is also a mother who loves her daughter, my question is why should the society deprive *me*, her mother, of identifying with her whiteness? They don't do this to black mothers who adopt biracial kids. Those black mothers are told by the society that they have a *black* daughter, or a *black* son. They aren't even asked to identify with the *whiteness* in the child," she exclaimed. "In fact, they are encouraged by the agencies and everyone else to forget that the child has one white parent." Turning to his wife, in a very understanding tone, Russ said, "Honey, everything you're saying is right, but it is also wrong. You are trying to isolate your children like every mother before you has probably done at one time or another. What do you think would happen if you reared Tara like a white girl? How are you going to comfort her when she comes home crying because one of her playmates has called her 'nigger'? We can't tell her that she should ignore it because she's 'integrated' or 'black-white' or some of those other names some of these white parents are calling their black children. That might even cause her more confusion because if you look back into history, the mulattoes and octaroons weren't looked on all that good. A lot of people still call these kids 'halfbreeds' and 'halfcasts.' If we lived in Brazil, what you're saying would be fine because that is a multiracial society. People are all different colors there. But the truth of the matter is that we live in the United States of America, where race is uppermost in everyone's minds. People see you in terms of whether you're *black* or *white*. Nothing else matters." Connie responded by saying, "I guess I am forced to agree with you even if I don't want to. I believe in an integrated society, and when people type you as being either black or white, they are reinforcing segregation instead of encouraging people to live together."

"I feel that everyone has to feel that there is someone who brought them into the world and that there was a reason for this happening," said Lee Simmons, a school principal who is the father of two mixed-race adopted sons and four biological children. Asserting that any identity crisis an adopted child goes through is a "cop-out," he said, "A lot of adoptive people who have reached young adulthood are now out looking for their 'real' parents. They tell themselves that 'If I could find my natural parents, maybe it would be different.' They aren't as interested in finding their real parents to resolve some identity crisis. They're using this as an excuse to avoid facing responsibilities in life. It's just another cop-out." Emphasizing that he and his wife teach their children a sense of responsibility, he added, "It's the same thing with the *biracial* identity. It could really hang somebody up, it could tear them up in little pieces. But if it did I would contend that there were other problems well in advance of this that caused it." His wife, Marie, a housewife, asked, "But what is causing all these people to go out searching for their biological parents? They must have a valid reason." Lee explained, "It has to do with a lack of knowledge of one's family. When people go looking for their other parents, their adoptive parents have not given them the secure identity so they would know who they are and where they came from, and of knowing where they are right now." Turning to the interviewer, he said, "As far as our adopted sons' identity is concerned, before they go to school [they are two and four], they are going to know that they are mixed racially. My guess is that they will have to come to the realization at some point, that they are half this and half that, and they will have to learn to live with this fact, to accept it and be responsible for their actions. Unless somewhere down the line there would be a new third, fourth, or fifth race created. But this would take hundreds of years." As an afterthought he said, "Maybe not that long. How long did it take, if you believe in Adam and Eve or evolution, for red men, white men, and black men to come into existence?"

The "Mixed Race" Child

Mary Conway, a young housewife, termed the legal designation of mixed-race children as black as a fallacious assumption and therefore rejected the black social workers' contention that such children belonged exclusively in black homes. "I think it is a ridiculous assumption for the black social workers to say that because Anita, our two-year-old, is one half black, one fourth white, and one fourth Indian. She is at least triracial, and who is to assume that the black part of her ancestry ought to be emphasized exclusively?" she asked. A father in St. Louis who adopted a mixed-race child acknowledged that he could understand why the black social workers view transracial adoptions as threatening of the black family, "But I personally don't agree with them," he said. "I just see people as people. Besides, it would take generations before any real threat could be posed against black people, before their race would be wiped out. These adoptions are so small in number that statistically they don't make any difference whatever. But if you consider it carefully, we're all mixed in some kind of way. I wonder if there is anybody who is pure pure. I'm part Italian and part Scandinavian, which is certainly a mixture. When my grandfather came to visit, he brought the family scrapbook and showed us pictures of his family. As a way of letting us know he approved of our adopting Kacey, he said that my grandmother's father had been black. We had always thought he was an Indian. This was something which had never come out in the family." He concluded by asking, "So who's to say where these children *absolutely* belong? Nobody in this society is *pure black* or *pure white*."

THE REJECTION OF BLACK IDENTITY

Black identity is rejected outright by some parents who view it disparagingly. They stress individual identity and maintain that their black adopted child should not be imparted a racial identity since they believe it does not have positive attributes. They often make the conscious decision to adopt a mixed-race child instead of one with two black parents. On occasion they are willing to admit that they would not have been able to bring themselves to adopt a dark-skinned child.

June and George Hobbs, who live in an upper-middle-class all-white suburban neighborhood, are such a couple. After the birth of their daughter, who is now three, June developed an infertility problem, and they decided to adopt a minority-race child after learning of the scarcity of white children. "A woman I know who is a member of the Open Door Society told me that biracial children are not undesirable anymore, and that people are actively trying to adopt them," said June. "So George and I talked it over for a few days and we decided that we had a legitimate right to a biracial child. We felt that whites should be responsible for them because whites are just as much a part of that child as blacks are." Since George, a research scientist, is away from home with his work a great amount of time, most of the childrearing is left up to his wife.

The Hobbs do not feel that children of mixed parentage should be classified "black" or that they should be given a black identity. "Basically we are not racial-oriented people," said June. "We think more in terms of personal identity," she explained. Before they adopted their son she explained that "I read [Erik] Erikson a lot to renew my faith. We felt that the development of the individual ego is much more important than the development of the racial identity. To tell the truth, we just can't take the concept of blackness too seriously, although I know it's important in determining what happens to people." June explained what black identity means to her: "It involves where you come from, what your racial origins have been, and what kind of people you sprung from, that go back to African societies. It is not a mystical thing but an enrichment part of your life. It's like any other culture." June emphasized that she and George do not look on blacks very favorably. "I think black people have a certain self-destructive element in their culture," June noted. "They have a self-denigrating view about themselves." Insisting that she doesn't want her son to identify with any of these "denigrating" aspects of blacks, she reaffirms her belief in the importance of a strong individual identity when she said, "We are not ashamed of our biracial child at all. I think we can and will give him a truly positive image of himself."

THE IMPORTANCE OF SOCIAL CLASS

For a few parents, social class takes precedence over race in their childrearing practices. They argue that theirs is primarily an upper-middle-class identification that their children are experiencing instead of one that is or should be black or white. Therefore, instead of trying to deliberately impart a racial identity to their adopted children, they insist that the overriding influence on the child's outcome will be that he or she has been reared as an upper-middle-class person, emphasizing high achievement values. They argue that, without regard for color, black upper-middle-class parents are just as likely to impart the same kind of socializing experiences to their children as they are. A mother remarked, "I think the problems that middle-class blacks have in raising their children and the kind of experiences their children have are by and large the same kinds of experiences that our children have. It's a middle-class experience." In summary fashion, a father noted, "When you reach a certain income and educational level, racial influences diminish, and the class you belong to has more of an impact on your attitudes, your values, and your overall lifestyle."

They also question whether it is realistic for others to expect them, as white upper-middle-class Americans, to be able to give their children a decidedly *black* identity. A father in St. Louis asks, "Is it really realistic to expect white parents to be able to incorporate any kind of blackness in their kids? My feeling is that they can't. It can only come from other resources." He also asks, "Is it necessary to have black friends and live in a biracial neighborhood?" This man, who adopted a child of mixed parentage, said, "At some point when we have acceptable answers for this question, we might have to move to a racially mixed neighborhood so that a major part of Jimmy's life will be involved with other blacks and the black community. But for the present, we'll remain where we are."

His concern with the racial composition of his neighborhood was expressed by many parents, who wondered whether their black child could grow up with a healthy black self-concept in an all-white or predominantly white suburban community. So strongly did some parents feel that their children would suffer identity problems that they moved from the all-white suburbs to more racially integrated communities, a few of which were located in the inner city.

To what extent has the adoption of a child who is designated *black* by the society forced these parents to confront some of their own racial prejudices and myths? A large number of parents admitted that this was one of the by-products of the adoption. As one father remarked, "You just don't grow up in America as a white person and not have some prejudices and racism."

Parenting a black child forces one to examine and analyze his or her own feelings and attitudes on a variety of issues, including race. It also produces an increase in self-awareness. One mother explained this personal transformation as the difference between adopting a black child into *your* white family where you continue to perceive yourselves as basically a "white" family, and being happy over the fact that your biological daughter is going to marry a black man. Another parent described it as the difference between the theoretical acceptance of black culture, and the practical aspect of having an equal number of black and white friends and living in a racially integrated neighborhood where you send *all* your children to school. "All of us as adoptive parents can be 'nice white liberals' as far as race is concerned," she said. "But the deeper and more important question is, How much have we changed for the better as a result of adopting a black child?" She explained, "Some parents I know feel they are giving this kid a chance in life that he never would have had if they hadn't adopted him. But they don't make the connection between what they've done and their own private feelings toward other blacks. The kid is kept neatly tucked away in their minds because he is 'different' as far as they are concerned. Just wait and let their daughter bring home a black boy friend. They'd hit the ceiling! It's like the movie *Guess Who's Coming to Dinner*." If parents teach their children racial equality, even in the theoretical context, they should not be alarmed if their children practice it.

Parents discussed a variety of ways in which their misconceptions of blacks had been altered or erased after they adopted. Racial myths notwithstanding, several parents maintain that their black child has more "natural rhythm" than their white children. One mother said all her myths were shed except one: "When the music starts, Donald gets up and starts swaying. My aunt says he has such natural rhythm," she said, as she echoed the sentiments of several others. Another mother said she always felt that blacks had a strong body odor until they adopted a black child. When asked if the adoption had dispelled any racial myths he had, a St. Louis father quipped, "His penis isn't any bigger!" referring to his three-year-old black son. On a more serious note, most of these parents have, at different times, been thrust into situations in which they were forced to raise questions about how they actually feel about blacks generally. One father said, "There is a difference between feeling sorry for the race and having one in your home. At some point your black child puts it in perspective." A mother said, "Every time we are out in public, we find people staring at us. That forces us to become *us* against *them*. If you find yourself defending your black child, you are bound to start questioning the things you were taught all your life about blacks."

Of course, there are many parents who say they had confronted and resolved all their myths and prejudices long before they adopted, while others said they could never recall having held any such racial stereotypes. As one mother explained, "I don't think I ever had any myths about black people. I don't believe in racial traits." Many are open-minded, flexible individuals who are committed to the goals of an integrated society.

Many of these parents said that in their pursuit of an integrated society, they had carefully examined their racial attitudes and purged themselves of any prejudices they may have had long before adopting a black child. Some had been involved in activist groups that promoted racial harmony. Adopting across racial boundaries was but another act in their long involvement. Thus they disagreed with the black social workers' charge that transracial adoptions were weakening the black family. Their belief in integration was antithetical to what they perceived as the social workers' desire for separatism. Jennie O'Donnell, mother of two biological children and an adopted child with two black parents, disagrees strongly with the black social workers. She and her husband, Harry, have enrolled their two older white children in a predominantly black Head Start school some eighteen miles from their home. "Because we believe in an integrated society, we have organized our lifestyle to reflect that belief," said Jennie. "Our two children are already reading materials on blacks, and we have family discussions on different problems that are related to race," she explained. "We also go to church in a black neighborhood, and we seek out black people through various organizations." When two-year-old Barbara is old enough, she will join her older brothers in the Head Start school where, according to Harry, "they are involved with black children every day of the week." In the meantime, Jennie spent a semester enrolled in black studies courses at a local university and she, with Harry, have participated in several black studies seminars.

The O'Donnells argue that the black social workers are actually contributing to racial polarization. "I'm all for the black family becoming a strong unit and I'm all for black communities pulling themselves together so they can combat racism," said Jennie. "But I see no need why it has to be a totally black effort because whites can contribute to combating racism." Harry agreed: "I think that a lot of the black social workers are also trying to establish a position for themselves. They seem to think that only they know what's important for the black community. They have an intellectual approach to blackness, and they forget some of the humanistic elements of the baby. I think the black social workers are more concerned about things that don't have anything to do with the babies. If in fact there were enough black families for all the black babies, that would be fine. I would like to see a lot of white babies adopted into black families, but there aren't a lot of white babies, but there are a lot of black babies." Jennie, however, was not so convinced. "I don't agree with everything you've said," she told Harry. "I think interracial families are very viable things. I don't think a black child has to be with a black family, nor do I think a white child has to be with a white family. I don't think the opinion of the black social workers is valid at this point in time because the fact is that there are not enough black homes or black people applying for the black babies. So the alternative is to either place them with white parents or leave them in an institutional structure." Harry said, "Maybe you're right. Too many blacks think that transracial adoptions are actually threatening black culture. But they aren't at all. I think the adoptions are promoting black culture and history because white families have more of an access to the various institutions which teach it, and in many ways, they can be more influential than many black people."

Jennie says that she has become more involved in black cultural activities since adopting Barbara. "I find myself demanding that the schools actively combat racism, and that's something very new to the educational institutions," says Jennie. "A white mother demanding that black culture be incorporated into the schools is unheard of. It's too bad that a white person has that much influence, but it's a fact. I think that transracial adoptions are a positive thing based upon the fact that you have people who are actively seeking out the black community and making them a part of your family. I think that the whole black movement is super!" she added. "The black intellectuals should get down into the dirt where, unfortunately, a lot of black people are forced to live, and stop worrying about transracial adoption. They should be out teaching more black culture to their own people. Then they would be doing more good."

The glimpses into the lives of the families described above indicate how varied are their perceptions of, and responses to, the problem of their black children's identity formation. These children's outcomes later in life will be determined, largely, by their parents' perspectives on this aspect of their psychosocial development.

9

TESTIMONY
Blacks Who Grew Up in White Homes

There are scattered throughout the United States a small number of blacks—adolescents and adults—who were reared by white parents. Some of these adoptions, which occurred as early as the late 1940s, were legal, and others were informal or nonlegal. As discussed earlier, until the 1960s it was illegal for parents of one race to adopt a child of another race in most of the southern states, and it was not an accepted custom in the rest of the nation, due to the prevailing segregation ethos. In those states where it was illegal for whites to adopt a black child, couples "informally" adopted the child by assuming the parental roles and responsibilities without fulfilling the legal requirements and without either parent or child enjoying the legal protections. In other cases the parents assumed responsibility without ever attempting to adopt the child. Perhaps in many cases they never had a desire to adopt. They became the guardians or permanent foster parents to these children. Of the black teen-agers and adults featured by Thompson, roughly half appear to have had relatively successful outcomes and the others had suffered various types of identity problems.

Most of the children in this study are either still under school age or in the early years of grade school. When the data were collected, few had entered grade school. Most parents wanted desperately to know more about what had happened to the small number of adolescents and adults who were adopted. What had been their experiences? These parents were preoccupied with this concern because they thought their parental roles and childrearing practices could be more successful if they could learn from the experiences of others. "If I could find out what the older children went through and how their parents handled it," said an apprehensive mother in Minneapolis, "I would feel far better prepared to plunge into the future with all the uncertainties of adolescence. It's hard enough to raise a teen-ager of your own flesh and blood, not to mention one who is *adopted* and *black*."

Many follow-up studies have been conducted on adoptees and their outcomes. The majority have concentrated on the young, healthy, white child. The determinants of success have been defined in various ways. The most elementary measure of the success of an adoptive placement is whether the parents kept the child beyond the probationary period required by state laws (usually ranging from six months to one year). If the adoptive parent or parents do not return the child to the agency due to a "breakdown" in the adoption, by the most modest evaluation, the placement would be deemed successful.

Beyond this basic criterion are other important measures of the degree to which the child whose adoption was legalized in the courts has successfully adapted to his or her familial and environmental setting, and the degree to which they have been able to develop a stable, integrated personality. In an assessment of outcome studies, Kadushin observed, "In general, background factors in both the child and the parents appear to have little relation to outcome. The child's background variables seem to have less and less significance as prognostic factors from placement to follow-up. . . . a tribute to the resilience of children in surmounting earlier developmental deficiencies, to the coping capacity of the adoptive parents, and to the rehabilitative potential of a good adoptive home."[1] A summary of outcome studies on agency and independent adoptions shows that the majority are successful: "Sixty-five per cent are unequivocally successful . . . 18 per cent achieve some intermediate level of success; 17 per cent are unsuccessful."[2] These studies included white, nonhandicapped infants.

Outcome studies have been conducted on nonwhite children by Raynor, Zastrow, Fanshel, Nutt and Snyder, and Grow and Shapiro. Raynor's study of nonwhite children adopted in Britain found that 83 per cent of the parents described the adoption as "very satisfying."[3] Zastrow's study of families in Wisconsin found that 88 per cent of the parents found the adoption "extremely satisfying."[4] A five-year longitudinal study conducted by Fanshel with parents who adopted American Indian children discloses that a majority described the adoption as "successful."[5] A longitudinal study by Grow and Shapiro of 125 black children and their white parents indicates a "success" rate of 77 per cent. All were at least six years old and had been in their adoptive homes at least three years. In this most comprehensive study of black children to date, Grow and Shapiro were encouraged enough with the level of success to recommend the continuation of transracial adoptive placements.[6]

One problem with assessing the outcome of transracially adopted children in these studies is that they have not reached adolescence—a critical phase of psychosocial development. In order to learn what happens in later life to those adopted, the researcher interviewed six blacks adopted into white families who were old enough to talk about their experiences. This enabled the researcher to bypass the parents altogether, and the adoptees spoke for themselves. (All interviews were conducted in privacy, and no parents or other relatives were present.)

The oldest was a thirty-six-year-old male who was adopted when he was thirteen years old. A twenty-seven-year-old black woman was never formally adopted but grew up under the guardianship of a wealthy white southern woman. Since they were "adopted" as older children, and because they grew up at a time when black-white relations were more segregated than they are today, their experiences and perspectives were, as expected, different from the large numbers of young children who were adopted since the mid-1960s. For this reason, I interviewed four younger children who are products of the transracial adoption movement of the 1960s and early seventies. All of these youths live in the Northeast; they are thirteen, twelve, and two are ten years old. While this is not a scientific sample, these case studies will give the reader insights into how these people have fared, what have been their experiences, how they have coped with racial and other problems, what kind of achievement motivation they have, and what their future expectations are.

RAY BROWN

"If I had been able to make the decision I think I would have preferred being adopted by a black," said Ray, a thirty-six-year-old college professor and father of eight- and six-year-old daughters. "Even though my parents tried to do as much for me as they could—they gave me all the amenities any child could ever want—as a black child you need people who are able to sympathize with you as a black individual. They tried, but they just couldn't play that role like a black person could.

"I was thirteen when I was adopted. My patterns were already set. But if you adopted a child at an earlier age—anywhere from eighteen months to about three years old—then you begin to set the pattern for him, you set his lifestyle. He doesn't really view himself as a black person in many ways. He sees his color as different. It can be very shattering for a black person who grew up in a white world or with white parents to be told they are black.

"The disadvantage of transracial adoption is that the parents do not have the ability to relate to the child as a black person would. Some white people say they can empathize with blacks, can feel what blacks do, but I don't think so."

Ray, who now lives on the West Coast, was adopted by a well-to-do professional couple in 1952. Born in Georgia as one of seven children, Ray's parents brought their children to New York when he was very young. The pressures of the city on this impoverished large black family resulted in permanent disruption soon after their arrival in New York. "My old man just disappeared and my mother wasn't able to take care of all of us. I guess that's why the agency took us away from our mother," Ray recalls. "I haven't seen him [his father] since then, when I was about eleven years old. My mother is still living. I guess that now that my sisters and brothers are grown up and on their own, some of them look her up occasionally." Ray has not seen either of his parents since he and his sisters and brothers went to live in institutions. Several of his siblings were also adopted, although none transracially, and all are now leading successful lives. Although he lives on the West Coast and they on the East Coast, he occasionally visits them.

When Ray was living in the city-operated institution, he and the other children were often taken to a nearby parish that served as the focal point for many community activities. "We were allowed to go to this church because there were so many things to do," he recalls. "Kids congregate at places where there are things to do. It was an inner-city church, and you could go to camp and on hiking trips." It was here that the minister and his wife, a young childless couple, took to Ray immediately and expressed an interest in adopting him. "They wanted someone to care for," he said, as he explained their motives for adopting him. "They had done so much in the community where I was adopted. They would always emphasize the fact that they wanted someone to love, and particularly a minority person." After a long pause, he said, "Looking back on it now I think they wanted to make up for what whites were doing to blacks. In many ways they felt guilt for their own race."

Ray lives with his wife of thirteen years, Marian, who is also black, and his two daughters, on the West Coast. The majority of their friends are black, although some are white. Their daughters are enrolled in a predominantly white school. Marian is a part-time student and is employed full-time. Ray has a quiet, easygoing manner. He seems quite well-adjusted, especially considering the fact that when he was growing up his adoptive family moved about the country continuously, making it impossible for them to put down roots in one place. The added pressure of being the minister's son, a role that could have caused Ray to have serious emotional problems, is a factor he fully recognizes. He remembers his growing-up years, frequently living in racially diverse communities, as very comfortable and secure, and always receiving whatever material things he wanted. He repeatedly speaks of the generosity of his parents, which persists today with the showering of gifts on him and his family. "I never wanted for anything. There was no lack; I had everything." In a rare moment Ray allows himself to question his parents' reasons for what he considered an abnormal pattern of giving: "I wonder if it was because of their guilt over being white."

Having been adopted into this particular family also provided Ray with privileges he is certain he would not have had otherwise. "As far as the advantages are concerned," he said, "I've had them all; more than I could have had in a black family unless it had been one that was quite well off." These benefits include attending a prep school, private college, vacations at their summer home, and travel. "I would say being adopted opened a lot of doors for me—doors opened a lot easier for me because of my adoption," he explained. When he was in college his parents adopted two Asian children, who are now grown. Since he was so much older, they never spent much time together, and they rarely see each other now.

Ray says there was a long period of time when he regarded himself "as a human being" because of the privileges of his upper-middle-class lifestyle, and although he was always fully aware of his blackness, he did not always strongly identify with it. Only after he was married and had set up his own household did he begin to seriously evaluate black-white relations. "When I was growing up, back in the late fifties and early sixties, some of my friends who became Black Muslims attacked me because of my white parents," said Ray. "I'd get on the defensive in most cases. Trying to protect my parents, and at the same time to keep the friends, I was really caught in a dilemma. I think in most cases I wound up just defending my parents. I had no choice. I lost some friends, but you can't love everybody."

He does not recall that his parents ever had to come to his rescue and defend him against racial hostility. He is certain that some of the church members put pressure on his parents, but they always shielded him from this hostility. "Oh, I'm sure they did. We spent time in a lot of places where there weren't many blacks. I'm sure there were many things they hid from me. I must repeat that I was always constantly aware I was black and equally aware that people didn't like me because I was black."

In his prep school he was the only black. There were isolated occasions when other students made derisive comments about him, calling him such names as "nigger." In his usual quiet manner, he either ignored them or responded in like fashion. On the whole he adjusted quite well and emerged as a school leader.

It was in the 1960s, after Ray was married and had set up his own household, that he began to seriously consider the implications of being a black. Always viewed as the "exceptional" who was different from other blacks because of his father's respected status in the communities where they lived, and never having had strong reason to experience a black identity crisis, it was only when the freedom rides began that he started to develop a black identity. He was further affected by the riots that started in Watts and spread to Newark and other cities. "Marian and I saw photographs of the riots in magazines. It was then that we became acutely conscious that we were black and knew we had to take sides," said Ray. "A lot of our white friends just turned away from us, and we were no longer on the party circuit as the only blacks in the group. We found ourselves having to side with blacks." With the increasing development of his black consciousness, he and Marian lived in the Caribbean and Africa, where they taught for several years before returning to the United States.

Ray describes his relationship with his wife as a very close one, admitting that she exerts a strong influence over him. In conversations, he constantly refers to her. "My wife sometimes tells me that 'those years you spent with your white parents may have done you more harm than good,'" says Ray. "She tells me that I am too much like my father—she says, 'You don't go at life the way most black people go at it. You seem to think that it's there for you.' She thinks I take everything in life for granted."

A problem with having been adopted by affluent white parents, Ray feels, is that he failed to develop the "survival skills" that black social workers mention so prominently. "I find myself really having to work hard to understand that blacks have to struggle for the things they get in life," he said. "My wife tells me that I have been raised to believe that things are going to be there waiting for me, whereas blacks are brought up to hope that it's going to be there. They never assume that anything is going to be waiting for them. I used to think the answer for all our problems in the United States was integration, because that was what I was brought up to believe in—that white and black would make it together. For a while in the sixties during the civil rights movement blacks and whites were doing it together. It was in 1963 that I could see that the whites were really taking advantage of us." During this period he had strong antiwhite feelings, going to the point of rejecting some of the whites he knew. "I began to generalize, and I would lump my white parents into the group with all other whites, particularly since it was some of their friends who were doing this to us." For a very short time he associated his parents with all other whites. "I went through a period in my twenties when I rejected my parents because they were white," Ray remembers. "It was difficult to rationalize. You begin to generalize your feelings on race. You try not to let that happen. You say to yourself, 'I don't hate *all* white people, because my parents are white. How can I?' Yet it's white that you're zeroing in on. I guess I had to suppress these feelings as much as I could, although I might have expressed my hostility in other ways. I might have been angry but did not say I was angry at them or at whites in general." At any rate, his parents' racial philosophy heightened his ambivalence: "I never broke contact with my parents, because my father was rather outspoken in the 1960s on the civil rights question. He wanted to send me into the civil rights movement as a participant. I guess in many ways his outspoken position helped me get through that period."

Today Ray maintains good relations with his parents and his only living grandmother, who often sends gifts to his daughters. Ray said, "We've had to explain to our daughters why my parents are white. They point out the difference between my wife's mother and mine. They say 'Grandma . . . I mean white Grandma.' Or 'white Grandpa.' But they accept them as grandparents." He continued, "They ask their grandparents, 'Why are you white when we are black?' My parents have no choice but to explain to them." His daughters are aware of the meaning of adoption. "I have never pressed details on them, but they understand what adoption means on a basic level," he explained. "For example, when they are playing with their black dolls we explain to them that they could never give birth to a white baby." In this way they learn that there are several ways in which one can become a parent.

In reflecting on the years when he was growing up, Ray says he often wonders why his parents always gave him so much. "Even when I was older I was still given, given. When I was going to graduate school and money was short, I always told them I would repay the loans they gave me, but it was always a gift. I am sure they wanted me to succeed. Now that I'm older and going through the crisis of having to state my beliefs or my loyalties . . . even now, looking back, I question the motivation. I suppose you get showered with so much. But I guess I've gotten as far as I have because of it. Dad once said, 'Maybe we did more harm to you than good.' But I guess he was joking."

With a bit of romanticism he said, "When I talk to black men his [father's] age, the fatherly figure, I wonder what it would have been like if I had been able to talk to my father this way or if he could relate to me the same way. However, at the time I was growing up we related to each other in a way that was fair."

JENNIFER ROBERTS

"The advantages I have now are the advantages of choice," says twenty-seven-year-old Jennifer. "I have some say in my own destiny. I don't have to be a welfare mother, I don't have to be a maid. I can choose what I want to do. Choice is a beautiful thing."

Jennifer was "informally" adopted by a wealthy childless southern white woman when she was five years old. Her biological mother, who worked as a maid on the estate, moved away immediately after consenting to have her employer become her child's guardian. Her guardian, an only child and heiress to a business fortune, had graduated from a well-known women's college in the East and was a widow. Her mother was dead, and her father never forgave her for bringing a black child into her home. Growing up as an only child in the midst of luxury, Jennifer remembers her guardian, which she calls her, as a very kind, warm person who introduced her to many exciting and intellectually challenging things in life that no black child in her community experienced. "My preadolescent memories are of a compassionate, perceptive, sensitive, intelligent, beautiful woman—just like magic," says Jennifer. "When I was growing up, she was just beautiful. She taught me how to high dive and swim when I was six; I was able to do gourmet cooking by the time I was seven, and to drive a standard-shift car by the time I was nine. So tackling the dictionary at eleven was really no big thing." Jennifer also expresses strong ambivalence and occasional hostility toward her guardian, resulting from a severe rupture in their relationship when she was sixteen. Her remarks about this woman are equally divided between laudatory and antagonistic.

Today Jennifer owns a consulting firm and is writing a book. She paints in her leisure time. Twice divorced, she has a ten-year-old son of her first marriage who is away in boarding school.

Jennifer recalls how she felt when she first went to live with her guardian. "When my mother first left, I was very unhappy and felt abandoned. Naturally I knew I was moving from the servants' house." With strong emphasis, she exclaimed, "Anybody would know that! But I didn't know why. And I didn't ask anyone. I was sad about it for a long time until it just didn't matter. At the time my guardian just didn't discuss it with me." In her own private way Jennifer came to understand and was able to rationalize this separation from her mother. "I once had a dream about Moses in the bulrushes, and how Moses' mother saw Pharaoh's daughter who was a barren woman with no children," mused Jennifer. "The mother more or less pushed the basket in that direction because she had planned that that would be the person who picked it up. It seems like my mother was, indeed, a beautiful, wise woman, and she knew what she was doing all along. I appreciate what she did for me because, naturally, my opportunities were greater than if I had stayed with her."

Jennifer's opportunities were indeed great. When she was ten her guardian took her to Europe for two years, where she went to school with the children of royalty, learned to speak several languages, and traveled throughout the continent.

"Most people in Europe didn't know that she was in a mother role to me," said Jennifer. "They thought I was some black potentate, and she was my maid. I loved it! I ate it up!" Upon returning to the United States she went away to a finishing school in the East.

During her growing-up years she never had friends come to visit her at the estate. "You had to go miles and miles before you found other black families to play with," explained Jennifer. "So I guess I didn't have friends to play with mainly because of our location. I was too far away." In spite of not having children her age to play with, Jennifer says she never felt lonely. "I didn't know I was being deprived of something because I had never experienced having friends to play with." Her guardian kept a busy schedule of activities for her at home, which filled all the leisure time she would have spent playing with friends. She went to an all-black school, having to walk a mile to the home of the bus driver. Her young playmates at school never questioned the fact that her mother was white. "There was something about the mother-daughter relationship in black communities in the South that nobody messed with, no matter if they were of different races," said Jennifer.

When she reached adolescence her guardian moved to a mansion in the city so Jennifer could be closer to school and friends. Jennifer remembers having slumber parties, attending parties and school dances, and going out on dates. When asked how her guardian related to her black friends who stayed over at slumber parties, she replied, "I had the whole upstairs suite. And the maid usually cleaned up after us so she didn't have to get that personally involved." This was also the period when she has her most bitter recollection of racial discrimination. Describing the times when they dined out, Jennifer said, "I always had to eat in the kitchen while my guardian and her friends ate in the restaurant. When we got to the restaurant we would split up; I went into the kitchen." When asked about her reaction to this discrimination, she replied, "I thought it was a drag. What hit me the hardest was the economics of the whole thing. They didn't charge any less for me to eat in the kitchen. I guess I became mercenary after a while, and started getting around more and more rich people and finding out how money works. That was just a bad use of money!" In reply to a query about whether she ever asked her guardian to explain why they couldn't dine together, she said, "I never had to ask; it was clear—because I was black and they were white. Different people reach different levels of social consciousness at different times. And that was the level of my guardian and her friends' awareness at that time. People do change."

In spite of the admiration she now expresses for her guardian, when Jennifer was sixteen, something drastic happened that caused a severe break in their relationship, and they were estranged for many years. Jennifer refuses to discuss what happened between them. Neither will she discuss her two marriages, which took place when she was sixteen and seventeen and a half. Her first husband, father of her son, was a local black disc jockey whom Jennifer considered "the epitome of manhood, a very light-hearted radio DJ." Her second husband, who was white, was a "wonderful person. I still think a lot of him. I still carry his name." Jennifer, now single, says she cannot imagine ever marrying anyone again, since she has already experienced it. Although the details are sketchy, somewhere during the time after she and her guardian parted when she was sixteen, she had a child, graduated from college, and supported herself through law school. With deep emotion Jennifer said, "After we had a serious falling out, I left her and she did not invest a cent in me. I struggled to make it on my own. I lived in a subbasement ghetto apartment with little food and practically no money, but I still made it." Expressing ambivalent feelings about the guardian to whom she was once strongly devoted, she explained, "I didn't think that much of her kind of wealth. The kind of money I feel good about is the kind of money I'm *making*. My guardian and other heirs and heiresses would have been rich even if they had spent their lives as babbling idiots. They were born right, not that they ever did a damn thing. Some of them I knew didn't do anything. But they still are going to be rich. And I didn't want that kind of money." Now that she has started her own business, Jennifer, who exudes self-confidence, replied to a query as to whether she wanted to become wealthy, "It isn't that I want to someday become wealthy, it's just that I'm going to."

Identifying herself as an assured *black* woman, Jennifer experienced much criticism and hostility as a teen-ager because of her unusual background. Her European accent and proper usage of English earned scorn from her black friends, who accused her of "talking proper." So humiliated was she by their criticism that she took to practicing the speech of her southern black friends. "It was very hard for me to find a world of my own because I wasn't accepted into a black world," said Jennifer, "not because I was Uncle Tomish or an 'Aunt Tomasina' but mainly because I am used to white people waiting on me. I certainly couldn't have been accepted by white people, and I couldn't fit easily into a black world because, even though I was trying my best, things still didn't work out." Over the years Jennifer has learned to cope with the ambivalence that comes from being caught between two cultures. "What I have done is to take the best from both worlds and made a third world—my world. The friends I have in my world are predominantly black, but there are also some white people. They are people with whom I feel comfortable."

During the 1960s with the upheavals between blacks and whites, Jennifer went through a period when "I totally rejected anything white, because I was trying to establish my identity." This rejection assumed a very personal dimension, because she found herself trying to justify why she was married to a white man. When the antiwhite sentiment was very high she never told her friends that she had been reared by a white guardian. "I left the South, I changed my name; no one knew. For a whole lot of years, I sort of went underground to the point that I was denying any white traits about myself and my entire existence. So I was gleefully joining in all the antiwhite diatribe. I used to say 'Get the honkies' like everyone else. But deep down inside I knew, and I guess everybody knows by now, that I didn't really mean that. I feel that those were my expressions or reactions to frustration. Now I feel that I've gotten close to approaching understanding and acceptance of change."

Jennifer said she never felt any antagonism toward her guardian because she was white. "It didn't matter that she was white. It was just that she was a mother image, and in a mother role to me. I thought that there was some point at which she had messed up that mother role, but it wasn't racial. I feel that my guardian and my natural mother made an awful lot of mistakes in bringing me up. But I feel that I'm probably making a lot of mistakes in bringing up my own child. And he will make mistakes. I tell my son that his measure as a person is not to remember how much I have messed up but what he does with his own life when he grows up. . . . My son is terrific. He's good-looking, bright, charming, marvelous; but then the fruit never falls far from the tree! It's just that there are probably little things I'm doing, little things that everybody does that can be considered acts of omission or commission." Her son spends his vacations with Jennifer's guardian and her natural mother. In recent years Jennifer has become reconciled to her guardian and has re-established contact with her mother. "I went to see my mother for the first time recently," Jennifer said. "I have eight sisters and a brother, and one sister wrote to say that mother was not doing well, so I went to see her. I've been trying to steer her away from telling me why she did things that perhaps caused problems for a long time, like leaving me and what I felt was abandoning me, and about how things were between her and my natural father at that time," said Jennifer. "But it's not even necessary for her to have to go through the pain of telling me, because I'm no longer hung up about it. There was a time when I would have fought to the death to keep anyone from knowing that I was illegitimate, yet it doesn't seem to matter that much to anybody. So it's started mattering less to me." During the years she spent with her guardian, her mother and siblings came to visit Jennifer on holidays, at the invitation of her guardian. "I didn't quite know how to ask my guardian if I could go and see my mother without making her feel I was unhappy with her, which was untrue," she said. She eventually lost contact with her mother, who moved to another state.

Jennifer disagrees with the black social workers' stance on transracial adoption. "The simple truth is that there aren't enough black families to go around," she said. "And if there is a capable, adequate white family that's ready and willing to adopt a black child, let that child be adopted." Jennifer explains her philosophy on child welfare: "When children are young they have very few needs. In the satisfaction of those physical needs they like to be fed, they like to be changed, and they need love. It doesn't really matter who loves the child so long as the child gets affection and feels secure. If a white family can provide that for the child, right on! If I had children and was considering adopting, I might give a white child such a break." She feels that children should go to integrated schools because they will have to live together when they are older. The philosophical, self-confident Jennifer quipped, "It's much easier to get used to each other at six than at twenty-six."

NIKKI CARTER

When Nikki was six months old, she was adopted by the Carters, a middle-class white couple. Bill, a college professor, and Jean, a part-time college instructor and editor, come from a long-standing radical intellectual tradition. Since they were college students they have supported leftist causes, at one time conducting an underground petition campaign to oust the late Senator Joseph McCarthy. One is impressed by their devotion to civil liberties causes, including equal rights, and prison reform. They are widely read and traveled, having lived in Europe, where Bill taught. When they were interviewed the family was about to depart for Africa for a year, where Bill was to teach. They are unusually Spartan in their lifestyles, as indicated by their sparsely furnished home—a home that did not include a television set.

When their daughter Susan, now a college student, was ten, and their son Matthew was three, they adopted Nikki, a beautiful, Afro-coiffed, dark-skinned, lanky girl. Nikki, who is now ten years old, had two black parents and had been released for adoption at birth. "We adopted Nikki the second time we applied to the agency for a black child," Jean explained. "Sometime earlier the agency had refused to allow us to adopt a black child." The agency had never made a transracial placement, and considered their request quite strange, but was eventually reconciled to the unusual application and agreed to allow them to adopt this little girl. The Carters adopted Douglas, a ten-year-old black boy, when Nikki was seven. (This will be presented as a separate case study.) Nikki, who is going through a tomboyish phase, is a very independent child, who tends to approach each problem and question philosophically. She has a fascination for trying to figure out the different angles of a subject. Before answering most questions put to her, she prefaced her remarks with, "I would want to know if such and such is the case before I . . ." or, "I would have to see . . ." Most of her friends are boys her age because they, more than girls, enjoy her major preoccupation: a fascination for trucks, which she has had as long as her parents can remember. Nikki said, "I didn't like to hear fairy tales when I was little. We had books about people like Hank Aaron, but I'd rather read stories about trucks." Nikki has the ability to recognize every single model of a motor vehicle. Her father said she can also recognize a particular individual's car after seeing it only once. "We have been in other cities and Nikki has been able to pick out a friend's car on the parking lot because she recognizes something distinctive about that particular car," he said. "It might be something you have in the window, a dented fender or whatever. She can always tell it, and she doesn't do it by noticing the license plates."

Nikki has model trucks and books about trucks that she checked out of the library all over her room. She said she has gone with the same boy friend for two years because he, too, likes trucks, and shares her desire to drive a tractor trailer and buy a pickup truck when they are older.

Nikki's preoccupation with trucks seems to symbolize a heavy interest in mechanical details and perhaps a sense of power. Her fascination with motor vehicle engines may well represent an interest in figuring out complex and sophisticated things. She approaches trucks with the same precision that she handles complex questions put to her.

For all of her life, Nikki has lived in a small college community that has about a 5 per cent black population. The vast majority of her friends and associates are white. She attends a predominantly white school, where she is a sixth-grader in an "alternative" program that is designed to give students more freedom and less structure in their learning environment. She does well in school, earning above-average grades. She is outgoing, and has many friends at school and in her neighborhood. The Carters are friendly with many of the blacks in their town. Bill teaches in a program that has a large number of black students, and Nikki knows many of them. For a time some of the black residents in their town sponsored a black culture program, and Nikki participated in it. The program was "for blacks only," and Nikki soon stopped going to the meetings because her mother was not permitted to attend. According to Nikki, this black culture program was primarily for entertainment and did not involve lectures on black history and the like, which is rather frequently the case with such enrichment programs. "We never discussed anything about black identity and Africa," Nikki explained. "It was for the kids to get to know each other. Maybe the grown-ups discussed black history."

Nikki said she has always been aware of the fact that she is black, and that her parents are of a different race. She said, "I never had to ask my parents about why we were different colors because I knew that God made people that way. All I notice is that people are people, no matter what color they are. They are all the same even if they are different colors."

Although Nikki has lived abroad (in Europe where her father taught), she and her brothers are approaching their impending stay in Africa with some hesitation. She isn't sure what will be expected of her in the African school, where French is spoken. She does, however, have some understanding of what it will mean to be in a country governed by blacks. "I won't be picked out of the crowd there like I am here because I am dark like them," said Nikki. She is concerned, however, that her white brother, Matthew, might suffer discrimination because he will be in the minority. This is a concern that Matthew does not share because he enjoys being different.

Nikki gets along well with her older sister, whom she adores, and her two brothers, who treat her as their "kid sister." Her sister, Susan, is away in college, so Nikki does not have daily contact with her.

Being an adopted child has had a strong impact on Nikki's ideas of what kind of family she would like to have. She said, "I want to adopt one child instead of having one. Besides, it takes too much time to have a baby." In keeping with her interest in trucks, Nikki said she wants to study auto mechanics in college and have a career in this field.

Nikki feels that she has encountered very little overt discrimination. She could not recall a single instance when she was rejected by whites because she is black. Matthew, her white brother, had experienced hostility from his white friends. Nikki recalled a recent incident involving a white boy she knew who asked Matthew, "How can you stand being the brother of two niggers? If I had a brother and sister that are niggers I'd lock myself in the closet and not come out because I'd be too embarrassed. One match and he wouldn't be my brother. I'd burn the [adoption] papers." Nikki said this white boy also wrote "nigger lover" on Matthew's linen at summer camp. This was surprising to them because the boy was Douglas's closest friend. Nikki was at a loss to explain this boy's conflicting behavior.

Nikki represents a multitude of paradoxes. While she appears to be a well-adjusted, average child, her compulsive fixation on trucks seems atypical. Trucks may well represent the powerful symbols of mobility. Huge trucks can be used to travel far distances away from her present environs. Her passionate interest in trucks runs counter to the intellectual interests and involvement of her college professor parents. Of course, it is impossible for the writer to go beyond speculation as to why a ten-year-old has invested so much in cultivating interests so unlike those values and interests to which her parents are committed.

Douglas Carter

Doug, thirteen, was born outside marriage of a white mother and a black father. At birth he was given up for adoption and went to live in a white foster home. His foster mother, who is of French-Canadian extraction, and his foster father lived in an all-white working-class community. Over the years they had cared for many foster children and had adopted their only son, who is now grown. Doug's foster mother had strong racial prejudice, but she always told him that he was "different" from other blacks—that he was an exception. Before she agreed to take Doug as a foster child, she polled her neighbors and asked them if they objected to her rearing a *black* foster child. The consensus among her neighbors was that it was all right so long as he did not have black visitors.

In order to compensate for Doug's "racial inferiority" and his temporary stay with her, his foster mother smothered him with love and affection and any material objects he desired. In this overindulgent mother-son relationship she imposed no rules and regulations over his behavior, allowing him to come and go as he pleased and to be friends with whomever he wanted to. Her strong antiblack feelings had a decided effect on Doug's developing racial identity. He began to take pride in the fact that his mother was white, and began to view himself as being light-complexioned, although he has medium-brown skin. Living in this all-white working-class, racially biased community, Doug began to develop antiblack sentiments, much akin to those of his foster mother. His foster mother's overindulgence and lack of rules and regulations also had an effect on his behavior. By the time he reached fourth grade he had been suspended from school because of his antisocial behavior, which worsened as he got older. Because his foster mother knew he would not always be with her, she lavished attention upon him, allowed him to watch television endlessly, and made no demands on his school performance.

When Doug's racial identity problems were recognized by his adoption worker, she arranged for him to participate in a Big Brother program. Unfortunately his Big Brother, although black, did not strongly identify with blacks, and had little to offer in helping to solve Doug's racial identity problems. His adoptive mother described Doug's Big Brother as having "very little black identity." In the meantime, Doug's foster father died. His foster parents' son was now grown and had moved away from home. He had few close associations with older male father figures, leaving him in the care of an overprotective and indulgent mother.

Doug's antisocial behavior at school became so severe that by the time he reached the age of ten, he had been suspended from school several times. Although his foster mother continued to indulge him, she found his behavior increasingly unbearable, as he made unreasonable demands on her. She finally called his adoption worker and asked her to remove him from her home. It was at this point that the agency put forth its first efforts to find him an adoptive home.

The Carters had already decided to adopt an older child when they first heard of Doug. He was the same age as their biological son, Matthew, so they could be playmates. They also felt it important to have another black child so Nikki could have a black sibling to identify with. Being thoroughly familiar with the difficulty of finding adoptive homes for older children, they were convinced that this was the right thing to do.

Doug's adjustment over the past three years has been extremely difficult for him and his family, especially his mother. Bill and Jean feel they made their first mistake when, out of sympathy, they allowed his foster mother to maintain contact with him over a protracted period of time. Until recently, when she moved to another state, she called continuously, they took him to visit her, and she visited them. Naturally, he was torn between the indulgent mother who showered gifts on him and demanded no responsibility from him, but who also rejected him, and the new parents whose lifestyle was the opposite in every respect of that which he had known. Whereas his foster mother had imposed few rules and little structure onto his life, his adoptive mother was highly organized, efficient, and demanded quality performance and a sense of responsibility for his actions. This has led Doug to describe his parents with ambivalence, for, in his words, they are "so-so." Had he had the choice to make, he is not certain he would have selected them to become his adoptive parents. He does not share their value for education very strongly. When asked what he wants to be when he is grown, he vacillates between wanting to become a chef and a farmer. He does poor to average work in school, does not like to read, and bemoans the fact that the family has no television set, although he has gotten used to it.

Doug is strongly influenced by peer group pressure. At this point in his development he is more concerned about being accepted by his peers than in establishing his own independence and individual identity. This particular problem creates many headaches for his parents. All of Doug's friends are white, with the exception of a black boy his age, whom he sees only once a year when this boy comes to summer camp. Doug perceives himself as light-complexioned, and frequently draws comparisons between himself and blacks who are darker than he. Although his closest white friend called his brother, Matthew, a "nigger lover," Doug refuses to dissociate himself from this boy because, Doug says, "He treats me well, and is nice to me at school."

It is apparent that Doug's early socialization received from his foster mother has left an indelible imprint on his self-concept and behavior.

Jean and Bill feel that his greatest adjustment problems stem from the fact that he was adopted as an older child. His personality and behavior patterns were so well formed that his parents have found the task of restructuring and modifying them a difficult one. Yet they have met with some success. According to Jean, "He has changed quite a lot since he became part of our family. We hope this will continue."

All of these problems have brought dissension into their household, causing Doug to sometimes play his parents off against each other. Jean and Bill, in the philosophical manner, have spent many hours discussing the implications of adopting an older child. At one point the pressures became so great that Jean left home for a few days. As a result Doug, recognizing the seriousness of his mother's leaving, immediately began to curb his antisocial behavior, since he did not want to be held responsible for disrupting the household. "With an older child, they come to you already formed," she commented. "You don't have anything to do with what they are when you get them. At least if you could change the child's name, you might feel that you are putting some imprint on his life. But here you take the child as he is."

Doug is quite aware of the problems surrounding his adoption, and those he has caused because of his different values and nonconforming behavior. When he grows up he says he intends to marry and have six children, two of whom will be adopted. He said, "I want to adopt babies because I know how hard it is to adopt an older child, I know how hard it has been for me and for my parents."

Doug has a good relationship with Nikki. They share mutual interests and are near the same age. They play together and seem to have an overlapping circle of friends. Because Nikki was adopted as an infant she has made a better adjustment in her family than has Doug. Yet there is a closeness in their relationship that seems to have bridged many potential barriers.

ANDREA AND SARAH NELSON

"If someone asked me to describe myself," says Andrea, a curly Afro-coiffed twelve-year-old, "I would say that I am brown, and that I am the adopted daughter of Mr. and Mrs. Gary Nelson. I would tell them that I intend to go to college when I grow up because I am not smart enough yet, and college will make me smarter. I want to study to be a herpetologist [one who handles and cares for reptiles and amphibians]." Andrea has great zest for life, with an easy smile and confident manner. She is somewhat large for her age, very articulate and precocious.

When Andrea was six weeks old, she was adopted by Gary and Carla Nelson, a young upper-middle-class couple who lived in a middle-sized town in the heart of the Midwest. Her father is a highly specialized physician, and her mother is a housewife, although she spends a great portion of her time with her music. Gary Nelson's quiet, subdued personality is the exact opposite of Carla's, who is a quite outspoken, articulate woman. They now live in a very comfortable modern house, surrounded by beautiful gardens, in a remote area of a small eastern town. An eighth-grader, Andrea is an honor student with a passion for her science courses and her musical interests. (Every member of the Nelson family plays a musical instrument.)

The Nelsons' second child, Sarah, is ten years old, and was adopted when she was six months old. She is of Puerto Rican descent and in many ways shares Andrea's enthusiasm, although she tends to be somewhat shy. The girls are very close, and get along quite well together. Sarah describes herself in the following manner: "I am the adopted daughter of Mr. and Mrs. Nelson. I want to become a model and a nurse." Sarah has a strong interest in clothes and wears them well. The diminutive Sarah has long blond hair and a warm smile. Although considered by agencies to be a transracial placement, Sarah's physical characteristics are strikingly Caucasian.

Andrea and Sarah give one the instant impression that they are very happy children. They laugh a lot, tell jokes, and play with their pet animals. Andrea has reached the age where her parents feel she has enough maturity to work as a baby-sitter in their neighborhood. They are thoughtful, with impeccable manners and decorum. Both girls quickly defer to the authority of their parents, as in the case when I asked Andrea when she expected to start dating. "It depends upon when my mother *tells* me I can," she explained, leaving the interviewer to understand that the serious events in their lives are decided, perhaps with the children's consultation, by their parents.

The girls and their parents are very close, and communication among them is free and open. Both share their mother's fondness for music. The family engages in a lot of activities together, including travel, entertainment, and the like.

Andrea and Sarah cannot remember ever having encountered racial discrimination. Because they live in an all-white community, their close friends are white. They both attend schools where there are other black children, and a large number of black teachers. Sarah has a black principal. However, Andrea said she has been called "nigger" by some of her schoolmates. This usually occurs when they are angry with her and use this as a means to get back at her for some specific act. Her way of handling these racial insults is to ignore them, a method she has found to be effective. Andrea says, "The white boys at school are harder to get along with than the white girls. The girls never say things about color." She attributes this to the fact that the boys her age are going through an "antigirl" phase, and tend to treat all the girls in her class with hostility. All the black children in her school are in higher grades than she. For this reason she is not close friends with them, although they do treat her quite well.

Andrea and Sarah expressed surprise when told that black social workers are against whites adopting black children. Andrea said, "They are? I don't know why they feel like that because it is better to be adopted than to grow up without a home and parents of your own." Sarah agreed: "I don't understand that at all. Why would they want children not to have a home? Children who have to grow up in institutions are so pitiful. I feel sorry for them." Both girls said they are glad they were adopted by their parents, and it is beyond their comprehension that anyone would oppose any form of adoption, so long as the parents love their children and take good care of them. "It is so terrible for a child not to have a home," said Sarah, whose expression showed her deep-felt sorrow for such children. "I am glad I was adopted so I don't have to grow up like that," she said as she and Andrea discussed what they had heard about children in foster care and institutions.

When asked how old they were when they first became aware of racial differences, Andrea replied, "I don't think I ever did because everyone is the same." At another point she wondered if I meant the difference among "Caucasoid, Mongoloid, and Negroid," differences that she was quite aware of. Although she and Sarah are quite aware that they are of a different race than their parents, it is of no significance whatever to them. Their parents have exposed them to various things related to their racial heritages. Their mother was at one time quite active in the Open Door Society. In their early years Andrea and Sarah participated in a black culture program sponsored by this group. They have taken vacations in several Caribbean countries, where they became aware of the fact that these are predominantly black countries. And, of course, they do the ordinary things such as reading books about blacks, they own a "black history" game, etc. These girls are unusually self-assured, adjusted individuals who are aware of their cultural and racial backgrounds. They do not view this disparagingly, nor do they find it necessary, at this stage of their development, to assert themselves as a *black* and as a *Puerto Rican*, or in other words, to assert an ethnic identity over any other.

When asked if she had a boy friend, Andrea, with her characteristic eagerness, said, "I knew you were going to ask that question. Yes, I have one." She explained, "He was my boy friend last year, and he is my boy friend this year. Our families are friends, so we see each other when our families get together." When asked if he was white or black, she looked questioningly, as if to say, Why does it matter? "He's white," she replied, "but it shouldn't make any difference because everyone is the same."

These adoptees have had experiences that cover a broad range. Each individual's lifestyle, personality characteristics, perceptions of their unique familial status—as an adoptee and of another race—also differ. Perhaps the glimpses into these persons' lives, and their problems and good fortunes, will provide parents of younger children with answers to some of their questions about what happens to the older child. No broad generalizations can be made about these six case studies.

10

KINSHIP
Grandparents, Siblings, and
Other Relatives

A young mother said that when she and her husband called his parents, who live in another city, to tell them they had adopted a black infant boy, her mother-in-law said over the phone, "O God! Please help me to overcome this tragedy which has struck my family." She told them that she would go to church to pray to God to help her over this hurdle they had put upon her.

An adoptive father said his parents were overjoyed when they told them they were adopting a black child. "They had waited so long for grandchildren," he said, "that they couldn't have cared less about the child's race. He could have been purple. Besides, my parents were out of a liberal intellectual background, and race was no problem for them."

Grandparents become most provoked by and involved in transracial adoptions. In all cases, they are the most outspoken in the wider family group, whether critically or accepting. Their reactions follow a consistent pattern: Most object to the adoption when it first occurs but eventually come to accept the child. It is easy to understand why grandparents get so involved in the adoption. They represent the forebears of a genealogy—or a social and biological bloodline. Acceptance or nonacceptance is never a factor in their relationships with their biological children. Such acceptance is automatic. Adoption is different, especially if the grandparents themselves have negative or ambivalent feelings about this family formation process. Not only must they have to contend with an *act* that they might oppose, but the child itself represents a departure from their expectations, especially since the child is of a different racial background. They are often concerned about the lack of firsthand knowledge they do not have about the child's background. For many grandparents the child is viewed as an alien being, and some are insensitive enough to regard the child as possibly having "bad blood," another example of their fear of and antipathy toward the unknown.

Therefore, it is not surprising that some grandparents view the adoption as an intrusion and see themselves as unwilling partners. They view the child as an intrusion into their consciously formed family unit. One grandmother put it this way: "I didn't have anything to do with this adoption. I wasn't called on to give my opinion on whether I thought it a good idea. Now they are upset with me because I cannot accept the adoption or the black child. But what do they expect? Don't I have the right to reject the child if I want to?"

In American society there have long been a great deal of antipathy and negative attitudes toward adoption. Many Americans, especially the aged, continue to have prejudiced and stereotypic ideas about adopted children. Even today, some people still have the notion that an adopted child has "bad blood." Others do not believe the child should have inheritance rights, a carry-over from an earlier legal practice in the United States. Some grandparents object to the family name being given an "outside" child, while others have a generalized feeling of alienation from the child, and will never accept him or her totally into the biological family unit. Obviously race exacerbates the problem in the sense that some grandparents might be willing to reconcile themselves to the adoption of a white child, but not to one of another race. Therefore some grandparents who favor adoption object to having a black grandchild. This attitude obviously reflects their personal racial attitudes.

Adoption, by its very nature, does not always afford the parents the opportunity to share their plans with their relatives and others who would be supportive. The element of uncertainty regarding when the baby is expected, what sex the child will be, whether he or she will bear physical characteristics similar to other family members and the like, often preclude adequate preparation for grandparents to enter this new, unexpected familial role. In comparing the differences between role preparation for biological and adoptive parenthood, David Kirk writes in his book *Shared Fate* that whereas "preparation for biological parenthood and parental roles is gradual . . . preparation for adoptive parenthood tends to be abrupt, with no clear-cut timetable by which the couple can share their feelings and thoughts about their hoped-for parenthood."[1]

Although Americans' attitudes toward adoption have probably generally changed since Kirk's work was published, for many adoptive situations his statement holds an element of truth. Indeed, there is a difference—a significant one for many—among parents and the wider family circle between biological and adoptive parenthood, including psychological, legal, social, and economic factors. For example, Kirk documents the fact that in adoptive parenthood there are no legal rewards, including a tax deduction for the expenses incurred in the adoption. Most states do not permit this as an allowable deduction.[2] Some parents regard this as an example of prejudice and discrimination against adoptive parenthood.

The majority of the parents in this study did not inform the grandparents of their plans to adopt until they had finalized their decision. Rarely did they consult with their parents and seek out their advice on whether they *should* adopt. Once they had made the decision, contacted the agency, and frequently, when a child was on the way, they announced this decision to their parents. A number of adoptive couples told the writer that they did not tell their parents until they *received* the child. Only in those cases where the grandparents could be expected to be supportive were they asked their opinions prior to the adoption, and in some of those cases they were not told because, in keeping with these parents' independence in decision-making, they felt it was not their parents' business.

Grandparents' reactions, upon being informed of the decision, were varied. They often received the opposite reaction they had expected from a particular parent. Also, in many cases a paternal grandfather might be eagerly accepting, and the grandmother might be hostile. Their reactions were frequently the reverse of what the parents had expected. A professional photographer for a large midwestern newspaper who has two adopted sons and a biological daughter described how he informed his parents:

> I told them afterwards. I still think that is the best way to do it because if a parent is going to react positively then it is just a nice surprise. If they are going to react negatively, they have less time to build up various reasons to construct support for the negative reaction. Besides, I firmly believe that it is an act that concerns the adopting parents only. And although it obviously affects their parents emotionally, I don't think they have any say at all. It's great if they like it, and if they don't, well, that's unfortunate.

His attitude was echoed by countless parents, who felt that it was their decision and theirs alone to make. There is a widespread feeling among these parents that to solicit any opinion from family members (especially their parents) might mean courting unnecessary hostility and opposition. Some say that the entire process is much smoother when it is handled completely independent of anyone's views except their own. This view was expressed by a housewife in the Midwest, who with her attorney husband adopted an infant boy:

> We decided not to talk to our older family about the adoption because they would be forced into having an opinion and would feel that they had to get it across to us. We didn't want them to participate in it. So when it was all decided and the baby was almost here, we told a few of our closest friends. But it wasn't until after the baby came that we told our family. Looking back, we did exactly the right thing.

A lot of adoptive parents said they knew their parents well enough to gauge their reactions. For some, conflict with their parents was nothing new. Their political and social views were very different from their elders', and they had clashed or disagreed on many other issues. As one father said, "My parents dismissed this as just another crazy thing we had done." They also knew what their parents' racial attitudes were. In these cases there was a tendency for them to take the position that they were simply living their own lives without parental influences or interference. In this sense they are probably not that different from the average young American couple who is trying to establish and maintain their authority and independence.

Numerous studies on transracial adoption emphasize the "social distance" that exists between the adoptive parents and the grandparents. They frequently do not live in the same city, see each other on infrequent occasions, and maintain a high degree of emotional independence, especially in decision-making. Therefore it was in keeping with their autonomy and independent lifestyles that the adoptive parents initiated and executed the actual adoption. Some adoption workers interpret this "independence" as rebellion and view it as a negative quality in an adoptive applicant, while others view it positively—as an indication of strength and courage.

To the degree that many of the adoptive parents conceal their intent to adopt transracially, a small group in this study made their intention known to their parents very early. Interestingly, some of them had experienced interracial marriages in their immediate families; they had grown up in racially integrated neighborhoods; and their *parents* had had extensive contact with blacks. A father of a racially mixed adopted son, living in the Midwest, describes how his family's previous experiences paved the way for the family's acceptance of the adoption:

My only sibling—a brother in Cleveland—married a black woman a few years ago. In some ways the black issue in my immediate and extended family was faced then. I was very pleased with the marriage. The issue of a black being accepted in the family was no real problem. The fact that we adopted didn't faze anyone.

Quite unusually, his wife's family experiences and lifestyle are quite the same, as she describes below:

My parents were not at all surprised that we adopted transracially. When we told them we were applying for adoption, they said they were a little surprised because they hadn't realized we had been trying to have children, but they weren't surprised that we were applying for a biracial child. My parents live in a community that is about 99 per cent black. They could sell and move somewhere else, but they like the neighborhood. My brother married a West Indian girl, so my brother and sister have been very receptive to our adoption. From what others have said, transracially adoptive families often face much bigger problems than we have had.

It should be noted that the familial experiences of this couple were not representative of the other persons in this sample.

There are other couples who have not had interracial experiences in their families before, but who also share their intentions with their parents. A Washington, D.C., mother recalled, "My parents were quite delighted. They were aware that we had planned to adopt from the very beginning."

Once adoptive parents decide to let their own parents know, the adoptive parents oftentimes treat the matter very delicately. A mother told me that she wrote her parents a seventeen-page letter "so there would be no question as to why we did it." A young father details how he and his wife revealed the news to his parents:

We told my parents over the phone that we were going to adopt. Then we wrote them a letter explaining the details—that we were adopting a black child. We wanted them to have time to think about it and not get mad. We didn't know what to expect because my father has lived most of his life in the Deep South. But we got back a really charming letter saying they thought it was a very beautiful thing to do.

The adoptive parents give top priority to finding the right situation, time, and place to inform grandparents of the adoption. Since the great majority of the adoptive parents in this study do not live in the same city with their parents, they usually write or call them to tell them about the adoption. One can only speculate as to how different the reactions would be if they were in closer physical proximity. Some take special precautions not to unnecessarily offend or threaten the health of an already ill parent with shocking news. Oftentimes ill grandparents are not told right away. A young physician and his wife were waiting to find the right time to tell his father, who was suffering from heart disease. However, on a few hours' notice his father, who was traveling nearby on business and who lived in another state, paid them an unexpected visit, which provoked an unusual reaction from them, as described below:

> My father-in-law was on a business trip. He called us and said he was bringing an old friend of his over to see us, when they were passing through the town where we lived. He had a weak heart, from which he later died, so we felt we couldn't shock him like that. So we hid Marvin for a few hours [one of the neighbors took him] while they were here. We wrote them afterwards and told them about the adoption.

She explains her husband's parents' reactions:

> He came around to the point where he wrote a letter to John saying he didn't understand what we had done. He realized that times were changing and young people are different and have different ideas. He said if we needed anything, he would always be there. Now his mother's letter was horrible. They curiously gave us the opposite reactions from what we expected. We thought his dad would be furious and his mother would not.

Rather curiously, both of her parents, who are far less educated, working-class people, were much more accepting of the adoption. Although they had initial reservations, Beth said, "They took time off work and drove to visit us [in another state] four days after our baby arrived. My parents immediately responded to him and have always treated him as their grandchild [and the three black boys adopted later]."

Roughly one fourth of the grandparents accepted the adoption as soon as they were told of the intent to adopt. They posed no problems and offered their total support. These grandparents seem to generally have a close relationship with their sons and daughters. They certainly are close enough for the adoptive parents to ask if they think the adoption can be a success, as some of them did. Unlike the large group of adoptive parents who conceal their intent to adopt until all plans have been made (and sometimes until after the child has been placed), they often share their ideas and more private concerns with their parents. This does not imply that they would not adopt if their parents were opposed to it. Many would undoubtedly do so because they are probably no less independent-minded than those adoptive parents described above. It simply indicates a "closeness" they share, which encourages them to confide, seek advice, and so forth.

Because acceptance is desired and is not problematic, adoptive couples are less likely to question *why* their parents accepted the adoption from the beginning. While even the accepting grandparents will warn the adoptive parents that they might be getting involved in a very challenging and sometimes difficult situation, the grandparents are nevertheless happy, supportive, and positive. They frequently visit the child, take him or her to their home alone for vacations, show them off to their friends and neighbors, and in one case, the grandfather took his grandchild to meet his supervisor at work. An adoptive father said his mother "uses the adoption as a weapon against her conservative friends," as a way of showing them how liberal her family is. As a result, she is placed in higher esteem by her peers for having such a unique family situation.

Then there is another small group of grandparents who accept the child initially, but view the child as an exception to or different from other blacks. They would not categorically endorse interracial adoption and racial integration. For them the child exists as a separate entity. They are able to love him or her because this is their grandchild. But they *do not* allow the child to symbolize blacks in general. One mother insightfully remarked that her mother "quite conveniently made Peter white in her mind, despite the fact that he is dark brown." Race is never dealt with or discussed openly by some of the grandparents. Perhaps if it were, acceptance would not come so easily. As one father remarked, "My mother was upset more about the idea than she was by Michael. They've accepted him, but I don't think they've changed their ideas about race. They would panic if a black family moved next door to them. . . . I think he's a different compartment in their minds entirely."

Others had similar experiences with their parents. Some even accused them of patronizing the child because they were too friendly, lovable, and accepting. A mother complained that her parents made such an effort to prove they were not prejudiced that it was all too apparent they were. She said, "It was simply disgusting. They showed him so much attention that they ended up discriminating against our other two children. We had to tell them to act normal—treat him like they had been treating the other kids."

It should be emphasized that in time the great majority of grandparents *eventually* accept the child, although in varying degrees. Other studies have reported similar findings. In many cases this eventual acceptance is total. For others it is not. For example, two or three grandparents might accept the child, and the others might remain silent or maintain a respectable and cordial distance. As time passes, acceptance increases greatly. Grandparents who expressed initial opposition to the *idea* of adoption before the child arrived, very frequently accepted the child as soon as they saw him or her. Typical comments are that they "mellowed" or "fell in love" with the child on first sight. A mother in Washington summed it up by saying: "When our parents saw our baby they were wiped out. All of their initial objections vanished."

Grandmothers, especially the maternal grandmothers, were far more likely to initially accept the child, whereas paternal grandfathers were the least accepting. This may be a function of the definition of the female sex roles that designate that American women always *accept* the maternal role, regardless of the circumstances under which it arises, whereas males are not so rigidly type-cast into the paternal role, and where allowances are often made for the nonacceptance or less than enthusiastic acceptance of the paternal role. For grandfathers, an important added dimension is that of *machismo*. The introduction of an "alien" biological person into the extended family is perceived by some fathers and grandfathers as threatening. (More will be discussed about giving the family name to the adopted child below.)

Perhaps it is only human nature for grandparents' harsh feelings and reactions to soften when presented with an innocent, loving, defenseless baby. Acceptance of the child is also a more calculated and logical choice for some grandparents. Not to accept the child ever could mean lifelong estrangement from their own children. How many grandparents are willing to endure the pain that goes with forfeiting permanent ties with their children because of the adoption? The grandparents' acceptance of the child becomes the most logical and painless course to follow. Surely few parents would give up their child because of the grandparents' refusal to acknowledge and accept him or her. As painful as it may initially be for the grandparents, they usually bring the adoptive child into the family circle.

For others it offers an educational experience. Open-minded grandparents might well see this as another rich and valuable experience that is broadening their horizons in their older years, when such experiences can be rare. Some parents said the adoption gave the grandparents a "boost" and a "new lease" on life, bringing to them much-welcomed joy.

Many of the grandparents, when first informed of the decision to adopt transracially, find themselves unable to immediately cope with and perform in this new role assignment. Their role handicap derives from several factors, including their antagonism and/or antipathy toward adoption, racial bias, and a concern with introducing an "unknown" genealogical element into a "known" and consciously formed family unit.

Although most grandparents in this study seem to have eventually overcome the initial role handicap, a small number never did so, as will be discussed below.

In the majority of cases where grandparents express disapproval of the adoption, their children make concessions, compromises, and try to lighten the impact. Although they have taken an independent, bold action, they nevertheless try to reconcile the differences that erupt, as soon as possible. Failing to do so, they are disappointed and unhappy. Many compromises are made in behalf of the grandparents, and much sympathy is expressed, especially in the early stages of the adoption. As one mother told me, "I know they are old and have set ideas about things. Therefore, we must be patient with them until they come around." Some wait patiently until their parents "come around," while others try to push the process along by being especially sensitive to their whims, hoping that acceptance of the child will come sooner. Because they know that this is a common reaction, based on other adoptive parents' experiences, they also know that acceptance will eventually be forthcoming in most cases. Therefore, biding time is a pattern typical to most. The wait is not always so bad, because they can usually predict a good outcome.

An important question the reader is likely to raise is: *Why* do grandparents object to transracial adoption? The most frequently raised concerns and objections are: What about the effect it will have upon the other children? What about the safety of the family? Is it fair to the adopted child? Why adopt when you can have your own biological children? How can you give the family name to a black child? How can you pass on your inheritance to such a child? How can you be sure the child won't hate you because you're white, once he grows up? Grandparents naturally tend to be very protective of their offspring. Although most adoptive parents do not dismiss their concerns and objections, they do try to convince them that things will not be as difficult as they imagine. In an effort to counteract or neutralize these concerns, they are careful to relate to the grandparents the happy experiences and kind words they get from strangers who take notice of the transracial adoption. A mother said, "My father doesn't worry so much now that he knows our house isn't going to be burned down, our kids aren't going to be beaten up because they have a black sister, and David is not going to lose his job because he has a black son."

It would be useful at this point to discuss in detail the specific reasons why grandparents objected to the adoption of black children. Some opposed *any* form of adoption. They could not understand why anyone, especially if he or she can have biological children, would want to adopt. They felt it wrong to bring into a homogeneous family a child who represents the unknown. For them, not only is the child black, but also his or her biological parents and lines of descent are equally mysterious and alien. They warn their children that the adopted might have "bad blood." They are frightened of the possibility that the child may later display some of these alleged negative traits, which he or she is thought to have inherited from their biological parents. One mother told me that when she told her mother-in-law that they planned to adopt, her only comment was, "Be sure to watch out for bad blood." In another case the grandmother kept watching for what she thought were the obvious signs of "bad blood" in the child. One day when the child was dancing to music playing over the radio, the grandmother said in a low voice to her husband, "You see, she's going to be fast just like her mother was," much to the consternation of the child's adoptive mother (even though the grandmother did not have the slightest idea as to who the biological parents were). The grandmother's fears and prejudices are indicative of the feelings a lot of people have about unwed motherhood. For many, to have a child out of wedlock is still a disgrace. They feel the biological mother who places her child for adoption has loose morals, and they sometimes doubt that she knows who the child's biological father is. Thus some "visit the 'sins' of the mother upon the child." Kadushin notes that "the attitude toward illegitimacy is related to family structure. Negative attitudes toward illegitimacy are designed to protect the monogamous family and associated marital family ties."[3] From the Middle Ages to the nineteenth century, attitudes and practices toward illegitimate children were very punitive. It was only in the "last hundred years [that] there has developed a more compassionate attitude toward the illegitimate child, a lessening of the distinction between the legitimate and illegitimate child, and a reduction in the discriminations against the illegitimate child. Changing attitudes are reflected in changing terminology—from bastard to illegitimate child to child born out of wedlock or the less frequently employed extramarital child and love child.[4]

It is significant to note that these changes in terminology and the birth status of the child are correlated with social class variables in the sense that today the lower-class female's child is far more likely to be labeled "illegitimate," whereas the middle-class (and especially white) woman's child might be designated a "love child."[5]

Adoption has traditionally conjured in the minds of many elderly persons the fact that the child was born illegitimately. For those who still adhere to the Puritan ethic, which cherishes the sanctity of "sex within marriage," to have a child outside marriage denotes a violation of one of this nation's most cherished values. Adopted children are often viewed as the end product of premarital sexual permissiveness. Grandparents and parents are challenged to come to grips with their moral attitudes toward illegitimacy, and on rare occasions, incest. This is especially important since a negative punitive attitude might cause the parents (and other relatives) to regard the child in an unfavorable light.

For other grandparents, adoption itself is an alien term. They are not necessarily prejudiced against the child and its out-of-wedlock birth status, but they are unable to separate their personal feelings on adoption from the act their children have committed. All they know is they would *never* adopt, so why would anyone else, as one mother in Washington, D.C., explained:

> My husband's parents weren't overjoyed. We're capable of producing biological children, and this is their biggest hangup. They want to know, "What's wrong with our genes that you don't want to have children?"

After explaining that she and her husband decided to adopt black children instead of giving birth, a mother said:

> The boom is going to be lowered shortly. Not only are we adopting another child, but I'm going in to have my tubes tied, and this is really going to be their biggest hurdle.

For all her life, according to her daughter, this grandmother was taught that she must have two children, as an expression of her wifely and motherly duties. In her generation the element of *choice* was nonexistent. Consequently, this mother bitterly recalls the emotional trauma she suffered while growing up, owing to the fact that her mother never *fully* accepted the parenting role. Another couple speaks to the same point, as the wife explains:

> My parents were horrified when they learned of the adoption. My mother could not understand why we would want to adopt, and also why we would want to cross racial lines. But since the adoption, she has come around beautifully.

And a similar reaction from grandparents on the East Coast:

> With the first adoption there was a negative reaction from my parents—just total adoption itself. My mother thought we should give birth to children, and we should not adopt a child of different blood, even though she may be white. It made no difference about race; they were just negative as far as adoption is concerned. With the second adoption, there was a strong reaction to crossing racial lines. Now that she has seen the child, I think she has totally accepted it.

A St. Louis mother put it even more bluntly as she described the reaction of her parents: "It was an insult to their genetic composition that we would go out and adopt a child. The fact that the child was so obviously not of their genetic composition—that he was black—was just rubbing it in further—compounding the problem." For those adoptive parents who already have children, grandparents ask them, "Don't you already have enough kids? Why do you want to adopt?"

There are some grandparents who simply could not understand *adoption*. An Atlanta mother explained, "My mother really had a hard time accepting it. She couldn't deal with adoption, period. She had ten kids of her own, and she can't conceive of the whole adoption thing." Another adoptive mother said that her mother-in-law "craved for biological grandchildren, and there is no question that they would have had a much more important place in her mind." An adoptive father told the interviewer he was certain his father "felt threatened by his only son having adopted a child" (without having had biological ones). The grandfather saw the adoption as an end to the family bloodline and family name.

Grandparents also base their objections on the negative effect they think this "alien" child will have on the biological children in the family, and feel that there is a possibility that the adopted child might be a bad influence on the biological children. Although adoption agencies generally provide the parents with all the background information they have on the child's biological parents (which is frequently substantial), there nevertheless remains the concern in the minds of many grandparents about the unknown. Perhaps this is an understandable reaction because secondhand information is never a substitute for one personally knowing the persons involved. Grandparents might feel more comfortable with an independently arranged adoption whereby the biological parents are *known* personally. One father said his father was very worried about the insults his two biological children might get from their playmates because of their black brother. No matter how much he tried to reassure him over the phone and in letters, it was only after the grandfather came for a visit and saw his three grandchildren (including the black one) playing quite normally with their friends that his fears were alleviated. Another grandfather, who had been reared in the Deep

South and eventually moved away, told his son that they were deliberately "living dangerously" and subjecting their biological children to violence unnecessarily. In his older years, he could not understand why they would "flirt with violence" and "ask for trouble" this way. This grandfather had experienced violent racial strife in his native Arkansas and sought to protect his son and his family from the same. "Is it necessary to adopt a black child?" this grandfather asked. "Can't you make a contribution to the civil rights of black people in some other way? I'm not against black people. For all my life I have always thought they should have the same rights as whites, but I think you're living too dangerously."

Most of the grandparents' fears of danger are unfounded. Very few families ever encounter more than hostile stares and occasional insulting remarks from strangers. And, contrary to many grandparents' worst fears and expectations, in the majority of cases the biological children are usually accepting and protective of the adopted child.

Giving the adopted child the family name provoked some of the strongest negative reactions among several grandparents. Ironically, in one case, they were quite fond of the child, but were unwilling for him to bear their name. Obviously their acceptance was very limited, and the child, regardless of their fondness, would always be considered an outsider. A father who had had this experience explained his parents' reactions to the interviewer:

> When we wrote and told my parents that we were finalizing the adoption, my mother wrote back and said, "Now, are you sure you want to give him your last name?" We were really shocked. We had thought the whole thing had been accepted . . . because they had previously appeared to have accepted the child. When they realized that we were going to legalize it, it was hard. They're ethnic, and the family name really means much more to them.

He goes further to interpret the meaning they attach to the family name:

> You have to understand their cultural standard and the attitude of the culture they were brought up in. My son would pick up my name, my father's name. In fact, I was given the middle

name of my father. It carries on to each generation. I am *not* going to have any more children. Tim is my son, and in a way the adoption is infringing on my father. It affects him in the sense that his name is now being carried on by someone who is not of the same blood, and with whom he cannot associate or relate to.

There are a few grandparents who feel the adoption is not in the best interests of the adopted child. They question whether it is fair for white parents to rear a black child, and go so far as to warn their sons and daughters that they are setting themselves up for a potentially explosive situation. However, some of the adoptive parents think this "concern" of the grandparents is a smoke screen that is concealing the objections they are fearful to express. A college professor expressed precisely this reservation about his and his wife's parents' "concern" for their adopted children's welfare when he said,

> The basic problem with both of them seemed a basic worry about the children, and how hard it would be on them as they are growing up. Whether that was a phony issue or not, I don't know. But we've had no acceptance problem with the children since they've been with us for a while.

Grandmothers expressed these concerns more often than did grandfathers. Several grandparents worried about what blacks would think about whites rearing their children. One grandmother, who had a strong Jewish identity, told her son and daughter-in-law that she was sure she would object to an "outsider" adopting children from her ethnic group. "Don't you worry that blacks would feel the same as I do?" she asked. "Would you mind if blacks were allowed to adopt our children? Now don't get me wrong," she continued, "because it is not a racial feeling I have at all. My years of experience make me feel that children should grow up with their own kind." Despite her protests and challenging queries, the adoptive parents were not dissuaded. The attitudinal differences between the parents and grandmother represent in microcosm the conflicts one observes between the two generations. These intergenerational conflicts are representative of the vast differences they have in political views, in religious tradi-

tion, and in ethnic culture. While the grandparents often interpret transracial adoption as a symbol of rebellion, the adoptive
parents merely regard it as their right and intent to live their lives
as they choose.

A different kind of objection to transracial adoption was raised
by a grandmother who operated a nursery school for many years
and taught black children in a Head Start Program in a large midwestern city. She accused her son and daughter-in-law of not being
black enough to rear the child, and to transmit a black identity to
him. According to her daughter-in-law, "My mother-in-law is into
this blackness thing. . . . She has a very emotional perspective on
black children. Of course, she was for the adoption, but then she
wasn't. *She felt that we didn't understand about blackness.* She
thought we didn't know enough about blacks to successfully rear
Mary. She thought she could do it better than we could because
of her emotional concern and her experiences with black children."

Still others voice their concerns on whether the child will remain loyal to the adoptive parents in later years. One parent said
her father and mother-in-law fear that one day my black son will
march off and join the black community." Such a deep-seated fear
is not one that can easily be overcome. It indicates how fearful
some grandparents are of the potential rejection the child might
have toward his or her parents—conceivably a fear that many of
the adoptive parents may eventually realize. It also evokes the
deep-seated reaction and arouses the grandparents' latent concerns
about the strife and rejection some of them have already experienced with their offspring. Thus they are speaking from the experiences of *parents*—parents who have felt the anguish and pain
that comes from seeing the values they have imparted to their offspring being rejected. It goes beyond a rejection of values, since it
also imposes upon the grandparents a set of roles they are unwilling or ambivalent about fulfilling.

When they are informed of the adoption, some grandparents
respond to the news with silence and a "wait and see" attitude.
They simply give no verbal response at all, with a few refusing to
allow the subject to be mentioned or discussed in their presence.
They ignore the adoption as though it never occurred, thereby not
becoming emotionally involved in what is for them a very painful

affair. A mother in the Midwest said her parents, after three years, still refuse to discuss the adoption with her, although they are nice to the child. Their behavior deeply perplexes and troubles her, since she does not feel they completely accept the child. Another mother describes the "silent reaction" she got from her parents:

> We don't know what my parents' reactions were because there was a silence, although now it's fine with them. I still cannot bring up the subject with them. For them, Johnny is fine, he's our baby. They are too smart to not accept him. They were very much upset. I know my mother was very upset, but my father hasn't yet said a word about it.

When asked if her mother discussed the adoption, she replied:

> She would not talk to me about it, nor would she let my sister talk to her about it. She had a lot of children and always treated us kindly. So I know she loves kids.

When asked if she thinks her mother is gradually coming to accept Johnny, she said, "Yes. She is an extremely intelligent woman, and a kind one. She has never had to deal intellectually or personally with racial hatred or discrimination on a hometown basis. The headlines, for her, are on the radio. In time I feel she will accept him totally."

Others feel that this silence and refusal to discuss the adoption prevents them from knowing what their parents' true feelings are. Therefore they speculate that the silence conceals grandparents' disappointment, disapproval, anger, pain, and trauma. Occasionally, grandparents will confide in other family members (especially their other sons and daughters) their true feelings, which are frequently conveyed to the adoptive parents. The silent response may indicate disapproval or uncertainty, while at the same time allowing them not to interfere in the affairs of their children.

The "silent treatment" has many side effects. While there is no open *opposition* involved, there is oftentimes no *acceptance* of the child either. This means that the child is sometimes silently but painfully discriminated against. Some grandparents show favoritism toward the biological children, while others ignore the adopted child as though he or she doesn't exist. They go so far as to refuse to regard him or her as their grandchild. The most extreme reaction is when grandparents refuse to see the child by making it known that the child is not welcome in their home. A mother talked about this problem:

> My parents are taking a lot longer than my husband's parents to accept the adoption. Eventually they may. They haven't disowned us or anything like that, but they don't call Freddie their grandson.

Another adoptive parent living in the Deep South tells the interviewer how he challenged his father, who lives in the East, to stop discriminating against his black son:

> Daddy does not share the same affection for Ronald that he shows for Kevin, his natural-born grandson. But I think he has come a long way from where he started. I feel free to speak to him if I believe that he is very badly showing discrimination or treatment of one of the children over the others.

Others describe, sometimes painfully, the difficulty their parents have had in relating to the child on any level. A few are even afraid to touch the child initially. One mother said her parents had never previously had contact with blacks. When her mother first saw the baby, she was very nervous and refused to hold her. She gradually warmed up to the child, with increased contact. Today one would never know she had once reacted that way, since she simply adores the child, oftentimes taking her home to spend vacations with her in a distant city.

A few grandparents express open hostility toward their sons and daughters for having adopted a black child. As one woman remarked, "My mother wasn't upset. She was terrified!" Grandparents often ask, "What are you trying to prove by doing such an outrageous thing?" They view the adoption in a very personal way, as an affront to themselves. Some are ashamed to face their friends and neighbors when they hear about the adoption. As one irate grandmother asked, "How can I ever face my friends again when they hear about this? Why would you do this to me? Are you trying to punish me?" Likewise, a grandfather who bitterly opposed his daughter and son-in-law adopting said he was stopped at the supermarket by someone conducting a survey on blacks. When they asked him how he felt about equal rights, he quipped, "Would you believe that I have a black grandchild?" Without any further explanation he walked to his car, with the surveyor wondering what he meant. One couple said that all four grandparents were very angry over the adoption. They asked them if they were crazy, and they wanted to know what were they trying to prove. The grandfather accused his son of being disloyal to all the family stood for—to all the family's sacred traditions. One of the most indignant responses came from the mother of a college professor in the East; the professor said:

> We have done the worst thing in the world to her. She said *we did it to get even with her.* My parents have no other grandchildren. She has seen him once. . . . I'm surprised that she got down here that one time. She says as lovable as he is, it's hard for her to kiss him. She's like half the people in the country. . . . My father gets along with him pretty good. He loves kids. But my mother really just can't take it.

As an afterthought, he said:

> Just the opposite of what you would think. My mother and father growing up and living their whole lives in New York City, and I have always gone to school with black kids.

Three of the couples in the study had undergone a severe rupture in relations with their parents as a result of the adoption. In one case a young father had come close to being disowned by his parents, as his wife explains:

> No one really liked the idea of us adopting a black child. My parents are liberals from back in the twenties and thirties. Therefore they couldn't make a significant protest. They said it would be difficult, but they would accept it, and they have. My husband's family is extremely Orthodox Jewish, and they found it very difficult. It took them three or four months before they could re-

solve whether they could accept us as a family. They decided they have. They haven't done real well yet on accepting our child, but they are trying.

For another couple, the break in relations with his family has been permanent. As his wife explains, "My husband's family asked us not to come back. Maybe of the twenty or twenty-five couples that we know who have adopted transracially, I think we're the only ones whose parents have continued to be as opposed to it as they were in the very beginning. We no longer communicate with them. As far as they're concerned, we're dead." As a result of the family problems they were having, she felt it a decided disadvantage to have adopted across racial barriers, and intimated that had they known it was going to destroy their relationship with her husband's parents, they never would have adopted. Presently they are trying to conceal this information from their children. Whenever their five-year-old daughter asks when she will be allowed to see "Granny," her parents make excuses. They realize that this pattern of evasion cannot continue forever. Another couple decided not to visit their parents anymore because the grandparents refused to see the child. In reflecting on this decision, this young mother said, "If they were to see Peter, I'm sure my mother would accept him. I don't know if my father would. We don't know if my father will ever see him, and I'm not going to press it. Really, it is not my problem."

In spite of the problems transracial adoptions cause for grandparents and their offspring, in most cases wounds are usually healed, and relationships get back to near normal. But until this happens, there is a lot of pain involved for all parties involved.

In addition to grandparents, the adoption of a black child has a strong impact on the biological children in the family, for they too are having their kinship structure altered in a profound way, since they must now claim kinship with an *adopted* sister or brother who is also racially different. This basic alteration in their nuclear family structure will have lifelong implications for them— interaction and family ties that will extend beyond their parents' life spans. This is a factor that few parents seem to have given enough careful consideration. As one mother said, "We must be concerned that all our children will remain a close family after they are grown, and even after my husband and I are dead. We have to try and build the strong family ties while they are still young children that will make it possible for them to love and respect each other as adults."

The decision to adopt is always shared with the biological children, regardless of their ages. One mother said the only way she knew how to communicate to her two-year-old that a new baby was expected soon was by laying out the baby clothes in front of her and saying, "This is what the new baby is going to wear." After doing this repeatedly, her son caught on and thereafter began asking each day, "Where new baby?" When his black sister arrived, so accustomed had he become to the idea that he started referring to his sister as "my baby." Another mother had to take the new baby (six months old) to her daughter's nursery school so her friends could see her adopted brother, whom she was so proud to show off.

Although sibling rivalry develops, the children share their parents' enthusiasm about the adopted child's arrival. One couple, whose infant son died a short time before they adopted, said they told their four-year-old daughter "everything about the adoption." Her father explained, "Karla knew we were going to the agency for conversations for a while . . . but there was a time when we were just waiting and nothing was happening. We took a drive to a small town and were in a general store when a woman came in with a baby. Karla asked, 'Daddy, are we still going to get a baby?' I reassured her that we were, but we had to wait until one was available. She thought we had given up the idea of adopting since she had not heard us discussing it for a while."

The presence of a black sibling in the home provides the biological children with a rare learning experience in race relations. Having a black sibling means they must try to comprehend the meaning of racial attitudes and behavior much earlier than most American children. They experience some things at age six that some white middle-class children may never experience as they are growing up. For example, they might have to defend themselves and their black sibling from the racial insults of cruel playmates, an experience that few white American children will ever have.

Many of the children tell their playmates and their teachers that their parents are adopting a new brother or sister "for them." And they oftentimes find themselves explaining the meaning of adoption to their peers, since many of these young children are unfamiliar with adoption. They also have to try to explain how and why they are getting a "black" brother or sister, since these young minds find it difficult to comprehend that you can have a sister or brother who does not look like you. A large number of the children questioned their parents about the adopted child's color. "Why does he have to be such a yukky color?" asked a five-year-old. The young children asked their parents why the baby was a different color; whether he or she had to be dark; and whether the baby would eventually turn white like they were. The older ones rarely raised such questions, because of their familiarity with racial differences. One mother said, "When we told our four-year-old that she would soon have a new sister, she was delighted because she would have someone to play dolls with. But when we told her that her new sister would be brown-skinned, she was neg-ative on that for a while, and we couldn't understand why. It finally occurred to us to ask her if she thought everyone in the family had to be the same color. That was what had been bother-ing her. We then pointed out some other transracial families to her, showing her that other families have mixed the colors to-gether. That made it okay." A midwestern couple said their two older children were confused by all the stares and questions they got from strangers because of their two adopted daughters. Mrs. Morton said, "We explained to them that people are curious be-cause they don't know where this brown child came from. . . . We discussed with them how some people don't know anything about adoption and that is why they ask us questions and stare at us. Before the arrival of our first black daughter, someone at school asked Harvey if his new sister was going to be a colored baby. I told Harvey to ask his friend what color they meant be-cause we all have color and pigmentation in our skin. He had quite a deal with his friends because they told him that white is not a color and they were white. . . . So we discussed some of the medical facts about color. . . . Hopefully they are getting a good experience from this all around, and not just in the family."

Some children were threatened by the adoption because it aroused deep insecurities within them. When parents explained to their young children that they would be getting a new sibling, quite often they were confused and upset over the adoption itself. A Washington, D.C., mother said, "Our two sons kept questioning us about a mother who would give up her child. It finally occurred to us that they wondered if we would give them up. I explained to them that Constance's mother really loved her but she couldn't give her a home and thought that adoption would be best for her. Once I made it clear to them that this was never going to happen to them, they stopped asking questions about it." Some parents said that once they explained the adoption to their children, they wondered if the "other mommy" would come back and take their sister or brother away from them. When told that this was not possible, they were reassured and their fears vanished.

In time adoption usually becomes a household word, especially as the children grow older. Some children become little authorities and can explain the meaning of adoption to anyone who cares to listen. A mother explained, "Our children have all grown up with the concept of knowing that you can have children two ways. You can have them born to you, or you can adopt them. . . . They are used to hearing the word 'adoption' used in a positive way. So when they hear ladies in the supermarket saying it with a negative ring, they wonder, 'Why is something different about this?' " Being sophisticated on the subject is but one way in which parents feel their children are having their knowledge expanded as a result of the adoption.

Once their strongest fears and anxieties about the adoption have been alleviated, some biological children become strong protectors and defenders of their black sisters and brothers. As one father said, "Adam now belongs to our two older children. When he cries, they get his bottle. When he needs to be changed, they try to diaper him. They spend a lot of time playing with him and entertaining him. You'd never know they felt threatened by the adoption before he arrived." Or take the case of the mother who said her four-year-old son was so excited about his " 'dopted" sister that she had to take her to his nursery school to show her off to his friends and teacher. "He beamed from ear to ear when his playmates saw her," said Mrs. Johnson. "He was the proudest little thing. None of the children seemed to mind that she was not white."

All is not always so positive, since the adoption frequently creates racial problems. There are many occasions for the siblings to defend themselves and their black sibling from racial insults. "When our little boy was called 'nigger,'" said one mother, "his older sisters and brother jumped on that little boy and scratched him up. Then they made him apologize and promise never to say that word again." Some of the older children have often had to go to the defense of their younger brothers and sisters when they are physically attacked and when they are called racial slurs. The older children often experience the taunts and cruelty of their playmates in the neighborhood and at school. A twelve-year-old girl who has several black brothers found herself constantly defending them and herself from the insults of other children. A favorite type of peer cruelty is that of snickering at the white child while making derisive comments such as, "There goes Sheila's black brother." One mother said several of her older son's schoolmates frequently jeered at him as they said, "Your brother is a 'coon! Your brother is a 'coon!" The child got in so many fights because of this that his parents eventually had a conference with school officials. They decided to allow their children to remain in the school only after the teachers and principal agreed to stop this hostility. While parents are usually upset over these conflicts and would prefer that they not occur, they tend to minimize their racial overtones and their seriousness. A typical response to the child is that the children who do such things are ignorant. They also maintain that ultimately it might prove to be a good and sobering experience for the children. "I think the experience has been good for Barbara," said one mother of her twelve-year-old. "She has much more openness and lack of fear." A father said the experience of defending his younger brother has "toughened my ten-year-old in ways that he would not have experienced otherwise."

Having a black brother or sister can also work to a child's advantage, especially if they live in an integrated neighborhood and attend a racially integrated school. Children frequently get singled out for special treatment by their black playmates. According to one mother, "My little boy's black friends think it's really neat that he has a black brother. They don't quite understand how it happened, but they like it. He is one of them." Other parents said their children's black playmates come to their aid when they are attacked by other kids, and in more pleasant situations they make many black friends.

Parents feel strongly that the adoption of a black child strengthens and expands the horizons of their biological children. "It makes them more aware of the many different people and things in the world," said a mother. For another, "My children are no longer provincial and limited, as they were before they got a black brother. They now have better relations with people of other races." A Washington, D.C., couple said their five-year-old son says his goal in life is to "grow up and get married and have ten children, five biological and five adopted, five black and five white. He says he is going to marry someone who already has a child or two because that would show that they really loved children." After adjusting to the adopted sister or brother, the biological children sometimes pressure their parents to adopt another child, an indication of how well the adoption has worked.

In most instances the relationship between adopted and biological children closely parallels that of all biological children in a family. Like ordinary children, they have their arguments and fights, as well as the peaceful and co-operative times. Many parents said that their younger children displayed jealousy over the new baby's arrival. The older the child, as in any other situation, the less likely he or she is to be threatened by the baby. "My three-year-old son absolutely went to pieces when we brought Betsy home," said a mother. "For several weeks I had to carry them both in my arms at the same time because he wouldn't let me put him down." Although some of these children temporarily regressed, it did not become a major problem in any of the families. Of course, this same jealous behavior frequently occurs when a baby is born into a family.

The reactions of other relatives to the adoption generally are far milder. While some openly object, their responses are not very consequential. They have less power and influence over the adoptive parents, and their approval is not sought after in the way in which the approval of the grandparents is. The reactions of their siblings, aunts, uncles, and cousins are just as unpredictable as their parents', but the other relatives tend to be far less involved. Other relatives do not influence the couple's decision to adopt. Moreover, they usually keep their feelings to themselves, and adhere to a "mind your own business" policy.

The data from this study indicate that there is, in the great majority of cases, an acceptance of the adoption among the adoptive couples' siblings. Other studies have also drawn the same conclusion. It is to be expected that one's sister or brother would be more in tune with, informed about, and sympathetic to current concerns and social issues such as transracial adoption than one's parents, grandparents, aunts, and uncles. The deference and tolerance that is shown one's parents and grandparents because of considerations of age, health, wisdom, and life experiences are not given to one's peers. Therefore adoptive parents are less tolerant of the objections and concerns of their siblings than of their mothers and fathers.

In the great majority of cases, this was the first transracial adoption to occur on either side of the family, although some parents indicated that other members of their family are now considering it. There were less than five exceptions. Most of the parents agreed that while adopting a black child is not something their siblings would consider doing, many nevertheless responded favorably, and were generally supportive. A few parents received the "silent treatment," and still others reported having heard, second-hand, that either a sister, brother, or one of their spouses raised objections. Rarely did these take as overt a form as did the objections of their parents. A mother complained that when she took her children to visit her family in Idaho, her sister-in-law refused to allow her son to play with the black adopted child. A father reported, "My one brother, whom we hardly ever see, is kind of a racist, and I suspect that he tags the adoption as another crazy thing to do since he generally disapproves of us." Still another parent said, "My sister's husband initially opposed the idea, but he wasn't very vehement." Finally, a mother from Missouri who adopted several black children described the reaction of her husband's brother and his wife:

They have a very bad attitude about the realities of oppression and other racial matters. I don't think they know what's going on. They were here a couple of years ago and they said that maybe the slaves really liked their oppression and were contented. They're not openly hostile about the adoption, though.

Another parent heard from a relative that her husband's sister "wondered why they are adopting a little pickaninny." These extreme reactions do not constitute the norm, although evidence indicates that the objections of other relatives are a problem. In a national survey conducted with white couples who had adopted black and mixed-race children, Nutt and Snyder found that the second highest source of opposition to the adoption was from relatives, who accounted for 8.7 per cent. Maternal grandparents comprised 11.3 per cent, and paternal grandparents were slightly higher, with 14.2 per cent.[6] No delineation was made by the investigators among cousins, aunts, uncles, sisters, and brothers, so one does not have a sense of which groups find the adoption least objectionable and which most objectionable.

The adoptive couple's grandparents also are an interesting group, in terms of their reactions to the adoption. Only a few reported what their grandparents' responses had been. Many, of course, were deceased. One mother said her step-grandmother had been very opposed to the adoption: "She lives in the South and thinks [George] Wallace and [Lester] Maddox are fine.* She used to go down to Maddox's Pick Rick Restaurant, and she would welcome everyone into the restaurant—a kind of unofficial hostess. She thought he was such a fine man." One other parent reported having received "absolutely the vilest letters imaginable from my grandparents—too vile to even mention the contents." Other grandparents pose no problem and are in favor of the adoption. A father in Atlanta laughingly described how happy his grandmother was that he and his wife had a child, that color and the fact that the child was adopted made no difference. In fact, because of her senility, she sometimes got her generations mixed up so that "she didn't know if it was me or Carmen that she was talking to" (a gap of thirty-five years!).

* George Wallace is governor of Alabama and Lester Maddox is former governor of Georgia. Maddox became famous for his segregationist policies.

The reactions of more distant relatives such as cousins, aunts, uncles, et al., were even less important to the adoptive couple. Generally, they are not very close to their immediate families. As previously mentioned, most do not live in the same city in which they grew up. This means that they are dispersed from their extended family members. Therefore the opinions of more distant kin had an even weaker impact. The exception, obviously, was with those few individuals who had close relations—for example, with a particular aunt, cousin, or grandparent.

Aunts, uncles, and cousins also, on occasion, express their views, but rarely. Again, the couple usually is not in close contact with these relatives, who are informed of the adoption by other family members or by formal announcement. One couple who sent out formal announcements, according to the father ("including the race of the child so there would be no response under false pretenses"), said one of the more interesting responses came from one of his uncles, who is about seventy years old. "He wrote us a long letter saying that when he first heard about it, he had to sit back and think for a while and wasn't sure about it. But now he thinks it's very nice." This same couple also were the targets of a vicious act by an aunt, who sent a New Year's card addressed to them as "Mr. and Mrs. John A. Smith and Susan" (their biological daughter), making certain that she excluded the adopted child's name from the envelope. It is quite possible that an equally large number of siblings and other relatives of the adoptive couple object, but because they do not have the right to interfere at all, one is far less likely to know how they feel. Only the strongest reactions become problematic.

There are many intrafamily problems created by the adoption, but the parents rarely talk about them. These parents cannot run the risk of appearing to fail in their duties and responsibilities toward their black children. If the adopted child—who is already considered by the agencies as a high-risk placement—appears to be the object of special treatment, it may well be that parents are more conscientiously going about their socialization tasks than would be the case if such a high risk were not involved. Parents are reluctant to discuss problems the adoption has created in their nuclear families, especially if these are conflicts between their biological and their adopted children. Since many people, including grandparents and friends, had raised questions about the advisability of the couple adopting across racial boundaries, and since the couples had proceeded to do so in spite of these cautionary notes of advice, their only option has been to prove that they have not failed. And in doing so, many have tended to ignore glaring problems in their families and to paint a rosy, optimistic picture to the observer.

11

THE SOCIAL MATRIX
Interaction with the Nonrelated

The views of friends, neighbors, and the strangers these families meet usually do not involve any of the intensity and rejection they experience with their families. The majority of these parents had encountered little *open* disapproval from their friends and neighbors, although many had questioned why they adopted and indicated they would not do so. Ordinarily there is a great deal of compatibility of interests, ideologies, values, and lifestyles among friends. Rarely do individuals maintain close relationships with people whose views are incompatible with their own. This is especially the case when the opposing views are verbalized and where little tolerance is shown for accepting differences.

When a couple in the Midwest was asked if they had lost any friends as a result of the adoption, the adoptive mother replied:

I don't think you lose real friends when you do something like this. You might lose acquaintances. People that I call friends usually have pretty much the same interests that I do—the same concerns and standards, or else they wouldn't be your friends to start with. You don't lose friends if you have another baby, so I can't see why you'd lose friends by adopting a child.

The opinions of more casual associates made little or no difference as one father indicated:

So far as our *true* friends are concerned, there isn't any problem. For those who weren't, it really didn't bother us one way or the other.

Another father remarked, "Our friends are the types who would do the same if they had the chance."

Since individuals are most likely to choose as their friends those persons with whom they have a lot in common, this perhaps accounts for the fact that transracially adoptive parents encounter little conflict and resistance from their friends on the adoption. Also, there is an additional important factor involved, which goes beyond *approval* or *disapproval* of the adoption. The initial impetus to adopt sometimes comes from friends. Falk found that over half the couples in his study said they had a friend who had adopted a child of another race—indicating that friendship played a role, if not in the decision to adopt, at least in attitudinal support following transracial adoption. It is for this reason that many parents asked the opinions and advice of some of their close friends before adopting and sought the advice of friends far more often than they did that of their parents. In a few cases these friends were black. They were especially interested to know how blacks viewed interracial adoption, how they felt other blacks would react to it, and how it would affect the child. "Should we anticipate a lot of problems?" a Minneapolis couple asked their black next-door neighbor. A St. Louis mother sought advice on whether they should adopt from a black professional couple with whom they had shared a close friendship for a long time. Although she felt their black friends might not be approving, they surprised them by saying it was a good idea. She recalled that her male friend posed the most important questions that she and her husband would hear from anyone when he asked:

Do you really have any idea of what you're getting into? Do you know that this is going to pose all kind of visible and invisible problems? Do you realize how "freaky" some people will think you are, and how others will call you "do-gooders"?

Satisfied that they could handle the problems, she explained, "We thought we had an idea of the kinds of problems we'd have to face, so in the end it seemed more important to do than not to do. And the hardest thing for us was talking in a vacuum, not about a child but the possibility of a child. As soon as he came and he was in our arms, that just put the whole human perspective into it. He was ours." Their experience is fairly typical of a majority of those couples who sought the advice of their friends. An adoptive mother said, "The one black gal I've had dealings with knew we were going to adopt, and she said, 'You're not being very choosy, are you?' I hardly knew what to say. So I said, 'Yes, we are, what do you mean?' I guess she thought we were reaching down and adopting beneath our standards. I tried to explain to her that we were not." After the adoption, this couple made an effort to make more black friends, and eventually formed a very interracial lifestyle. After another mother told a black friend about their plans to adopt, she got a disappointing reaction:

I was so hurt when this great black gal I know, who has been a friend for several years, told me she strongly objected to the adoption. She said, "It's one thing for us to be friends but it's another for you to take that friendship to extreme lengths by taking into your home one of 'our' children." Although we have continued to see each other, our friendship is not as strong as it once was.

The reactions of black friends are by no means uniform. Some are very supportive and others express strong opposition. Those who have blacks as close friends generally are supportive. Although the blacks might question the couple's ability to withstand the difficulties that they feel lie ahead, they usually accept the adoption and are helpful in recommending black literature, teaching them to comb and braid the child's hair, trying to sensitize them to a black perspective, etc. A St. Louis mother who has a large number of black friends told the interviewer, "I don't know if we just have 'Uncle Toms' as friends or not, but they have all been positive toward the adoption." A father commented that, "None of the blacks we know were opposed to the adoption. Some kind of cynically looked at it as the 'liberal way.' And some thought it was really neat. We didn't feel we had to explain ourselves, but after talking about it with our friends, they were more positive toward it."

Occasionally black friends of the couple sharply criticize the adoption. A few questioned their motives, and accused them of being paternalistic. Some were cynical and felt that the couple was condescending by having adopted a black child. They wondered if they had settled for what they considered the "second best" upon learning there were no white babies available. This was especially the reaction to those who adopted mixed-race children. Blacks were quick to question whether they preferred a white child, and after being unable to get a "blue-ribbon" baby because of the scarcity in the market, settled for a mixed-race child with Caucasian physical characteristics. Some blacks were resentful of these prospects because they felt the child should be a first preference instead of a substitute for something the couple was unable to get. Many younger blacks whom they personally know often impute sinister motives to the adoptive parents, while others are openly cynical. There are also those who simply cannot *understand* why any white person would want a black child, or vice versa (if there was such an occurrence). Others say that blacks whom they know wonder "what we are up to" by adopting across racial lines. A father who lives in a suburb of Washington, D.C., described an encounter he had on his job with a woman whom he described as an "independent African nationalist," who was very involved in various nationalist activities in her community. He describes their encounter:

> She was sort of silent for a while. She was shy and it was hard to get to talk to her. But finally we got to talking about it and she just wanted to know what was going on in a white person's head who adopted transracially. I think she finally accepted it and thought it was a good idea.

A father who is a social worker in Atlanta spoke of the same problems when he said, "Some people in my job see it as plain sad news for a white to be raising a black child. And a lot of white families we meet also respond negatively to white families adopting black children."

Friends, and to a lesser degree neighbors, provide the least overt problems for the adoptive couple and child. In a study conducted by Simon, only 9 per cent of the adoptive couples' friends had negative reactions, while at least 25 per cent were approving. Over half (58 per cent) were neutral, "which in behavioral terms means that the couple did not notice an increase either in positive or negative affect directed toward themselves or any of their children."[1] Simon notes that slightly fewer neighbors expressed positive reactions, with about the same number of neutral responses.[2] In a national survey conducted by Nutt and Snyder, very few friends (2.1 per cent) and neighbors (4.4 per cent) had negative reactions to the transracial adoption of the child in their study.[3]

A great number of parents in this study reported having at least one friend who questioned whether they knew what they were getting into. Others simply wanted to know *why* they were doing it. Many others understood why one would want to adopt, but they asked, "Why a black child?" A Washington, D.C., mother said that although her friends generally approved the adoption, practically all of her girl friends wanted to know her reasons. She said, "As far as I am concerned, they simply wanted to know what was going on inside my head, because although they knew they had an awful lot in common with me, this was still something they would never have thought of doing themselves." Still other friends had negative comments about the adoption, expressing their opinions to the couple and to mutual friends. While the majority of friends were supportive or at the very least pleasantly neutral on the subject, some friends voiced strong disapproval. An adoptive father, who works as a civil servant in Washington, D.C., found much antipathy among his male friends and colleagues. According to one of his friends, "I always thought we had practically everything in common, but this adoption—it is not something I can understand."

Although it is somewhat rare, there are occasions too, when friends make it known to the couple that they do not approve of the adoption. A father in Maryland reported, "We did have one friend who was very honest and said she didn't like it. We have drifted away from them somewhat, but not just because of this. Their whole lifestyle has become different from ours." His wife added, "It is probably better that they let us know what they were thinking because it would have been bad for us and our chil-

dren if we had continued to try to be friendly with all their pretense. We have a right to live our lives any way we please, and
that includes the right to adopt our black son. If they had the
nerve to tell us they didn't like what we'd done, then we had the
obligation to drop them." He added, "Maybe we should really admire them for having the courage to be honest instead of accusing
them of being bigots. After all, they have a right to their opinions
too."

Other friends generally accept the adoption but with some reservations. For example, a mother in St. Louis noted, "Our
friends in the neighborhood probably wouldn't want their children marrying a black, but they are happy to have us as friends."
When the adoptive families join the Open Door Society, Council
on Adoptable Children, or a similar parents' group, they have
more frequent contact and support with other families who have
adopted black children, and children of other races. Some of the
associations developed in these groups become supportive alliances and friendships, and the parents no longer experience isolation and total disapproval, since they have now broadened their
social network to include persons with whom they share a great
deal in common.

Some parents accuse their neighbors and friends of patronizing
the adopted child. A mother in Washington, D.C., recalled how
one of her friends "goes out of her way to praise the beauty and
intelligence of our two black children." The mother continued,
"This friend was even telling people what wonderful liberal people we were. She couldn't conceive of ordinary people like herself
adopting. She treated us and our children like we were 'super' people—like we were unreal." Her husband added, "A lot of people
either think you're 'great' or that you're 'crazy.' They refuse to accept you as their equal." Whatever disagreeable thoughts neighbors have they usually keep to themselves. As one mother said,
"They don't usually say anything to your face, but I'm sure there
is a lot of over-the-fence 'tongue-wagging.'" Most adoptive parents appear to be especially sensitive to those friends and neighbors who must constantly remind them that they have committed
a great deed by adopting a black child. Most would prefer them to
express their approval by accepting it without fanfare. One
mother said she has a next-door neighbor who always felt obli-

gated to let her know how great she thought they were for having adopted. The mother recalled, "My neighbor has a friend in another state who adopted an American Indian child, and I hear that from her all the time. She's patronizing. I wish I could find a great line to come back with. Not to be cruel, but just to let her know that I'm not too pleased about her reactions." Another mother related that several people have said to them, "Gee, you've really done a wonderful thing, and we admire you for your courage." However, she says, "They obviously wouldn't have said that to us had we adopted a *normal* child" (emphasis added). Ironically, while this mother does not hesitate to criticize her neighbors' patronizing reactions, she does not regard her black adopted daughter, although mentally and physically normal, as *normal*. Neighbors occasionally make disparaging remarks about the adopted child. One mother recalled that a neighbor inquired of another neighbor if "the Martins have received their pickaninny yet." A father in Virginia recalled that one of their neighbors was so stunned to learn they had adopted a black child that she intimated to a neighbor that "the leases in the neighborhood all said that you cannot sell to a black family, when they were drawn up twenty or thirty years ago." According to this parent, "our neighbor was concerned that the neighborhood would 'deteriorate' because of our black child's presence." One of the most interesting accounts of neighbors' negative reactions was related by a couple living in a suburban town of a large midwestern city. They had lived for several years in Africa, and upon their return often entertained Africans in their home. According to Mr. Markham, "We've gotten a lot of scuttlebutt from neighbors because they didn't know our visitors were Africans. They assumed they were American blacks. But what difference should that make?" he asked. "They're people, and just because we choose to have friends who have black faces come to visit shouldn't affect the neighbors." His wife added, "We had a next-door neighbor who wanted to get a lawyer and get us out of the neighborhood because of our black visitors. But none of the neighbors would have supported him on that because that was going a bit too far."

A few of the parents who had adopted children had not made it known to their neighbors that the child was Negro. Because of these mixed-race children's physical characteristics, the neighbors (and occasionally friends) were allowed to think the child was white. One mother insisted that she does not feel it is anyone's business what race her child is, while several others indicate that the circumstances had not arisen where it was necessary for them to know—that is, no one ever asked because they assumed the child was white. If these parents do not clarify the racial status for the child, it can eventually be psychologically damaging. On some occasions friends and neighbors were very supportive and accepting in a quite normal fashion. For example, there was the time when a group of neighborhood friends in a Maryland surburb, upon learning of the impending adoption, called the agency and found out when the child would be placed. With the co-operation of the agency, on the day of the arrival they threw a surprise baby shower for the mother. There are some families who live in neighborhoods with a diverse mixture of persons, including racially mixed marriages. They rarely experience hostility from neighbors and are less likely to draw attention to themselves because they are different. They simply become part of the scenery in the community.

The most threatening persons these parents must deal with are the strangers they meet in public places. Mothers are more likely than fathers to have the unusual, friendly and unfriendly, encounters with strangers because they do most of the shopping, chauffering of the children to and from nursery and kindergarten, doctors' offices, day camp, and a variety of other places. Most families had had unpleasant experiences with strangers. They are frequently the objects of curiosity as people stare relentlessly at their unusual-looking family. All of the mothers whose children were visibly Negro reported having encountered hate stares on at least one occasion, but usually more often they got the impression that they were being personally scrutinized, since strangers often thought the child was the product of a mixed marriage of which the adoptive mother was a part.

There are several types of reactions they get from strangers. For the purpose of simplification, "white" strangers will be discussed in the following section, and later, "black" strangers will be dealt with. There are some strangers whose facial expressions betray strong surprise or immediate shock. Occasionally they make inquiries into the child's racial background. For example, a St. Louis mother said a woman stopped her in the supermarket and inquired, "Is your husband dark?" to which she replied, "No." The adoptive mother said she then proceeded to explain to this stranger why her son "looked a little darker" than other babies. "The stranger was kind of taken aback," she said. "She didn't know what to say when I told her Ryan is part black. Ryan doesn't look different enough for it to be obvious that he's Negro. People don't know how to categorize him when they find out that his father is black."

Occasionally parents form friendships with some of the strangers they meet as a result of the adoption. A Washington, D.C., father noted: "We have become friends with some people who are really interested in seeing how this works and what actually happened. He continued, "We have had people who were acquaintances come up to us and say, 'Oh! I want to tell you that my children are adopted too.' We didn't know this because it wasn't common knowledge in the community. We became friends since that time mostly because of the adoption, not because of the transracial aspects, but just because it's another family who has gone through this and is being supportive."

There are some strangers who immediately show the parents their approval by smiling at the child and by telling the parents what a great deed they have done, or by offering the child candy or other kinds of treats. Frequently they are elderly women in supermarkets, department stores, and other public places. Parents are usually happy to hear what appears to be a sincere sign of approval, although every parent probably wishes they could go completely unnoticed. But if strangers must react to them, they certainly prefer approval over disapproval.

At other times parents express disapproval of outward signs of acceptance because it draws "special" attention to them. Some parents say the strangers treat them like missionaries, an attitude they strongly dislike. Also, they are not always certain that these "kind" remarks are being made with sincerity. For some, it represents a racist reaction formation in which the approving strangers are attempting to convince *themselves* that they really do not dislike blacks, nor do they consider them inferior. These attitudes are more to the stranger's benefit than the family's. It is similar to the attitudes expressed by those grandparents who are amazed at the high intelligence of the child, as though it is not to be expected that he or she would be normal. A father in Minnesota explained it this way:

A lot of people want to talk to you about the adoption, but I think that's counterproductive. They want to make much more of a deal out of it than I prefer to make it. I think to a large extent COAC and Open Door make too much of a deal of it. Maybe that's one of the problems. The more of a deal you make of the adoption, the more you are pointing the finger to the fact that you have done it and the child becomes conscious of it. There are a lot of more subtle ways that can intervene into the social relationships with your children, and I would prefer just to forget it.

Others were not prepared to undergo the stares and curiosity, although often well-meaning, they received. In fact, two couples said they probably would not have adopted had they known it would be this way. As one disenchanted mother said, "We had absolutely no idea that we would be singled out by every stranger we meet simply because one of our children is a Negro. I was definitely not prepared for all the stares and whispering people do when they see us coming. I doubt seriously that I would have adopted a Negro kid had I known we'd have to go through this." On several occasions I interviewed friends of some of the adoptive couples informally, in whom the parents had confided that the adoption was a mistake. Among the reasons cited were an inability to cope with the stares, the hostile remarks, the exclusion by their families, and the occasional conflict between the adopted child and his or her biological siblings.

Finally, there are some strangers who are openly hostile. They glare hate stares and make insulting, derogatory comments about the child and the mother. One mother reported that she had had several such encounters, the worst of which she describes as follows:

There was this little old white lady who came up to me in the store and said in a very nice voice, "Is this your daughter?," pointing to Jessica and, "Is she adopted?" When I said "Yes," she just clicked and became a mass of hate. As she turned to leave, she said, "Just you wait until she is grown up. Then you'll see what a whore she is."

Although this was an extreme reaction, others had also had insulting encounters with total strangers who viewed the child as symbolic of all blacks whom they were prejudicial against or feared. It is inconceivable to them that any "normal" or "average" white person could make a black child a part of their family. A fairly typical reaction is that strangers assume that the mother is married to a black man, which provokes a wrath all its own. In fact, some of the most insulting comments come from people who make this assumption, and usually the mother becomes the target of the verbal abuse instead of the child.

The classic, highly publicized case of overt hostility directed against a white couple who adopted a black child occurred in 1966, when Rev. David Cohen, a civil rights activist, and his wife, Ann, with four children of their own, adopted David, a mixed-race infant. Rev. Cohen participated in civil rights demonstrations in Mississippi and Alabama, and worked for better working conditions for migrant laborers in his home state of California. Adopting young David was but an extension of his involvement in and commitment to human rights. Soon after David arrived, neighbors expressed shocked negative reactions. The Cohens were constantly stared at, and after the Watts riots, garbage was thrown on their lawn. Someone painted "Watts" on their door. Speaking to *Newsweek* magazine, Rev. Cohen said, "I've usually been able to complete what I undertake . . . but we couldn't go any further."[4] The Cohens then made the painful decision to return David to the adoption agency.

It is only natural that the abuse the parents receive from strangers causes them to be angry, and also evokes emotional trauma and pain. One mother said, "If only I could strike out and tell them off instead of ignoring the hostile stares, the nasty remarks, and the cold, impersonal looks on the faces of people who consider themselves too intelligent to stoop to revealing what dirty things they're really thinking. I would relieve a lot of anxiety if I could strike back."

Generally whites are said to be more hostile than blacks. Only a few families had firsthand encounters with hostile blacks, although most described their reactions to the generalized hostility that they know is held by black social workers and other opponents of transracial adoptions. One father summed it up when he described the experiences he had had with blacks who are critical of his having adopted transracially:

> It is very painful for me to listen to blacks criticize me for what I have done, even if I know they don't personally know *me*. I used to dismiss their criticisms as trite, irrelevant, and irresponsible. But I began to listen to them more carefully. One day I asked myself, "How would I feel if I were them?" I then realized that I could understand their anger and frustration, even when I also know that many of these children wouldn't have homes if whites had not adopted them.

For the most part, the parents felt that the ordinary black stranger they meet does not display the hostility described above, especially older blacks. Most parents make a distinction between the outspoken black opponents and the black "man on the street." Invariably they see the average black person as warm, friendly, and sometimes admiring of their having adopted a black child.

Although they too are very curious, the parents feel they are more willing to accept them at face value without questioning their motives. And they certainly are less likely to intellectualize the process, by casting it into an ideological framework. For many of the black middle-aged and elderly strangers these parents meet, the only strong sentiment they feel is a tenderness toward a child whose welfare is being cared for by caring parents. Racial considerations are cast within the realm of the less serious, and usually do not go beyond raising curiosity. Their curiosity is sometimes overwhelming. A mother said she and her two black sons and white daughter were at a suburban shopping center when they passed two elderly black men. Both turned abruptly when they saw her and the children approaching. One turned to the other and said, "Did you see that?" to which his friend replied, "Yeah, man, I saw it, but I don't believe it!" Their shocked reactions are understandable when one considers that a very large proportion of the black masses probably have never heard of transracial adoption. The majority of American blacks probably have never seen such a family. When I asked one parent if she thought blacks are generally more friendly toward transracial adoption than whites, she replied:

Absolutely, and I don't understand it. If I were in a strange neighborhood, I would rather run into a black person than a white person, because the reactions I've had have been warmer. . . . About the only blacks I know who are hostile about this whole thing are the black social workers.

A mother in the South said she had not encountered any hostility from blacks. "The black community we live in has a lot of rural people here. They are much more accepting of white people, whereas in New York, where we once lived, there was much more hostility toward white people adopting black children."

It is impossible to determine precisely why the average black person appears to be more receptive to the adoption than others cited above. They seem to be less inclined to impute motives than an intellectually informed group such as social workers. It has been established elsewhere that low-income blacks have a high rate of informal adoption, and traditionally have placed a high value on children. Perhaps this is one of the manifestations of their value orientation. It also speaks to the somewhat informal lifestyles and attitudes that one finds in these people. As an elderly Alabama black put it, when questioned about his feelings on transracial adoption, "Who can find fault with somebody taking on the burden of raising somebody else's child? Me, myself, I don't judge people. The good Lord said that whoever is without sin cast the first stone. Now you're telling me that some of our folks think these are mean and evil white folks. Well, I can't see it that way, because nobody made them take these little babies and raise them. They aren't even kin to them. When I was growing up, white folks were mean to colored people. They didn't do things like this for you. Maybe I could've got an education if some of the white people I worked for as a boy had helped me—had sent me to college."

Few of the adoptive parents reported having experienced discrimination in their places of employment because of the adoption, although some related small incidents involving insulting remarks made by coworkers, as well as the same curiosity they encounter elsewhere. The adoption also remains an unknown fact to many of their employers and coworkers, not because of deliberate concealment but because there has not been a reason to make it known. There is also the attitude that it isn't anyone's business. The majority of the working parents are employed in large metropolitan centers, where one's personal affairs are not as likely to be known, nor do others particularly care to know them.

While the fact that one has adopted across racial lines only occasionally influences one's friends or neighbors to do the same (only five reported cases in this study), most parents feel that the adoption has served a good influence in other ways. "The exposure to an interracial family," according to one father, "is a good lesson in better human relationships." For a mother in a suburb of a midwestern city, "It gives many people the chance to see that ordinary persons like ourselves do this sort of thing. Contrary to some of their wildest imagination, we're not wild-eyed radicals or way-out hippies. Just folks."

Most adoptive parents seem to be pleased that their neighbors and friends, regardless of their personal feelings on the adoption, continue to accept them and respect their rights to practice any lifestyle within limits they choose, including adopting black children.

There is a peculiar responsive chord that transracial adoption strikes in a broad cross section of the American population. Since it is such an atypical racial pattern that most Americans have probably never observed at a close distance, the most natural reaction is one of curiosity, bewilderment, or shock. Then, beyond the initial reaction, are a second set of more deeply laden ones that people express, and that are based on their personal values, orientations, and beliefs. The very inner feelings of many Americans are that transracial adoption is a private "trouble." It deviates from their values and beliefs on what are appropriate standards and practices in race relations, in family formation, and in child welfare practices, child socialization, social policy, and the like. Therefore the adoptive parents are often on the receiving end of a variety of reactions from their nonkin. What may give the appearance of being a simple racial reaction may be much more than that, since it may also evoke the observers' feelings on adoption, the values they place on "sameness," and their disdain for the potential for "bad blood" in the *unknown* child to one day come lurking forward. Of course, these are more general negative reactions, since they may be directed against *any* adoptive parent. Then there are also the clear-cut racial reactions. When a stranger approaches a mother in a supermarket and asks her in a negative tone of voice if she has had a child by a black man, there can be no mistake that this is a racist reaction. Or if previously friendly neighbors stop allowing their children to play with the adoptive couple's children *after* they adopt the black child, the racial implications are quite clear.

The web of social interaction among families who adopt a child across racial boundaries and their friends, neighbors, and the strangers they meet in public places is complex. While the reactions of these people can be and often are provocative, they should be kept in perspective—that is, parents must be careful to display strength and courage when faced with the hostility and to learn to expect the congratulatory comments as natural reactions from people who have been conditioned to view such a practice in this manner.

12

THE POLITICS OF CHILD WELFARE

Adoption Agencies and Social Policy

There were at least 26,000 children in New York City in 1975 who were wards of the city and state and were being cared for by private and public child-care agencies.[1] An investigation of the problems many of these children suffer found that "the vast majority of these children are being placed in private child-care agencies that regularly deny them that opportunity to gain a permanent home. Most . . . remain locked in foster care for years —many for the balance of their adolescent lives, while the private agencies to which they are assigned collect millions of tax dollars each year for their maintenance. . . ." The interest in finding adoptive homes is so low that 47 of the city's 77 private agencies offer no adoption services at all.[2] In 1974 only 3 per cent of the children in the care of these agencies were adopted.[3] The study reports the following as examples of the victimization of New York City's homeless children: In 1974 one agency with 326 children placed none for adoption; an agency with 577 children placed only 4 for adoption; an institution with 725 children in care placed 1 child for adoption. One agency, which has been in operation for 84 years, has never made an adoptive placement or made a child legally free for adoption.[4]

It is widely felt that the primary motivation for the institutionalization of foster care is an economic one. In a unique arrangement, the New York City government pays private agencies fees reportedly as high as $1,000 per month for the care of these children.[5] So long as they remain in permanent foster care, the private agencies are able to sustain their existence: They can pay their overhead, personnel salaries, and other expenses while frequently skimping on the quality of care offered the children they are paid to keep.

The majority of these are older black children. There are also Hispanic and older white children, and the handicapped of all races. Many have not been legally freed for adoption, and agencies have made little effort to rehabilitate the parents so their children can be returned to them. They have also done little to get the children freed for adoption.

Foster care, according to the Child Welfare League of America, is "a child welfare service which provides substitute care for a planned period for a child when his own family cannot care for him for a temporary or extended period and when adoption is neither desirable nor possible."[6] Kadushin categorizes foster care, adoption, and institutions as substitute child welfare services. As the "third line of defense [they] are used when the situation is so damaging as to require either a temporary or a permanent dissolution of the parent-child relationship."[7] In an ideal sense, the intent of foster care is to eventually reunite the child with his or her parents or to find adoptive ones for them. Obviously, as Kadushin notes, these two alternatives are not always possible, and many children are relegated to the permanent status of living in foster homes or institutions.

Child welfare agencies have failed miserably to achieve the goal of rehabilitating parents so they can be reunited with their children. Instead of reuniting families or working to free the children for adoption (especially when they are still quite young and more adoptable), agencies have created a permanent foster care system —a system whose goal oftentimes is to keep the child in care from the time he or she enters until adulthood. Thousands of such children have been moved by agencies from one foster home or institution to another, thereby never achieving a necessary degree of permanency in their lives.

The failure to find adoptive homes due to the institutionalization of foster care has created the present crisis in child care in New York City and in other urban centers throughout the nation. It is clear from the New York case analysis that some private agencies have never seriously undertaken the responsibility of finding homes for black and other "hard to place" children. It could be forcefully argued that these children acquired the "hard to place" label from adoption agencies not because of the disinterest in or scarcity of minority families ready to adopt them; rather, they became "hard to place" because of the insensitivity of the agencies and their lack of care and concern with finding *adoptive* parents. As a result, foster care became economically profitable, administratively efficient, and philosophically expedient.

Of course, child-care agencies never could have created and executed such policies toward the "hard to place" child had it not been sanctioned by the legislative bodies who make the appropriations and who are empowered to monitor the conduct of the agencies. The lawmakers' insensitivity parallels that of the child-care agencies. Most adoption agencies have always had a notorious reputation and tradition for discriminating against black children in their care, and against black applicants seeking to adopt them. It has already been established in this book that adoption agencies came into existence for the purpose of supplying babies to white middle-class couples who were infertile. This has given priority to finding the best child for the family who wanted one, rather than finding the best family for the child who needed one. Traditionally, agencies set up basic standards that parents were required to meet before they could be approved to adopt. Although there was some variation among agencies, most adhered to the following requirements:

- declaration of religious faith; husband and wife must be of the same faith
- husband and wife of same racial background
- good physical and mental health
- husband must be employed
- wife must be a housewife and not otherwise employed
- proof of infertility validated by a medical doctor
- the couple must have a middle-class income and lifestyle, including a separate room for the child
- they must apply for a child of their own racial and religious background

- they must not be too old nor too young
- they should not be too intense about their desire for a child,
  nor too uncaring

Adoption agencies, by setting up such rigid and unreasonable eligibility standards, had a practice of "screening out" instead of "screening in" applicants. Certain groups of persons automatically fell victim to the agencies' bureaucracy, middle-class bias, racism, and overall archaic philosophy. Blacks, other minorities, the white poor, single persons, the middle-aged, and couples with biological children were either not encouraged to apply or not permitted to adopt outright. Childless couples who applied often found themselves at the mercy of agency bureaucracy and their adoption workers' whims. Agency policy notwithstanding, so many of the experiences applicants had were highly personalized and based heavily upon the personal attitudes and philosophies of the caseworker. Parents in this study often regarded their worker as either a highly efficient, empathetic angel, or an awful, incompetent, unsympathetic person who should not be allowed to place children. Adoption workers usually evoke strong reactions in the applicants because of the personalized relationship between the two parties. Because the agencies have always wielded such strong power over childless couples seeking a baby at any price or cost, very few protested the policies and practices. This is understandable in view of the fact that if one is desperate enough for a baby, he or she is not likely to jeopardize that opportunity by noncompliance with the agency's eligibility requirements. Thus couples have been eager to comply with some of the most outrageous requirements, even those they strongly opposed. Their attitude has been, "Why try to challenge them when you know it will mean an automatic rejection and they'll deny you a child?" One couple said they objected to their agency's requirement that one be a regular churchgoer. As avowed atheists, they were at first willing to take the agency to court in an effort to get the law changed, but later changed their minds because they decided they'd rather have a child even when they had to comply with a rule they were strongly opposed to. The wife's comment was, "Once we filed suit against the agency, we would have been branded by every adoption unit in the state, and they wouldn't have come near us." The possibility of being able to adopt a child was of such urgency that personal objections were dismissed or overlooked.

Many applicants complain about the insensitive questions the caseworker asked in the process of conducting the home study. The home study is the investigative process conducted by agencies of adoptive applicants. The parents must submit to interviews and provide legal documents, including their birth certificates, divorce decree (if previously married), references, and documentation of income (frequently, the W-2 form is requested) and other wealth. It is upon the basis of the home study that the agency is able to make an assessment of the applicants' fitness to parent. The screening process is designed to determine their mental and economic competence, and their overall maturity. In the process of conducting the home study, parents frequently feel that their very private lives are being revealed to a virtual stranger—the adoption worker. Many of the questions the workers ask can be sensitive and embarrassing. Some parents particularly objected to the questions involving their intimate relationship. A young woman in Chicago said, "A caseworker who looked old enough to be my grandmother asked me how often I had sex with my husband. I got so angry that I snapped back at her, 'Probably twenty times a week more often than you do. This is none of your damn business, and it has nothing to do with my ability to be a good mother.' I was so angry that I stormed out of her office, telling her in the process that I didn't think she was even qualified to make adoptive placements, since she probably hadn't changed her line of questioning since she started working there, probably before I was born. My husband and I applied to another agency, and we told them voluntarily why we withdrew our application from the other agency. Fortunately they were more modern in their thinking, and we got a lovely little four-month-old girl from them. Susan is five years old now."

Many adoption agencies are getting rid of these kinds of embarrassing and irrelevant questions and procedures. They consider the sex life of the applicant to be important only insofar as it might provide some insight into other areas of the couple's overall compatibility. Indeed, there are agency workers who do not even pursue this line of questioning in their interviews at all. Still there are perhaps hundreds of elderly women working in agencies scattered throughout the United States who are still evaluating applicants' eligibility to adopt by the same standards they used twenty or thirty years ago, when they considered the only motive for anyone wanting to adopt to be infertility. Preoccupation with a couple's sexual relations might have been somewhat justified then, but certainly not today, when the motives have broadened and changed. Unfortunately, the elderly, traditional adoption workers probably will not change very much. They continue to cater to their traditional white middle-class infertile clientele, and perceive all other applicants to be an aberration of this ideal.

Because of race and poverty, a disproportionately high number of blacks have had an exceedingly difficult relationship with agencies. Several studies have documented their high withdrawal rate from the agency adoptive process, as well as why a majority still adopt informally or independently.[8] The adoption agency symbolizes for many blacks an indifferent white bureaucracy that has little awareness of their needs. This image has been reinforced by the firsthand accounts of those who applied and had negative experiences with the agency. One study concluded that blacks viewed the adoption agency as "forbidding, threatening, rejecting, as 'screening out rather than screening in,' as demanding perfection in adoptive parents, as 'holier than thou,' as sitting in judgment with power to give or withhold." Their overall view of the agency was that of having a "middle-class bias, a white orientation and a readiness to reject."[9] Festinger found that blacks withdrew their initial applications for adoption because they objected to the agencies' financial requirements, rules and procedures, and miscommunication between them and the agency."[10] Billingsley and Giovanonni found that blacks objected to the fee charged because "they find the idea of 'buying a child' reminiscent of slavery and particularly repugnant."[11] The fertility tests were particularly objectionable to black males, many of whom have a high degree of *machismo*, which is perceived as the ability to father *biological* children. To be subjected to a fertility test is tantamount to having one's manhood called into question. Some applicants drop out at this stage, often refusing to discuss why they did so.

Another screening-out device was that of excluding working mothers and individuals who were previously married. Agencies assumed that a "good mother" was one who spent her time as a housewife and was available to the child at all times. They were unconcerned that many mothers who can afford to stay home with the child really did not prefer doing so, or they were not necessarily the ideal mothers simply because they were there. Obviously this criterion eliminated any woman who could not or did not want to become a housewife, especially the poor. Divorced persons came under severe scrutiny. Agencies assumed that such persons were too unstable to be trusted with an adopted child. Some workers also held strong moral feelings against divorced persons because they believed that individuals should remain *legally* married, regardless of circumstances. This attitude probably had its origins in the traditions of the upper classes, who abhorred divorce and perceived it to be a characteristic of the lower classes. Many black applicants, especially the poor and working class, were rejected because they were "guilty" of some of these practices.

The bureaucratic red tape that dominates agency practices has always acted as a great deterrent to many black applicants. For example, low-income persons who work an eight-hour regularly scheduled day are frequently unable to take the time off during working hours for the required interviews. To do so may well mean taking an entire day off and losing badly needed income. It would also require explaining to one's supervisor why he or she must take the time off. A lot of people do not want others to know they are trying to adopt. The poor do not have the flexibility of persons working in professional and semi-professional occupations.

Income and home ownership also acted as screening-out devices. By virtue of being low-income, many black applicants were unable to meet these eligibility requirements, since they probably rented their apartments or houses, were not college educated (and frequently had not gone through high school), and did not earn a middle-income salary. These applicants simply could not understand what importance the agency's questions and requirements had to do with adopting a child and to being good parents. As one black woman in New York said, "None of my friends or family own their homes. All of them work in blue-collar jobs, and some of them have been divorced. But they're good parents, and they love their children. So when the agency told us that we couldn't qualify because we didn't meet their requirements, I just figured they didn't even know what they were doing with these little children. They don't even need these babies in their custody. I could do a better job than they're doing, and I don't even have any social work training." (She was referring to a private agency.) Needless to say, none of these rigid agency requirements have any direct relationship to one's ability to be a good parent.

In view of this history, it is not surprising that black social workers—individuals who are quite familiar with the practices of these agencies—would become bitter critics of their policies and practices toward other blacks. Their primary contention has been that adoption agencies have not been concerned with the social welfare needs of black children and prospective black parents. Audrey Russell of the National Association of Black Social Workers stated, "The transracial adoption movement is designed to meet the needs of the same group that the American adoption movement met—the white middle-class couple who now find themselves unable to adopt a white infant because of the shortage of such children. As an alternative, they are willing to adopt a child of mixed parentage. As an absolute last resort, they will take a black child."

Black social workers also charge that transracial adoption is an expedient to eliminating the white infant shortage. Some social workers and other outspoken persons criticize the adoption agencies for meeting the needs of white parents at the expense of acting in the best interests of the child. As healthy white infants became scarcer and scarcer, the black social workers contend, these white middle-class couples pressured agencies to alter their traditional "matching" policies, allowing them to adopt black and mixed-race children.

A black social worker activist gives voice to her group's anger when she commented, "The supply of white children has dried up and their human desire for parenthood is being realized through this psychological bastardization of our children."[12]

The black social workers attacked the agencies for refusing to expand their programs to include black applicants and for placing black children in white families. These must be understood as two separate but overlapping issues. They argue that it is impossible for the agencies to sufficiently concern themselves with placing black children in black families unless the agencies transform the structure and character of their operations. They must also transform their image from that of a white middle-class institution whose sole concern is that of meeting the needs of white parents, to one of serving all the population, with a priority on the minority child's needs for a permanent home. They must eliminate their restrictive hiring practices and include blacks in their organizations in administrative and staff positions, and on their boards of directors. It is important that black social workers and sensitive white social workers do the initial screening of black applicants, since they are likely to be more familiar with why applicants might appear hesitant, nervous, or might manifest any other problem.

The agencies, it is argued, must also make more vigorous efforts to recruit blacks by going into the black communities of the cities in which they operate. "They must go to the people," said a black social worker, "instead of waiting for the people to come to them. Most blacks I work with don't even know the agency exists, and some may have heard of it, but they don't know where to find it." Her point is to be taken seriously because there are literally thousands of blacks throughout the nation who would probably welcome the opportunity to adopt a child if they knew of the need, and if they knew how to do so with relative comfort and ease, in an unthreatening situation.

A successful adoptive recruitment program for minority-group parents is being conducted by the Spaulding for Children Agency, which specializes in finding adoptive homes for "hard to place" children. The most productive recruiter, who has acquired a legendary reputation for his superlative skills, is Kojo-Mbogda Odo, a consultant to the Spaulding agency. Kojo, who as a single parent has adopted three sons, was recruited to find homes for black and Hispanic children. After canvassing bars, pool halls, speaking to ministers and their church groups, women's clubs, and simply stopping people on the street to talk to them about his recruitment efforts, Kojo has been extremely successful in finding applicants for the so-called "hard to place" children.

There are other model programs that have pioneered, with great success, in the placement of black children. In 1967 the Los Angeles County Department of Adoptions set up a branch in Compton for the explicit purpose of recruiting black parents. This agency was physically located in a black community so as to make it accessible. The Harlem-Dowling Adoption Service, a component of the prestigious Spence-Chapin Agency in New York, was opened in 1969, and is black-sponsored and black-staffed. Harlem-Dowling is well known for its special drug unit, which treats addict mothers and places their children for adoption. Homes for Black Children in Detroit came into existence in 1969. It too is staffed and sponsored by blacks. A more recently organized group is the Black Adoption Program and Services of the Kansas Children's Service League. There are also numerous small programs, such as the Harlem Adoption Movement, which seek to inform and recruit prospective parents. All of these agencies and groups have had great success in recruiting black parents. Indeed, at the National Association of Black Social Workers' meeting in Detroit in 1975, the director of Homes for Black Children, Sydney Duncan, reported that her agency had found black homes for all the babies available and had a waiting list of black families willing to adopt. Black social workers and other concerned persons argue that adoption agencies could use the above-mentioned as models for their own operations.

There are, of course, many historical precedents for dealing with the problems of black orphans. Billingsley and Giovanonni document the history of black orphanages operated by black church groups, women's clubs, individual philanthropists, and fraternal organizations. A number of these institutions are still functioning.

Some adoption agencies made attempts to recruit black parents as early as the 1950s. The National Urban League Foster Care and Adoption Project was established in 1953. New York City organized an Adopt-a-Child Program in 1955. The purpose of Adopt-a-Child was to develop and implement methods of recruiting adoptive families for children of black, Puerto Rican, and mixed racial ancestry in New York City and the surrounding areas, and to co-ordinate interagency co-operation. Through lack of funds, the agency was terminated after five years of operation. The Minority Adoption Recruitment of Children's Homes (MARCH), already referred to in a previous chapter, was organized in San

Francisco in 1955. Although the original intent was to find minority parents for these children, a small number were adopted by whites. Minneapolis created Parents to Adopt Minority Youngsters (PAMY) in 1961. This project was perhaps the most widely known, and laid much of the foundation for transracial adoption, since many of the children were adopted by white parents. Also, the United States Bureau of Indian Affairs, in conjunction with the Child Welfare League of America, sponsored an Indian Adoption Project in 1958, some of whose findings have been reviewed elsewhere in this work.[13] While all of these special efforts or campaigns met with some success, they did not make a major impact on reducing the tens of thousands of black and other minority children in need of permanent homes. These early efforts, although well intentioned, were too little and too late.

In addition to these special programs, individual agencies, slowly recognizing the need to alter their racial policies, simultaneously recruited social workers and administrators to their staffs and named blacks, usually well-known personalities, to their boards of directors. In some cities the news media provided free space to advertise for black adoptive parents. Radio, television, and the press ran pictures of orphaned black children who were available for adoption. Some of the parents in this study said they originally became interested in adopting a black child because they saw a picture of a particular child in the media in the "Sunday's child" campaign. Quite often they do not adopt that specific child but another available one. Of course, this practice of advertising children has come under sharp attack by those critics who compare it to merchandising human beings. Others contend that the ads oftentimes portray pitiful-looking children who evoke nothing more than sympathy in the applicants, and arouse within them a "rescue fantasy."

Some agencies have made alliances with black church groups, social clubs, and fraternal organizations in an effort to facilitate black adoptions. Agencies and adoptive parents' groups have also set up speakers' bureaus for the same purpose. They have printed and distributed pamphlets designed to answer the interested person's questions regarding eligibility to adopt. Such questions as "Do you have to own your home?" or "Can the wife work if you adopt?" are answered in concise language, with the intention of destroying some of the outmoded ideas regarding eligibility. These have been widely distributed in black communities in some of the larger cities; for example, the Atlanta Chapter of the National Association for the Advancement of Colored People organized a project designed to increase the number of black adoptive parents. They held conferences, conducted an attitudinal survey to determine how blacks felt about adopting, and printed and distributed literature on adoption, including the names, addresses, and phone numbers of adoption agencies in the metropolitan area. Most impressive was a bibliography of references on adoption, which could be obtained from the public library.

Similar practices have occurred in other cities, and the impetus has not always come from agencies, as indicated in the Atlanta example, but from community groups. One of the most impressive organizations that has worked extensively with black adoptions is the Black Child Development Institute (BCDI), located in Washington, D.C. The BCDI has conducted regional black adoption conferences that have facilitated the formation of local groups, distributed literature on black adoption, and formulated social policy in this area. Before the end of the Vietnam war they sent a task force to that war-ravaged country to investigate the plight of orphans fathered by black servicemen. Their firmly maintained position is that black children should be placed in black homes.

The "politics of child welfare" are clearly indicated in the adoption of black children by white parents. The dynamics between the white applicants on the one hand, and the adoption agencies and their personnel on the other, deserve some discussion, since they often involve sophisticated maneuvering and manipulation. Such an analysis is also illustrative of the private images and personal assessments the white parents who adopted have of those agencies that provided them with their black children.

Some parents in this study said they went to several agencies before they were permitted to adopt a black child. They were turned down because they did not qualify, but eventually found an agency whose eligibility standards encompassed them. It is within this context that many parents active in the transracial adoptive movement are quite sophisticated about agency rules and regulations. On both formal and informal levels, they are usually very familiar with the ways in which each agency in their area operates. Thus they can assuredly tell anyone who inquires that "X agency's director does not allow transracial placements; Y agency has a policy of permitting a token number; but Z agency is a breeze. We recommend that you apply to Z." Oftentimes they are equally familiar with individual workers, with familiarity with their temperament, the kinds of questions they are likely to ask, and how one should answer them. In some cases, workers are active members of the Open Door Societies (ODS) and Council on Adoptable Children (COAC) groups. In at least one case, an ODS was founded by a black social worker. However, as a rule adoption workers maintain a distance from these groups but recommend that adoptive parents join them. Some agencies seem to expect COAC or ODS to do much of the postadoptive counseling that should be the task of the agency.

Just as some agencies acquire the reputation for being inclined to place black children in white homes and others not, some workers earn the reputation for being friendly or very hostile toward this type of placement. In almost every city the writer visited, there was at least one worker who was regarded by the parents as "awful," as "one to stay away from if you want a black child," and, in a few cases, as "black racists who follow the philosophy of the black social workers' statement." If possible, these workers are avoided by parents seeking to adopt. What this implies is that these groups have fostered a close cohesiveness in which they share their experiences regarding individual agency performance, and they also conduct more formal investigations of the agency's policies. For example, when an agency in the Midwest decided to put a moratorium on further placements because they felt they had not been careful enough in their planning and organizational policy, an angry group of parents went to the agency for a confrontation with its staff, demanding to know why they had chosen to halt the practice. They attempted to intervene in an effort to reverse the policy and lift the moratorium. When they were unsuccessful in influencing the agency, they began to perceive it as one that was hostile toward its aims.

Parents are equally likely to evaluate the agency's performance toward them as individual applicants. The couples in this study had equally mixed reactions to their experiences with their agency. Roughly half commended their worker for the way she or he handled the home study, offered beneficial advice and suggestions, and made their preplacement period as easy as possible. The others expressed dissatisfaction, ranging from mild to harsh. They disapproved of such things as agency bureaucracy, incompetent workers, invasion of privacy, and excessive fees. Many complaints focused on the haste with which the agency handled transracial placements. Parents complained that the private and public agencies, especially the former, spent far less time conducting a thorough home study for a transracial adoption than with the adoption of a white child. For example, a few couples said they received a child a month to six weeks after they initially applied, even though they had never previously adopted from that agency. On this point, one father remarked, "They definitely don't study you enough." Another said, "We thought it was going to be a long, drawn-out process, but it took us a little less than two months from start to finish to get Edie." Social workers are accused of being naïve, too trusting of the parents, and unwilling to invest the necessary time to understand and analyze the motives of the white applicants. One mother likened it to "the blind leading the blind," since the workers often were as naïve and inexperienced in matters of race as the parents. This probably accounts, in part, for why so many people were allowed to adopt these children, who, by their peer evaluation, should not have been. They very probably would not have been allowed to adopt a white child, had one been available, since stricter imposed criteria are used for such placements.

A good example is the case of the Robinsons, a couple in their early thirties, who have two biological daughters and a two-year-old black son. Jim Robinson, a college professor in the Midwest, and his wife, Mary, a housewife, adopted Freddie after they had a second daughter. They decided not to risk having a third child, because it may not be the son they wanted to round off their family, and felt it would be "socially useful" to adopt because of the population explosion.

Mary grew up in a small upper-midwestern town in a middle-class family, and her contacts with blacks were limited to the four in her high school. In college, her friends were from small-town middle-class backgrounds like her own, and did not include blacks or any other minorities. Jim comes from an upper-class family in the Northwest. His father is a wealthy businessman. "There were blacks in our town but I didn't know them," Jim commented. "This might sound racist and I don't mean for it to, but my only black friend was my nanny. She was a great woman and was with our family for as long as I can remember. It wasn't that I disliked or liked blacks. In my world they just didn't exist."

They moved to an all-white suburb, Mary said, "because of its quality schools and pleasant people. It never crossed our minds to live anyplace else." When informed by three adoption agencies that no white infants were available, they considered adopting a child of mixed parentage. The Open Door Society referred them to a "friendly" agency in which they could be assured of a speedy placement. They received a four-month-old black boy within nine weeks.

Today, their lifestyle remains unchanged. Freddie, who is two, is enrolled in an all-white play group, and he has not been exposed to any blacks. "Why should we punish ourselves and our daughters by moving to the city, where the schools are bad, the housing is deteriorated, and the crime is awful?" asks Mary. "Maybe Freddie should be exposed to black people, but I don't see this as a problem now or in the future," Jim remarked. In the meantime, Freddie's complexion has darkened considerably since infancy. They emphasize to anyone who asks that he is biracial (his biological mother is white), and according to Mary, "his father was a mixture of black and Indian." Although she admitted that the agency said that Freddie's biological father was black with perhaps a strain of Indian blood in his ancestry, when the writer discussed this placement with the worker who made it, she said, "At the time we placed Freddie, they seemed like such a loving nice couple who had so much to offer a child. It never occurred to me that it was important to find out more about their inner feelings on race, and how their parents and friends would react. I accept it now as something that cannot be undone. They have sheltered him too much. . . . I've learned my lesson too. I just wouldn't place another child with this kind of family because I have learned that love is not enough."

It is widely believed by parents and critical social workers that there are different sets of criteria used by agencies to evaluate white parents who want to adopt transracially and those who want to adopt white children. The feeling is that lower standards are accepted for the transracial placements. A parent complained that agencies will allow any whites to "go slumming around for black kids when they wouldn't dare let them have one of their 'blue-ribbon' babies."

Many workers, however, feel that love is a sufficient criterion for one to be a good adoptive parent, and other considerations should be secondary or unimportant. An adoption supervisor in a private agency on the East Coast expressed a familiar sentiment adhered to by some of her peers: "We feel that the most important characteristic our young white parents who want to adopt black children should have is the ability to *love* a child different than themselves. A lot of people criticize us for our position, but our reply has been that if you can conquer love, you've achieved a lot, because love isn't so easy. Everyone can't handle that." This agency had the reputation among parents for making hasty placements and for not "hassling" the applicants.

There are, however, a range of practices used by adoption agencies. All agencies have not been so negligent in their handling of black children. Indeed, many have acquired reputations for being tough and challenging in making transracial placements. Although they make them (some deliberately make very few), they do so only after the greatest caution has been exercised. They deliberately "screen out" instead of "screen in." Their primary concerns are motivation for wanting to adopt a child so dissimilar to oneself; the ability to accept the child for his or her *differences*; the degree to which the applicants are able to cope with the objections of family, friends, and neighbors; how well they can handle the curiosity and hostility of strangers; the possible degree to which this unusual request is related to "acting out" and rebelling against their own parents and others; whether there is some degree of masochism involved; whether they are anxious to draw attention to themselves and perceive this to be a proper medium to do so; whether they are trying to assuage their guilt over white racism; whether they are trying to "uplift" the black community by adopting one of its children; the flexibility of their lifestyles; whether they are willing to make changes in their residence, school, church, etc., in order to properly expose the child (and themselves) to a black cultural setting; whether they have close black friends, and whether they are willing to identify with blacks generally so as to avoid the social and psychological isolation of this child from other blacks. These are some of the most frequently cited questions for which these social workers want in-depth and thoughtful responses.

One worker said she always asked the applicants, in accordance with their feelings on race, if either would be willing to marry a black. Such a question, she felt, penetrates the core of their innermost feelings on this subject. An adoptive mother said that many of her friends, while having adopted a black child, say they would never consider marrying a black man. "How can you even think of adopting a black child, a black son who will eventually grow up to be a black *man?*" she asked. Of course, this has strong implications for how the parents will be able to handle these children as adolescents and young adults. It certainly exposes some of their potential weaknesses in rearing these children to have healthy self-concepts.

A black woman who heads an adoption agency said she immediately eliminates all applicants who say they want to do something "useful." She argues that children should not be used this way. She said, "I want to know when and how they arrived at the point where they feel they want to adopt a black kid. If they tell me that they didn't know any blacks before they came into the agency, or that they just realized how hard it is for blacks to make it and decided to adopt one of them, I ask them why they didn't take a stand in some other way. I ask them if they ever stood up against injustice, or if they spoke out when they saw someone being discriminated against. If they say 'No,' then I ask how it is that they expect to all of a sudden take on this awesome responsibility." Many parents are unable to answer these questions to the satisfaction of the workers, because this agency makes few transracial placements.

While some workers are inclined to admire the independence of adoptive parents and are not bothered by the social distance they maintain from their own parents, others want to know if they are adopting because they are rebelling against their parents' ideals and values. These workers refuse to consider placing a child with a couple who do not intend to inform their parents of their intent to adopt a black child. "How can they ignore what their parents think about such an important matter when these are going to be that child's grandparents?" a worker asked. "Instead of ignoring what they are likely to think about it, they should be trying to get acceptance as early as possible." In one agency, grandparents are asked if they would be willing to rear the child in the event something happens to the parents. According to a worker, "Some aren't willing to do so. We always want to know who will be the backup person. Some list the sister or brother, and some don't list anyone. They are the ones we study longer, as with any adoption."

Adoption workers are also concerned about the emotional impact a transracial placement will have upon the biological children in the home. A social worker described it as a "heavy burden" on the other children, while another said it was "unfair" for them to be forced into this role. She said, "We assume the child will say, 'I love my brother,' but when he realizes that his brother is black, will he love him then? Will he resent the heckling and insults he gets from other children, and will he take it out on his black brother or sister?" This remains, for many adoption workers, an unanswered question. Most workers, however, seem to feel that there won't be any long-range racial problems between siblings.

It is difficult to assess the overall success of transracial adoptions. The workers know little about their outcomes, since no official follow-up is conducted beyond court termination. (The findings of a longitudinal study by Grow and Shapiro have already been discussed and will not be analyzed here.[14]) Also, the agency is unavailable to provide any further postadoptive services the family might need. Although the agency has no legal right to involve itself with the family once the adoption has become final, it does have a moral obligation to follow it up and, if possible, it should maintain some kind of informal contact with the family. One has to recognize that these are atypical adoptions that require atypical methods for handling them.

Some workers wondered how well the transracial (and other) placements they made were going. A few were suspicious about possible problems with particular families. One worker recalled a highly unusual experience she had with an adoption that failed. She placed a black infant girl, whom we shall call Abby, with an upper-class childless couple. They could not have children of their own. About three years after Abby had been in the home, the worker received a call from the parents asking her to come to get Abby, since they had changed their minds and no longer wanted to keep her. When the worker drove to their home to pick her up, they sent her to a nursery school. Upon arriving there, she inquired about Abby, but was told that there was no such pupil by that name registered. She then told them the child's parents' names, whereupon the director of the nursery conceded that she did have such a child registered, but they never called her by her given name. They called her "Pick," an abbreviation for "Pickaninny." The worker remembered that this little frightened, rejected girl was glad to be rescued by her, a virtual stranger. Hopefully, the overwhelming majority of the adoptions have been more successful than Abby's was.

In order to provide the reader with additional insights into the way adoption workers' personal values and attitudes, combined with the organization's policies and practices, influence the adoptive process, excerpts from an interview with the director of adoptions in a public agency will follow. She has had extensive experience in adoptions and is one of the few blacks in such a post in a large city. The primary purpose for including these excerpts is to illustrate how *one* worker in a single agency functions. However, this case study does present some of the somewhat typical attitudes and responses expressed by other workers interviewed in this study.

INTERVIEWER: Do you feel that black children should be placed in white homes?

RESPONDENT: I don't feel that we should go out and recruit white homes until we've done some recruitment of black homes. Whites tend to be more knowledgeable about agency services. If their supply of white babies has dried off and they want black kids, that shouldn't be the only criterion for them being allowed to adopt a black child.

INTERVIEWER: Do you encourage whites to adopt black kids when they come here?

RESPONDENT: We don't feel we should convince them. Adoption for us is a very personal, individual thing. What the parents need and value is important, and it is not a question of what we need and value. We don't want to be moving these kids out of the agency and then having to bring them back in. Placements work out better when they decide on their own that this is what they want to do.

The bulk of the transracial placements I've seen involve people who are always on the move. I can't evaluate them because they move around a lot. Many families want to congregate and be together. They display a strong effort to organize. You don't see this in traditional adoptions because they are not searching for identity and togetherness. This has always bothered me about the transracial adoptive families. Any adoption has enough means to establish one's family identity. Racial differences shouldn't be brought out to increase the problems parents have to cope with.

I don't think that white parents, regardless of the love they give the black child, can answer the question the child will raise with his parents: "Why did you adopt me?"

The parents are going to be constantly faced with the choice of dealing with what the child is like, what he wants to be like, and what he isn't.

When a family has to rely on outsiders for answers to these questions, they lose control over their family, and the family becomes disorganized. You can't pick people for a child to emulate. Some white parents name these kids after famous blacks such as Martin Luther King. When blacks named their kids after these people we weren't that concerned because you could say we haven't had names that long. But when a white names his kid Malcolm or Martin Luther when later on the child might want to be called Michael or Benjamin, I always feel that the group they're looking for the child to be a part of is not the one the child necessarily wants to be a part of. This means they're throwing in another barrier for the child to have to face.

INTERVIEWER: Do you feel that a black child can gain his black identity in a white home?

RESPONDENT: No, I don't feel he can. Often the white family starts off wrong by whom they invite to their home. They shouldn't have to point out to the child who the blacks are who attend their home. But they seem too anxious to get their kids to identify with the few blacks they have around.

Another problem is that they don't know how to teach the kid to identify with blacks. Why do you tell a child that he's black? Do you tell him that you adopted him because he is black and poor? Why not tell him that you adopted him because you love him? These families can't remove the aura of negativism that surrounds them. The child is the reverse of something that they don't like to think about. Something that is not wanted. In a lecture I gave I told a group of these parents that if they are interested in black kids they will lobby for the legislation of subsidized adoptions; they will go into the black community and inform our people about the agencies and their work; and I told them that if we fail after this has been done, then we'll look at your white homes.

INTERVIEWER: What else should agencies do to solve the problem?

RESPONDENT: Agencies should hire black social workers if they're afraid to go out into the black community to find homes.

One of the myths I'd like to speak to is that some people say that the racially mixed child is hard to place. This is not true. It depends on the kind of recruitment program the agency conducts. If the agency perceives this to be a hard-to-place child, then it is hard to place the child. The agency shouldn't wait on the people to come in and look for a child. It should go to them. The community is not always aware of services the agency can provide. Part of our success in finding black homes is that we've tried to get to the grass roots in adoptions.

INTERVIEWER: What are some characteristics of white parents who adopt black children?

RESPONDENT: First, they are highly intellectual [said with great emphasis]. Second, a large percentage have had biological kids, usually two or more. Third, the woman usually stays home; some are smothering the kids with too much attention. More should get out and work or volunteer. Fourth, they are people who have gravitated to a very cosmopolitan or "now" way of living; they are modern thinkers. The "banner carrying" ones are very submerged. You don't see too many of them. One of the questions I ask them is, "Who are your friends?" I usually find that the blacks they know aren't on their socio-economic level. They are either higher, or they'll bring in a few blacks who are on a lower level than they are. Their peers aren't their equals. They are people they're using for identity purposes. When questioned about their black friends they will say, "I live in an inte- grated neighborhood, but I don't know the people well." You don't get the feeling that they have an everyday peer relationship with blacks. It is improvised out of necessity. You get the feeling that they think the agency is going to expect them to have black friends, so they cultivate short friendships at a distance, that don't go back to, nor last more than two years at most. Fifth, their families aren't with them in this venture. If one parent says, "I'm not for your adopting this kid," they must be willing to take the risk. I have never observed a family when all grandparents are 100 per cent supportive of the adoption. One grand- mother stopped visiting and refused to go back to the home anymore. I remember a case where a child was returned in three days. The grandmother looked at it and immediately rejected the child. Those were three tormenting days, so they returned the child. Sixth, they are involved in social is- sues. Some tutor in the ghetto; others have home visiting or exchange programs with blacks. Most I have noticed have never been involved with blacks before. . . . Finally, they want children who are going to be high achievers. They want the "cream of the crop," even though they say the child's background is not important. We once placed an in- fant girl with a white family, and there were many un- knowns in the child's background. She started out making very slow progress, but later it increased normally. She was placed in a home of high achievers. At first they said that her low achievement didn't bother them. They later began to press us about her behavior, her language development, and her socialization. They were exposing her to a higher level than she'd been exposed to in the foster home, and they expected too much of her. One time one of the workers came back to the office and told me that they had seen the child dressed in gloves and a hat in July. I became very con- cerned because these gloves were not related to the child's warmth. At about the same time she began to refuse to go near the sand pile to play. All kids need to be able to feel free to play in sand. At age three she had begun to change because they were trying to remold her into something they wanted. This was a well-educated couple with one biological child. They had traveled internationally; they were a very cosmopolitan family, highly verbal, and had been given well-rounded exposure. The first strange thing about them is that they moved as soon as we placed the child. We began to wonder about them then. One of their parents didn't visit for three or four months, whereas they had previously been very close. This was one of those unfortunate placements. . . .

One of the things that bothers me is the heavy burden on the biological kids in the family. No one examines this. The parents try to buffer these things for the other children, but do the children really want to do it? No one ever asks them. The young child will have a heavy load to carry when he gets old enough to realize that his brother is black. Kids get into fights with other kids about this. Is this something you want to subject your children to?

I want to know from those who apply to adopt what they know about black culture. That is where you pick up your greatest leads about their sincerity. They've read everything on blacks, more books than we have, but it shows in their actual life experiences that they don't have sincerity about it because they don't socialize with blacks.

I am interested in what happens to the child in a white home at puberty. What will be his relationship to his parents? I had a worker tell me that she would rather see a child be able to go to the Smithsonian and art galleries and know about caviar and filet mignon than to play in the park and eat neckbones. My response was that I ate a lot of neckbones and they didn't do me any harm.

Whites don't know what they should about black culture. The hair and skin care are very important. It is important for the worker to orient the white parents to these things. I had a client whose kid's skin kept cracking. She thought the child had a disease, but the kid was just ashy. One client didn't know how to braid the hair, so she kept cutting it from the time the baby was three months old. I told the worker who reported this to go back and find out why. She found that the child's hair got tangled and the mother didn't know what to do with it, so she cut it. She kept shampooing that child's hair so it would dry quickly. These are some of the reasons why I think follow-ups on transracial adoptions should be pushed.

INTERVIEWER: What do you think will happen to these kids in twenty years?

RESPONDENT: Some will be confused. With what's going on in the society today, the kids will feel that something is wrong. I talked to about twenty-five couples, and none convinced me that they've had positive reasons for adopting. As whites drain off black kids, they leave fewer for blacks to adopt. They also want the cream of the crop. They are very concerned about the health of the child. Recently some have been scared about sickle cell anemia. In spite of their saying that they aren't concerned about the background of the child, they are. They want the agency's reassurance. They feel that the agency has protection for them.

There are larger problems of social structure that must be dealt with if the crisis in black child care is to be resolved. Adoption agencies and institutions in large urban areas have increasingly assumed responsibility for the lives of black children as the once-strong extended family has become weakened. Informal adoption, once a widespread, accepted tradition even in the cities, is no longer highly adaptable to central cities such as Chicago, New York, Detroit, and Los Angeles. Urban housing patterns, geographical mobility, and economic deprivation have contributed to the present decline in the role of the extended family in childrearing as well as the impact it has had upon the pattern of informal adoption. Informal adoption does not appear to be designed for the large urban center because family contacts are oftentimes distant, and neighbors are not as likely to express great concern for the welfare of someone else's child. Moreover, the extended family has been greatly altered as young parents no longer find themselves living in the midst of their parents, grandparents, aunts, uncles, cousins, and friendly neighbors, who could always be depended upon to offer assistance when needed. The end result is that there are an estimated 120,000 children available for adoption. A majority are black, Puerto Rican, and American Indian.[15]

The Child Welfare League of America (CWLA) states that two thirds of children born out of wedlock are not adopted and must spend their youth in foster care, in institutions, or being reared in one-parent homes. They also note that some 266,000 children are presently in foster family care. The cost per child is over $60,000 during their childhood. The CWLA feels that one third could be placed in adoptive homes if there were enough child welfare workers to find homes and help free them legally. These statistics provide indisputable evidence that it is more expensive to maintain children in foster care and institutions than to find adoptive families for them. It is also more psychologically damaging for the children to remain in this precarious situation, which provides little stability in their lives. In addition to serving the best possible interests of the child, it would also save taxpayers hundreds of millions of dollars annually if these children were adopted. Therefore, the most viable alternative is for agencies to recruit *legally* adoptive parents for these children, making use of adoption subsidies wherever available and whenever necessary.

Today there is a crisis in child welfare, especially among minority youth. Although changes are being made gradually, agencies are still placing too few children in permanent homes. The racism and middle-class bias that have long dominated the practices of agencies cause them not to perceive black children to have the same welfare needs as do white children. Agencies have been content to leave these black children in temporary care, virtually forgetting them as they proceeded toward adolescence and adulthood. The longer they stayed in this temporary position, the more fixed did their status as "hard to place" and "unadoptable" become. The fact that agencies did not make any great efforts, until recently, to enable foster parents to adopt children in their care allowed thousands of black children to grow up in this temporary and unstable situation. As social workers shuffled papers, kept neat files on the children, and observed the agency's bureaucratic routine, the needs of the real children—the human beings—were put in the background and sometimes forgotten. They became faceless, invisible little creatures insofar as agencies were concerned, and their futures were viewed as precariously as their fateful growing-up years. It is no small wonder that the large cities of this nation have produced thousands of antisocial blacks, especially young males, whose lives have been destined to poverty, misery, crime, and other activities that have caused more young black men to enter prison annually than to enter college. Thousands of these persons were brought up in institutions or have been shuffled from one foster home to another. The fact is that black children have historically been one of the most powerless groups of Americans. And the tradition of America's child welfare institutions has been that of ignoring, discriminating, and giving second-class services to these children.

Undoubtedly the present crisis in child welfare could have been averted to some extent if adoption agencies had encouraged foster parents to adopt the children to whom they had become attached and desired to make their own. Traditionally agencies have had separate criteria for *foster* and *adoptive* parents. Foster parents, as second-class citizens, were usually not expected to have the same material resources, and were not required to meet the other rigid eligibility standards as were adoptive parents.

There is a note of condescension in the attitude agencies have taken toward foster or temporary parents. While they have been confident in the foster parents' ability to nurture infants and to socialize older children, they have not considered them to be "good" enough to become the permanent parents. There is a bit of irony in this situation, because thousands of children have remained in the same foster home for most of their lives. Some have entered a home in infancy and stayed with the same family until they reached adulthood. One wonders why an adoption agency, in such a case, would not encourage that the family be allowed to adopt the child. There are numerous examples of agencies deliberately moving the child to another foster home when the parents and child became too attached to each other. Whose welfare is the agency concerned about? Perhaps more its own than that of the child or foster parents who would like to be able to make him or her a part of their legal family unit.

Because the foster child and foster parents know that the all-powerful agencies and courts can exercise their power to remove the child at will creates a hazardous psychological condition that both must endure. Paradoxically, the traditional policy of adoption agencies has been that of discouraging foster parents from becoming attached to the child. While they expected foster parents to be "good parents," they simultaneously discouraged them from becoming too attached to the child. One could infer that agencies expected the parents to provide for the children's physical needs, while remaining emotionally aloof. When foster parents became emotionally attached to the children in their care, agencies frequently removed them. This grim picture is slowly changing today, since many agencies are encouraging foster parents to adopt and to use the subsidies available.

One encouraging development is that a large number of states now have adoption subsidies. Although some of these are limited to covering medical expenses, others grant a monthly allowance to a family who, although having adopted a child, would find it difficult to adequately provide for his or her economic needs. These subsidies have greatly benefited poor parents of all races who, without the subsidy, may not have been able to adopt the child. Social workers tell many success stories associated with subsidized adoptions. Some foster parents have been allowed to adopt the child in their care, while other families have accepted the subsidy until their economic situation improved. A social worker told me about a family who adopted two foster children and were enabled, through the subsidy, to get a much-needed larger apartment. In another case, a medical subsidy allowed the parents to adopt a child who needed costly surgery. Clearly this is the progressive type of legislation needed. Many experts feel that subsidized adoption, if adequately funded and carefully administered, would provide the most important breakthrough in this field of all modern innovations.

Other reforms are also needed to solve this crisis in child welfare. The federal government should offer subsidies to parents who wish to adopt and who meet eligibility standards. An alternative to the adoption subsidy is a tax rebate to adoptive parents whose low-income level would allow them to qualify.

Legal reforms are also desperately needed. The courts have been grossly derelict in their responsibility to the children. The "divine rights" of birth parents precluded any significant changes in these children's lives. So long as they had not been surrendered for legal adoption by their birth parents, regardless of the fact that many parents had long since surrendered them psychologically and no longer provided for their physical maintenance, the child could not be provided a permanent home in an adoptive family. Legislative bodies could be more conscientious about the welfare of these children by revising the termination of parental rights laws, making it easier for the courts to free more children sooner for adoption.

White parents who adopted black children in the past, did so for the most part in good faith, in that they desired to have a family. Contrary to speculation by some critics, there is no evidence to support the theory that most whites adopted to fulfill some kind of perverse fantasy. That adoption agencies should not have placed children with some of these families has already been demonstrated. Since these placements were made, the trend has shifted, and there is general agreement among agencies, adoptive parents, and black social workers that black children should, if at all possible, be placed in black homes. In 1973 the Child Welfare League of America revised its standards for adoption by stating:

> It is preferable to place children in families of their own racial background. In today's social climate, children placed in adoptive families with similar racial characteristics can become more easily integrated into the average family group and community. If adoptive parents of the child's own race are not available in the agency, use of local, regional and national adoptive exchanges should be used.[16]

However, they are aware that this might not always be a possibility, and they make allowances for these exceptional cases:

> In any adoption plan, however, the best interest of the child should be paramount. Children should not have adoption denied or significantly delayed when adoptive parents of other races are available. In most communities there are families who have the capacity to adopt a child whose racial background is different from their own. Consideration of these families as adoptive parents should include awareness that appropriate resources should be reasonably available to these families after placement to help them and the child with issues of cultural heritage and identity.[17]

A majority of white parents in this study adhere to the CWLA's standards and contend that they will never consider adopting another black child, in view of the opposition against this practice. Many are convinced that these children will be better off in black families. Therefore, the activities of such groups as the Open Door Society and the Council on Adoptable Children have redirected their efforts away from transracial adoption to other areas, including encouraging blacks to adopt, lobbying for adoption subsidies, parental surrender, and other legislative reforms; the adoption of older white children, and children with medical or emotional handicaps; and campaigns for agency reforms. Their scope of involvement has broadened considerably, and while their activities originally focused heavily on transracial placements, now such placements play a minor role.

In view of the trend toward agencies seeking out black families for orphaned children, it seems reasonable to urge that this practice be continued and vigorously expanded. Every effort should be made to eliminate the restrictive practices of public and private agencies in their dealings with black applicants. In accordance with my belief that *every* child in this society has the right to a permanent home, I feel that the concept of group homes* with a small number of children should be encouraged. If agencies put forth their best efforts to locate adoptive homes as early as possible, then the institutionalization of foster care will slowly disappear. There will of course continue to be situations in which children must be placed in temporary and long-term foster care—in those cases when agencies and the courts have not been successful in terminating parental rights, when no adoptive homes can be located, etc. With the available human and financial resources at the disposal of agencies and the courts, more alternatives should be created to replace the institutions in which too many children remain for too long a period of time. Many institutions have become nothing more than dumping grounds for children when agencies didn't know what else to do with them. No one

---

* Group homes are those in which several children are placed in foster care with the same family. This might include sibling groups or nonrelated children. This is viewed by many agencies as a viable alternative to the larger, impersonal institutions.

can dispute the fact that a great number of these institutions were started by benevolent individuals and groups who were committed to providing homes to orphaned children. Today, however, most have outlived their usefulness and should be discontinued. Children of all ages need more individualized care that is, by definition, impossible to get in an institutional setting.

There will also, of course, continue to be very special cases in which transracial adoptions can and should be made. I agree with the CWLA position, which states that no child should be denied a permanent home when parents of another race are available. If agencies, after extensive search, have not been able to locate a black family for a child, then transracial adoption might be considered. It would become but one alternative, instead of the primary mode for disposing of black children. Even in the most desperate cases, however, agencies must take special precautions in screening white adoptive parents. The child should not be used by the adoptive couple to prove a point, whether it is to prove their independence from their own families, to prove their liberalism, to expiate racial guilt, or whatever. Also, a black or mixed-race child should not be resorted to as a last choice, after the white applicants find that there are no white children available. The child should not be used as a substitute, or regarded as second-best. The parents should consider such a child their first choice, so much that they would want to adopt across racial boundaries even if there were an abundance of white children available. In view of the naïveté of many of the parents in this study, I strongly advise that whites not be allowed to adopt black children if they have not already had interracial experiences. All too often such contacts do not begin until after the adoption, when the parents frantically find themselves seeking ways to form friendships with blacks, and do not quite know how to go about doing it. The adoption should be an extension of, instead of the beginning of, their other interracial involvements.

These parents must also live in integrated neighborhoods and be willing to send their black child to an integrated school, preferably where there are a large number of blacks. This will prevent the child from being the lone black, where special attention is constantly drawn to him or her. The parents should also become

involved in institutions and organizations (churches, neighborhood associations, etc.) in which there are other black
members. This does not mean that a parent who, under ordinary
circumstances, is not a "joiner" should suddenly be thrust into
groups solely because there are black members involved. Obviously, many people are not joiners and will find alternative ways
to become involved with blacks on a sustained level. But they
must make every effort and sacrifice to do what is in the best interests of the child.

As stated earlier, transracial adoption suffered a downward trend
from 1972 to 1975. The 1976 Opportunity Survey indicates that
transracial adoptions are now on the increase. But agencies are not
likely to again risk raising the wrath of antagonistic blacks. Being
highly susceptible to public pressure, they will probably continue
to take the path of least resistance by making very few and carefully
adoptive placements. In order to remain viable, they will probably
concentrate increasingly on finding black adoptive homes for this
plentiful supply of children, and on international adoptions, as well
as the placement of older children and the handicapped. However,
there are many skeptics who feel that only an insignificant number
of agencies will seriously assume the task of finding homes for black
children. They are quick to buttress their argument with examples
of those agencies that expanded their services into areas unrelated
to adoption instead of embarking on a serious program of black
adoptions.

One final observation on the politics of child welfare. Children
do not vote. They do not pay taxes or have taxes withheld. They
do not manage organizations. And by and large they do not exercise the kind of power in their own behalf that is so highly respected in American society. Public policy advocates on their behalf have not been strong, well organized, consistent, or selfless in
their advocacy. Consequently, as Kenneth Clark, the eminent psychologist, has observed, children are among our most powerless
citizens. And in this society black children constitute a disproportionately large number of the most powerless and dispossessed.
Therefore, their needs are often not addressed adequately. Social
change in this regard requires change in the power and influence
relationships and values in the larger society. Even much of the

highly vaunted permissiveness of recent years may have its origins not so much in a genuine child-centeredness in the society but more in self-centered parents and others reluctant to exert themselves in the best interests and needs of children.

13

THE FUTURE

Some idealistic transracial adoption advocates feel that transracial adoption has the potential for transforming a racially divided American society into a racially integrated utopia. The foes perceive this phenomenon as one that is designed to usurp the powers of blacks to care for children of their race. Actually, transracial adoption has neither the potential for creating a utopian society, nor does it pose a threat to the stability of the black family. It is estimated that there are at least fifteen thousand black children adopted into white families in the United States and Canada today.[1] This represents a mere fraction of the total number of black children in this country, and a tiny percentage of those available for adoption. That transracial adoption is a rapidly declining phenomenon whose chances for being revived are dim, has already been demonstrated.

Therefore, the more important concern is what the future will be like for those children who have already been adopted, and secondarily, what the prospects are for those black youngsters who will be adopted in the future. Beyond the controversy over transracial adoptions and the social policies lies the basic consideration of what is in the best interests of the child. This very important element has often been obscured, as the various forces have become embattled in a bitter confrontation and power struggle. The interests of the warring adults—adoptive parents, agencies, and black social workers—have been served to the detriment of the child's welfare.

I should state my own values and preferences. I firmly believe that every child is entitled to a *permanent* home and parents. The permanency that the home offers enables the child to develop a secure sense of self, a stable identity, and the confidence that will enhance his or her ability to function, to perform adequately, and to meet the challenging tasks in life. There is an abundance of evidence that suggests that children who grow up in institutions and foster care frequently do not develop adequately psychosocially because of lack of permanence in their lives, which often leaves lifelong scars.[2]

The sparse amount of available data on the outcome of transracially adopted children is far from conclusive. Although the data are unanimous in reporting that up to this point, the children and their parents are adjusting quite well, the pitfalls are obvious. The children are still too young and have not yet faced certain inevitable problems because of their ages. One can only anticipate hopefully that they will continue to adapt and adjust to their adoptive statuses as well in the future as they are presently. There is a great need for follow-up studies that will monitor their psychosocial development as they go through adolescence.

The outcomes of those children who have already been adopted poses many serious and challenging concerns. While few parents have had serious problems as a result of adopting a black child, they nevertheless look to the future, especially adolescence, with great hesitancy. Even the more idealistic parents acknowledge that the problems will increase as their black child begins to interact more with the outside world on his or her own. Ordinarily, the onset of these problems occurs when the child enters grade school and is exposed to racial insults from peers, deferential treatment and reverse discrimination by teachers, and hostile encounters with strangers. It is at this stage that he or she begins to understand some of the important implications of their adoption, and the time when they have to explain to other children why they are black and their parents are white. One mother said, "My black son always had me around to explain the adoption to all the curious people who questioned me about it. It was only after he went to school that I realized he was going to get these questions. So we decided that we had to teach him how to handle the situation himself. That was when it hit us that we couldn't be there for the rest of his life to protect him." Another mother described entering school as the time "when my black daughter broke out of her cocoon and began to meet the blows of life on her own." Parents with school-age children frequently cite incidents in which their children have met with discrimination, sometimes overt but more often in a subtle and insidious form. Oftentimes it is only after the child comes home to report an incident to his or her parents that they are hit with the recognition that others do not perceive their children in the same way they do. Their belief in racial brotherhood is not necessarily shared by people with whom the child comes into contact, very often not even by his or her very young playmates, whose attitudes reflect their parents' racial philosophies. Indeed, the black social workers' warning that "these children do not remain cuddly babies forever" takes on new meaning for some parents, as they observe the transition their children make from the relatively innocent, unthreatening, and lovable stage of infancy to that of older black children whose very color alone provokes racial discrimination.

The Montreal Open Door Society addressed this problem by writing,

> . . . We see among [some parents] what we believe is a dangerous idealism which refuses to see that the unbiased world which we, our friends and relatives present to our children is not the same as that which our children will meet in our society. . . . It can be very painful, if not emotionally crippling for our children to meet this racism without some preparation from us. . . . Some way must be found by each of us to tell our children that the hostility, false cordiality or injustice they meet in this racist world is not as a result of some serious fault in them but rather a fault in those expressing these sentiments. . . . The important thing is not our children's race nor the hostility it can bring to them, but how we teach them to feel towards both these factors and towards themselves.[3]

Unfortunately, there are a few parents who do not alter their perceptions nor their childrearing practices even after their child begins to encounter discrimination. They contend that the society's

hostile attitudes do not matter. One mother echoed their sentiments when she explained, "We teach our children that one day
those evil people will change to think the way we do, so just *ignore* them." One has to raise serious doubts as to whether these,
or any children can go through life simply *ignoring* the verbal insults and discrimination they encounter. At some point, the average child can be expected to exercise some kind of defensive tac-
tics in his or her behalf.

This is what the black social workers refer to as survival skills,
an attribute they feel every black child should have to cope with
racial discrimination. On the other hand, it can be a temptation
for such parents to interpret each incident their child encounters
as having racial overtones, when this is not always the case. Parents must be cautious that they maintain a balanced view and not
err too much in either direction—that of being oblivious to racial
considerations, nor overly sensitive so that they view their child's
entire existence through the prism of race. Occasionally parents
overreact to slights their children receive from other youngsters—
slights that are frequently unrelated to the fact that the child is
black. In their book titled *Black Child Care*, Comer and Poussaint caution black parents against overreacting each time their
child is bullied with racial slurs by a white child. They warn, "If
the parents' only response is to tell the child to 'knock him off his
block,' it might achieve the desired response, but fighting is not
the best solution to the problem—even if your child wins the
fights. Win or lose, nothing has happened to change the other
child's attitude about using racial slurs. . . . If he must fight physically every time an act of racism occurs in America, he could become too busy to do anything else."[4] Instead of reacting violently,
these psychiatrists instruct parents to try to use these experiences to teach their children to understand the meaning of prejudice and racism and to help the other child handle his or her feelings better. "Remember that most seven-year-old white children
are not diehard racists. They are often repeating what they have
heard—sometimes from people other than their parents. They are
usually trying to handle their feelings as best they can. Without
help in coping with their feelings, it is easier to become a diehard."[5] They feel parents should teach their children to view this
as the white child's problem of insecurity, and to confront the

white child by insisting that he or she has a problem if they have to call playmates derogatory names. This approach often has the desired effects.

Adolescence, regarded as the period when American youngsters search for their identities, is one that arouses anticipatory anxieties in most of these parents. They feel that their children are likely to experience the typical rebellion and self-discovery and, additionally, a "black identity" crisis. Some fear that, in the process, their children may reject them for no reason other than the fact that they are white. One mother said, "I don't know if I will be able to cope with my black child rejecting me when she gets to be a teen-ager. I won't know if it's because I'm white or just because I happen to be her mother, the authority figure. With my white kids, it will be more clear-cut. I'll know their rejection isn't racial." A mother who has a teen-age black foster son said their entire family went through a very difficult period when he decided to become a black nationalist. "He acted like he didn't want to be seen with me," she said. "Every time he came home from one of his black history courses, we got into deep arguments. For a time he considered me to be one of the white oppressors." Her foster son said he saw her "as just another racist because she was white. I used to call her 'honky,' and I stopped allowing her to go anywhere with me. I didn't want my friends to know that I had this white foster mother." Their relationship has since returned to normal and he's no longer hostile toward her, although he is still hostile toward other whites.

Parents wonder what form the adolescent identity crisis will take with their black children. "Will my daughter be ashamed to have me go to PTA meetings?" one mother asks. Will they refuse to allow their black friends, and boy friends, to visit them at home? Will they turn against their white siblings? One father asks, "Will my black son refuse to communicate with me, and will he reject all of my values solely because we are white and he is black?" Perhaps most difficult of all is the question a small number of parents ask, as eloquently voiced by a St. Louis mother: "Will Anna hate us for doing this to her? Will she accuse us of twisting her life into a web of confusion? Will she ever hold us responsible for creating a freak out of her because she is caught between the white world and the black world? I pray to

God that we are doing the right thing by her and that we will never have to answer to any of these charges." But what if some parents do have to answer to these charges? Will they have done so poorly with their childrearing that their children will, justifiably, accuse them of these things? If more adoptive parents seriously confronted themselves with the potential for such problems arising in their children's adolescence, then perhaps they will more carefully examine the values they are now imparting to their youngsters and the possible outcomes their childrearing practices may bring about.

Dating poses one of the most serious concerns to these parents. Some feel that it is, potentially, the most troublesome problem they may experience. Even when they do not consider it problematic, their relatives and friends often raise questions concerning dating. As one mother said, "The first thing our friends asked us when they knew we had adopted a black baby was, 'Who will escort her to the senior prom?' " This irate mother asked, "Can you imagine the gall they had. Here is a six-months-old baby, and the only thing they can think of is who is going to take her to the senior prom. Their attitude was ridiculous." These friends were sure that white boys would never consider dating her, and they did not consider it advisable to encourage her to date blacks.

Dating conjures up deep-seated fears and emotions within parents because it symbolizes the child's disengagement from parental authority, and it may also be viewed as a rite of passage in which one may have first intimate experiences. It is a period preparatory to adulthood. Parents who are ambivalent are forced to confront their deepest racial feelings when their black child begins dating. They wonder, "Will my daughter prefer dating whites or blacks?" If she prefers dating whites, does this mean they have not given her a black identity? And if she dates blacks, they will quite likely have to examine how they feel about the possibility of having a black son-in-law and black grandchildren. There are, of course, additional implications for her dating blacks. For example, will this practice have any effect on her white siblings? As one father noted, "A lot of people continually ask me if I would allow my *white* daughter to date a young black man, since they assume that this will automatically happen because we also have a black child." While some parents may be willing to accept their black child dating and eventually marrying a black, it is another matter for them to entertain the notion that their white children may also end up dating and possibly marrying across racial lines. Some parents are not willing to extend their beliefs in racial brotherhood this far. Many parents will undoubtedly wonder why they should be expected to approve of their daughter or son marrying across racial boundaries, simply because they themselves adopted a black or biracial child. This is especially true for those parents who have compartmentalized the transracial adoption, and who believe that its effects will not have an influence on the rest of their lives. Parents who deny that their children are black and who refer to them as having a human identity and socialize them to have a human identity that is devoid of color are most likely to be unwilling to accept interracial dating, or to be able to cope with their black children's adolescent upheavals. Of course, there are those parents who do not consider the above-mentioned factors to be problems. Since adopting a black child was merely an extension of their commitment to integration, it does not matter to them if their children date and marry blacks, whites, or whomever. They are quick to criticize those parents who find these concerns troubling because they do not feel they should have adopted a black child if they find it difficult to accept other blacks into their families.

White parents who adopt black youngsters must also be willing and able to identify not only with their black children but also with blacks generally. They cannot be permitted to isolate their child and view him or her as "different" from other blacks, but rather they must perceive their child to be an extension of other blacks.

To adopt a black child means that these parents have forfeited their rights to be regarded as a "white" family. They cannot try to continue to fit the role of the idealized white middle-class nuclear family who happen to have a black adopted child. Therefore they will never be able to successfully retreat into their previously protected all-white enclaves without risking psychological harm to the child, to their biological children, and to themselves. Some parents have already been confronted with social problems related to or resulting from the adoption. For example, an Open Door Society chapter in a northeastern town had a bitter conflict and split into two groups as a result of the open housing issue in their town. Some adoptive parents felt it incumbent upon themselves as parents of black children to fight for an end to housing discrimination. Other parents refused to join this campaign, since they saw no relationship between open housing and parenting a black child. They did not feel that their parenting responsibilities should become "politicized" and saw no differences between discharging their parental roles to a white child or to a black child.

It is important that white parents expose their black children to a variety of role models in all walks of life. It is necessary for these black youngsters to see black "success" models, as well as people functioning in ordinary roles. Children should be exposed to and interact with blacks—adults and children—instead of being aware of their existence vicariously, through children's story books on black heroes, eating "soul food," and on other indirect ways.

Many parents feel that if they love their adopted child and provide for his or her physical needs, then there should be no serious problems ahead. The notion that love is sufficient is indeed naïve. That most of the parents who adopt these children love them is probably indisputable. But whether they understand what their differential needs are and will be as they grow to maturity is a more important question. Are they willing to transform their white suburban middle-class lifestyles to accommodate the child's needs, which, ultimately, are their own needs? Many parents have not been willing to do so, even though they love their child and provide for all of his or her physical needs. That they have been insensitive to certain psychological and emotional needs he or she will have—needs that are related to their identity—is most important.

I fully recognize that there are many whites who are capable of rearing emotionally healthy black children. In fact, some of the parents in this study appear to be handling this sometimes difficult task quite well. Such parents, however, must have an abundance of positive characteristics that one rarely finds in a married couple. They must be idealistic about the future but also realistic about the society in which they now live. To deny that racial, ethnic, and social class polarization exists, and to deny that their child is going to be considered a "black" child, regardless of how light his or her complexion, how sharp their features, or how straight their hair, means that these parents are unable to deal with reality, as negative as they might perceive that reality to be. On the other hand, it is equally important for parents to recognize that no matter how immersed they become in the black experience, they can never become black. Keeping this in mind, they should avoid the pitfalls of trying to practice an all-black lifestyle, for it too is unrealistic in the long run, since their family includes blacks and whites and should, therefore, be part of the larger black and white society.

Parents cannot insulate their child from societal forces. Although it is a natural instinct for parents to want to protect their children from the harmful acts others would inflict upon them, the child must be exposed to those things in their environment, positively and negatively, and they must be equipped with strong individual and racial (communal) identities and coping skills that will enable them to protect themselves when necessary, and to function adequately in two worlds. White parents have a special responsibility to teach their black children that the outside world is very different from the idealism of their home environments. Somehow the child has to be taught to understand and appreciate the differences between the two. He or she certainly must be taught to function in this marginal, bicultural role.

When an examination is made of the problems faced by parents and children beyond adoption, they are very much the same, in many ways, as those faced by birth parents in their childrearing. Adoptive parents have the same expectations of their children as do birth parents. Both groups equally want their children to be successful, healthy, upwardly mobile individuals, whose behavior is a reflection of their socialization. Yet there are some problems that adoptive parents must face that do not confront birth parents. The adoptive parents must come to terms with their own feelings about illegitimacy (and, occasionally, incest), and they must be able to transmit to the child a wholesome attitude on these subjects.

Of equal importance is that parents feel comfortable about the adoption itself. They should not have frequent second guesses and ambivalence about having adopted—regardless of the child's race. It is of the utmost importance that parents be confident that their decision to adopt a black child was the correct one. At no time should they convey to the child—by word or deed—that they now question the wisdom of their actions.

In a similar manner, parents must be willing to discuss the adoption with the child, informing him or her at the earliest age possible that he or she was adopted. The child has a right to know his or her background, and parents should try to avoid the "genealogical bewilderment" the child might face by being open and honest about their roots. This information can be conveyed in a positive manner in which the child will feel secure in the fact that he or she was adopted. Parents must not feel threatened when their child, especially as he or she grows older, begins to raise more pointed questions about their biological parents, especially the often heard one, "Why did my other mama give me up?" Rather, parents can be helpful to the child by explaining in their own manner the circumstances surrounding the adoption. Adoptive parents need to be exceptionally strong, well-adjusted, independent-minded, confident individuals who are more prepared for failure in their childrearing than are birth parents. The added dimension of transracial adoption is obvious. It requires courage, commitment, independence, and sensitivity to undertake this awesome responsibility in bringing up a healthy black child. While they share the objective characteristics of the American white middle class, one parent stated, "We are the same, but we're different too."

Ultimately, the future of transracially adopted children, as with all children in the society, is inextricably linked to the future of the American people. Their growing-up years can be as problem-free or as problematic as the majority of Americans decide. The racial attitudes and behavior as well as their attitudes toward adoption itself will, more than anything else, determine these children's outcomes.

Notes

INTRODUCTION

1. Joseph Goldstein, Anna Freud, and Albert J. Solnit, *Beyond the Best Interests of the Child* (New York: The Free Press, 1973), p. 22.
2. Joyce A. Ladner, *Tomorrow's Tomorrow: The Black Woman* (Garden City, N.Y.: Doubleday & Company, 1971).

1
THE FAMILIES
A Look into Their Private Worlds

1. The data presented in this chapter are taken from interviews with the subjects in the study.

2
FAMILY DYNAMICS

1. For a discussion of pluralism in family forms, refer to Arlene S. Skolnick and Jerome H. Skolnick (eds.), *Family in Transition* (Boston: Little, Brown and Company, 1971), pp. 1–32 and Marvin B. Sussman, "Family Systems in the 1970s: Analysis Policies and Programs, *Annals of the American Academy of Political and Social Science,* 1971, Vol. 396.
2. Fleur Conkling Heyliger, " 'The Answer' (to an adopted child)," *Saturday Evening Post* (Apr. 5, 1952).
3. The following studies provide data on background characteristics of families who adopt transracially: Gerald Pepper, "Interracial

Adoptions: Family Profile, Motivation, and Coping Methods," unpublished Ph.D. thesis (University of Southern California, 1966); Gerald St. Denis, "Interracial Adoptions in Minnesota: Self-concept and Child-rearing Attitudes of Caucasian Parents Who Have Adopted Negro Children," unpublished Ph.D. thesis (University of Minnesota, 1969); Charles H. Zastrow, "Outcome of Negro Children-Caucasian Parents' Transracial Adoptions," unpublished Ph.D. thesis (University of Wisconsin, 1971); Lawrence Falk, "A Comparative Study of Transracial and Inracial Adoptions," *Child Welfare*, Vol. XLIX, No. 2 (Feb. 1970); Thomas E. Nutt and John A. Snyder, *Transracial Adoption* (Cambridge: Massachusetts Institute of Technology, 1972); Rita J. Simon, "White Parents of Non-white Children: An Analysis of Transracial Adoption," (University of Illinois, 1973) (mimeograph); and Lucille Grow and Deborah Shapiro, *Black Children–White Parents* (New York: Child Welfare League of America, 1974).

4. Nutt and Snyder, ibid.
5. Thomas E. Nutt, "Adopting the Hard-to-place: System Change in a Public Service," unpublished Ph.D. thesis (Massachusetts Institute of Technology, 1973), p. 24.
6. David C. Anderson, *Children of Special Value–Interracial Adoption in America* (New York: St. Martin's Press, 1971).
7. Colette Taube Dywasuk, *Adoption–Is It for You?* (New York: Harper & Row, 1973), p. 135.
8. Ibid., pp. 136–37.

3

The Motivation to Adopt

1. Andrew Billingsley and Jeanne Giovanonni, "Research Perspectives on Interracial Adoption," *Race Research and Reason: Social Work Perspectives*, ed. Roger Willer (New York: National Association of Social Workers, 1969).
2. Grace Gallay, "Interracial Adoptions," *Canadian Welfare*, Vol. 39, No. 6 (Nov.–Dec. 1963), pp. 248–50.
3. Lawrence L. Falk, "A Comparative Study of Transracial and Inracial Adoptions," *Child Welfare*, Vol. 49, No. 2 (Feb. 1970), pp. 82–88; Thomas E. Nutt and John A. Snyder, *Transracial Adoption* (Cambridge: Massachusetts Institute of Technology, 1973); Charles H. Zastrow, "Outcome of Negro Children-Caucasian Parents' Transracial Adoptions," unpublished Ph.D. thesis (University of Wisconsin, 1971), and Rita J. Simon, "An Assessment of Racial Awareness Preference, and Self-identity Among White and Adopted Non-white Children," *Social Problems*, Vol. 22, No. 1 (Oct. 1974).
4. Falk, ibid., pp. 82–88.

5. Nutt and Snyder, ibid., p. 82.
6. Gerald Pepper, "Interracial Adoptions: Family Profile, Motivation, and Coping Methods," unpublished Ph.D. thesis (University of Southern California, 1966).
7. Drew Priddy and Doris Kirgan, "Characteristics of White Couples Who Adopt Black-white Children," *Social Work*, Vol. 16, No. 3 (July 1971), pp. 105–7.
8. Ibid.

4

BLACK/WHITE ADOPTION IN HISTORICAL CONTEXT

1. Alfred Kadushin, *Child Welfare Services* (New York: Macmillan, 1972), p. 519.
2. Robert Hill, *Strengths of Black Families* (New York: Emerson-Hall, 1972), p. 6.
3. Andrew Billingsley and Jeanne Giovanonni, *Children of the Storm: Black Children and American Child Welfare* (New York: Harcourt Brace Jovanovich, 1972), p. 36.
4. Ibid.
5. See Bowers Swithen, "The Child's Heritage—from a Catholic Point of View," *A Study of Adoption Practice*, Vol. II, ed. M. Shapiro (New York: Child Welfare League of America, 1956); also refer to Kadushin, op. cit., p. 586.
6. Los Angeles *Times* (July 9, 1975).
7. New York *Times* (March 25, 1972).
8. Era Bell Thompson, "The Adoption Controversy: Blacks Who Grew Up in White Homes," *Ebony* (June 1974), pp. 84–94.
9. Ibid., p. 94.
10. Interview with Laura Gaskin, director, Hennepin County Department of Adoptions (Nov. 1972).
11. Billingsley and Giovanonni, op. cit., pp. 139–73.
12. Ibid.
13. Ibid.
14. "Progress Report of the Montreal, Canada, Open Door Society" (1963).
15. Drew Priddy and Doris Kirgan, "Characteristics of White Couples Who Adopt Black-white Children," *Social Work*, Vol. 16, No. 3 (July 1971), pp. 105–7.
16. Hill, op. cit.
17. W. E. B. DuBois (ed.), *Efforts for Social Betterment Among Negro Americans*, Atlantic University Publication No. 14 (Atlanta University Press, 1909), p. 10 (New York: Russell & Russell, 1969).
18. Charles S. Johnson, *Shadow of the Plantation* (Chicago: University of Chicago Press, 1934), pp. 64–65.

19. Ibid., p. 71.
20. Hortense Powdermaker, *After Freedom: A Cultural Study in the Deep South* (New York: Viking Press, 1939), p. 201.
21. Ibid., p. 203.
22. Hylan Lewis, "Agenda Paper No. V: The Family: Resources for Change," Planning Session for the White House Conference "To Fulfill These Rights" (Nov. 16–18, 1965), Washington, D.C.: Government Printing Office, p. 15.
23. Billingsley and Giovanonni, op. cit., p. 86.
24. Billingsley and Giovanonni, op. cit., pp. 45–59.
25. Hill, op. cit., p. 8.
26. Ibid.
27. "Survey of Transracial Adoption," Opportunity, a division of the Boys and Girls Society, Portland, Oreg.; although this is the only national survey of black children adopted since 1968, it must be noted that their sample is not totally representative because many agencies did not respond to the questionnaire.
28. Leslie Aldridge Westoff, "Kids with Kids," New York *Times Magazine* (Feb. 22, 1976), p. 14.
29. "Child Welfare League of America Statistics, June 1974 Compared with July–December 1973, Summary of Findings" (Oct. 1974) (mimeographed).

5

VALUES IN CONFLICT: I

Black Autonomy

1. Richard C. Fuller and Richard R. Myers, "The Conflict of Values," *The Study of Social Problems*, ed. Earl Rubington and Martin S. Weinberg (New York: Oxford University Press, 1971), pp. 87–88.
2. Earl Rubington and Martin S. Weinberg (eds.), *The Solution of Social Problems* (New York: Oxford University Press, 1973), p. 143.
3. Ibid.
4. Alphonso Pinkney, *Black Americans* (Englewood Cliffs, N.J.: Prentice-Hall, 1975), p. 193.
5. William N. Newman, *American Pluralism* (New York: Harper & Row, 1973), p. 182.
6. Stokeley Carmichael and Charles V. Hamilton, *Black Power: The Politics of Liberation in America* (New York: Random House, 1967), p. 44.
7. Michael Novak, *The Unmeltable Ethnics* (New York: Macmillan, 1972); Andrew Greeley, "Making It in America: Ethnic Groups and Social Status," *Social Policy* (Sept.–Oct. 1973); and Nathan

Glazer, *Affirmative Discrimination: Ethnic Inequality and Public Policy* (New York: Basic Books, 1975), Chap. 5.

8. Alphonso Pinkney, *Red, Black and Green: Black Nationalism in the United States* (New York: Cambridge University Press, 1976), p. 10.

9. Ibid., p. 11.

10. New York *Times* (Apr. 3, 1972).

11. "Position Statement on Transracial Adoptions," National Association of Black Social Workers (Sept. 1972).

12. Ibid.

13. New York *Times* (Apr. 8, 1972).

14. The following black publications carried feature stories on transracial adoption: *Ebony* magazine (June 1974); *Encore* magazine (Oct. and Dec. 1972 and Jan. 1973); *Muhammad Speaks* newspaper (Aug. 17, 1973); *Black World* (Nov. 1972).

15. "Position Statement on Transracial Adoptions," op. cit.

16. New York *Times* (Apr. 22, 1972).

17. Ibid.

18. "Should Whites Adopt Black Children?," *Encore* (Jan. 1973), p. 18.

19. "Position Statement on Transracial Adoptions," op. cit.

20. Op. cit.

21. "Should Whites Adopt Black Children?," *Encore* (Oct. 1972), p. 27.

22. *Encore* (Jan. 1973), op. cit., p. 19.

23. Op. cit., p. 19.

24. Robert Blauner, "Black Culture: Myth or Reality?," *Afro-American Anthropology*, eds. Norman Whitten and John Szwed (New York: The Free Press, 1970) and Robert Blauner, *Racial Oppression in America* (New York: Harper & Row, 1972). Leon Chestang, "Dilemmas of Biracial Adoption," *Social Work* (May 1972). Lee Rainwater, "The Crucible of Identity," *Daedalus* (Winter 1966). Sam Yette, *The Choice: The Issue of Black Survival* (New York: Putnam, 1970).

25. Blauner, "Black Culture: Myth or Reality?," op. cit., p. 358.

26. "Position Statement on Transracial Adoptions," op. cit.

27. Rainwater, op. cit., pp. 194–95.

28. Blauner, "Black Culture: Myth or Reality?," op. cit., p. 358.

29. *Encore* (Jan. 1973), op. cit., p. 19.

30. Chestang, op. cit., p. 103.

31. Ibid.

32. Maye H. Grant, "Perspective on Adoption: Black into White," *Black World* (Nov. 1972), p. 74.

33. "Position Statement on Transracial Adoptions," op. cit.

34. Ibid.

35. Interview with Wendell Rivers, professor of clinical psychology, University of Missouri at St. Louis (June 1972).

36. Interview with Alvin F. Poussaint, black child psychiatrist and co-author, *Black Child Care* (New York: Simon & Schuster, 1974).

37. Interview with James P. Comer, black child psychiatrist and co-author, *Black Child Care.*

38. Interview with Robert Williams, professor of psychology, Washington University, St. Louis.

39. Interview with Andrew Billingsley.

40. Interview with Louise Beasley, op. cit.

41. Interview with Cenie Williams, past president of NABSW.

42. Interview with Audrey Russell, member, NABSW Task Force on Transracial Adoption.

43. Interview with Louise Beasley, op. cit.

44. This figure is based on a survey conducted by Opportunity, a division of The Boys and Girls Society, Portland, Oreg.

45. *Encore* (Jan. 1973), op. cit., p. 18.

46. *Muhammad Speaks* (Aug. 17, 1973), p. 11.

47. Ibid.

48. Audrey Russell speech presented to NABSW Conference (Apr. 1972), p. 2.

49. *Encore* (Oct. 1972), op. cit., p. 27.

6

VALUES IN CONFLICT: II
Racial Integration

1. Thomas E. Nutt and John A. Snyder, *Transracial Adoption* (Cambridge: Massachusetts Institute of Technology, 1973), p. 29.

2. Ibid., p. 36.

3. *Encore* (Jan. 1973), p. 18.

7

RACIAL IDENTITY

1. Erik H. Erikson, "Youth: Fidelity and Diversity," ed. Erik H. Erikson, *Youth: Change and Challenge* (New York: Basic Books, 1963), p. 11.

2. Kenneth B. Clark and Mamie P. Clark, "Racial Identification and Preference in Negro Children," *Readings in Social Psychology*, ed. T. M. Newcombe and E. L. Hartley (New York: Henry Holt and Company, 1947), pp. 169–78; Erik Erikson, "A Memorandum on Identity and Negro Youth," *Journal of Social Issues*, Vol. 20 (Oct. 1964), pp. 29–42; Erik Erikson, "The Concept of Identity in Race Relations: Notes and Queries,"

Daedalus (Winter 1966); Mary Ellen Goodman, *Race Awareness in Young Children* (New York: Macmillan, 1964); and Judith Porter, *Black Child, White Child* (Cambridge, Mass.: Harvard University Press, 1971).

3. Abram Kardiner and Lionel Ovesey, *The Mark of Oppression: Explorations in the Personality of the American Negro* (New York: W. W. Norton & Company, 1951), pp. 302–3.

4. Jean Smith, "I Learned to Feel Black," repr. *The Black Power Revolt*, ed. Floyd Barbour (Boston: Porter Sargent, 1968); Joyce A. Ladner, "What 'Black Power' Means to Negroes in Mississippi," *Trans-Action* (Nov. 1967); Alvin F. Poussaint, "The Negro American: His Self-image and Integration," repr. *The Black Power Revolt*, ed. Floyd Barbour (Boston: Porter Sargent, 1968).

5. Alphonso Pinkney, *Red, Black and Green* (New York: Cambridge University Press, 1976).

6. Interview with James P. Comer (Nov. 1973).

7. Rijo Suzuki and Marilyn Horn, "Follow-up Study on Negro-white Adoptions" (Los Angeles, County Bureau of Adoptions 1965) (mimeographed).

8. Rita J. Simon, "White Parents of Nonwhite Children: An Analysis of Transracial Adoption" (University of Illinois, 1973), p. 13 (mimeographed).

9. Lawrence Falk, "A Comparative Study of Transracial and Interracial Adoptions," *Child Welfare* (Feb. 1970), p. 87.

10. David Fanshel, *Far from the Reservation: The Transracial Adoption of American Indian Children* (Metuchen, N.J.: Scarecrow Press, 1972), p. 21.

11. Ibid., p. 337.

12. "Some Experiences in Interracial Adoption by Members of the Open Door Society, Inc.," ed. Margaret Edgar (Montreal, 1963), pp. 2–3. (Mimeographed paper.)

13. These results were presented in a speech by Margaret Edgar to the Washington, D.C., Chapter of the Council on Adoptable Children (Nov. 1972). Mrs. Edgar works in adoptions and has also adopted several minority children.

14. Ibid.

15. Rita J. Simon, "An Assessment of Racial Awareness, Preference and Self-identity Among White and Adopted Nonwhite Children" (University of Illinois, 1973), p. 20 (mimeographed).

16. Ibid., p. 20.

17. Ibid., pp. 20–21.

18. Lois Raynor, *Adoptions of Nonwhite Children—The Experience of the British Adoption Project* (London: Allen and Unwin, 1970), p. 191.

19. Charles H. Zastrow, "Outcome of Negro Children-Caucasian Parents' Transracial Adoptions," unpublished Ph.D. thesis (University of Wisconsin, 1971), p. 137.
20. Fanshel, op. cit., p. 323.
21. Ibid., p. 323.
22. Lucille Grow and Deborah Shapiro, *Black Children—White Parents* (New York: Child Welfare League of America, 1974), pp. 12–15.
23. Ibid., p. 239.
24. Simon, op. cit., p. 20.
25. Clayton Hagen, "Placement of the Minority Race Child" (Minneapolis Lutheran Family and Children's Services), p. 32 (mimeographed).
26. Ibid.
27. Interview with Charles Olds, director of Pierce-Warwick Adoption Agency, Washington, D.C. (Mar. 1972).
28. Lawrence A. Scyner, "Looking Ahead to Youth and Adulthood," *Children Who Wait* (Proceedings of the Second International Conference on Transracial Adoption, Boston, 1970), p. 69.
29. Fred Hobby, "Transracial Adoption: A Political Threat or Social Movement?" (Washington University, St. Louis: Mo., 1972) (unpublished paper).
30. Interview with James P. Comer (Nov. 1973).
31. James Curtis, "Point/Counterpoint: Should Whites Adopt Black Children?," *Encore* (Dec. 1972), pp. 14–15.
32. Mae Neely, "Point/Counterpoint: Should Whites Adopt Black Children?," *Encore* (Oct. 1972), p. 26.
33. Interview with Kenneth B. Clark (Jan. 1974).
34. Interview with Charles Prudhomme (Apr. 1974).

8

Who They Are
Case Studies

The data presented in this chapter are taken from interviews with the subjects in the study.

9

Testimony
Blacks Who Grew Up in White Homes

1. Alfred Kadushin, *Child Welfare Services* (New York: Macmillan, 1973), p. 581.
2. Ibid., p. 570.
3. Ibid., p. 574.

4. Ibid., p. 574.
5. Ibid., p. 574.
6. Grow and Shapiro, op. cit., p. 239.

10

KINSHIP

Grandparents, Siblings, and Other Relatives

1. H. David Kirk, *Shared Fate* (New York: The Free Press, 1964),
   p. 7.
2. Ibid., p. 12.
3. Alfred Kadushin, *Child Welfare Services* (New York: Macmillan,
   1973), p. 478.
4. Kadushin, ibid., p. 480.
5. Joyce A. Ladner, *Tomorrow's Tomorrow: The Black Woman*
   (Garden City, N.Y.: Doubleday & Company, 1971), p. 238;
   and Kadushin, op. cit., p. 480.
6. Thomas E. Nutt and John A. Snyder, *Transracial Adoption* (Cambridge: Massachusetts Institute of Technology, 1973), p. 82.

11

THE SOCIAL MATRIX

Interaction with the Nonrelated

1. Rita J. Simon, "White Parents of Nonwhite Children: An Analysis of Transracial Adoption" (University of Illinois, 1973), p. 8
   (mimeographed).
2. Ibid., pp. 8–9.
3. Thomas E. Nutt and John A. Snyder, *Transracial Adoption* (Cambridge: Massachusetts Institute of Technology, 1973), p. 82.
4. *Newsweek* (Apr. 4, 1966), p. 32.

12

THE POLITICS OF CHILD WELFARE

Adoption Agencies and Social Policy

1. William Heffernan and Stewart Ain, "Big Money, Little Victims:
   Kids in City Care Denied Homes," New York *Daily News*
   (May 13, 1975), p. 3.
2. Ibid.
3. Ibid., p. 19.
4. Ibid.
5. Ibid.
6. *Standards for Foster Family Care* (New York: Child Welfare
   League of America, 1959), p. 5.

7. Alfred Kadushin, *Child Welfare Services* (New York: Macmillan, 1973), p. 29.
8. Trudy Festinger, *Why Some Choose Not to Adopt Through Agencies* (New York: Metropolitan Applied Research Center, 1972); Robert Hill, *Strengths of Black Families* (New York: Emerson-Hall, Inc., 1972).
9. Elizabeth Herzog, Cecelia Sudia, Jane Harwood, and Carol Newcomb, *Families for Black Children* (Washington, D.C.: U. S. Government Printing Office, 1971), p. 16.
10. Festinger, op. cit., p. 57.
11. Andrew Billingsley and Jeanne Giovanonni, *Children of the Storm: Black Children and American Child Welfare* (New York: Harcourt Brace Jovanovich, 1972), p. 195.
12. Audrey Russell, speech presented to the Workshops on Transracial Adoption at the Annual Conference of the National Association of Black Social Workers, Nashville, Tenn. (Apr. 1972), p. 9.
13. "Adopt-a-Child, Adopt-a-Child—A Midpoint Report" (New York: Jan. 1955–June 1956) (mimeographed); Arnold Liplo, "The Indian Adoption Project," *Child Welfare*, Vol. 40 (May 1961); Billingsley and Giovanonni, op. cit., pp. 139–73.
14. Lucille Grow and Deborah Shapiro, *Black Children—White Parents* (New York: Child Welfare League of America, 1974).
15. These estimates were made by the United States Department of Health, Education, and Welfare. See the Washington *Post* (Apr. 8, 1975), p. A14.
16. *Standards for Adoption* (rev.) (New York: Child Welfare League of America, 1973), p. 92.
17. Ibid.

13

The Future

1. Opportunity Survey of Adoption of Black Children, Portland, Oregon, 1977. It's likely that there are more than 15,000 transracially adopted children in the U.S. since the Opportunity Survey relies on voluntary participation of reporting agencies.
2. Droza Kline and Helen-Mary Forbush Overstreet, *Foster Care of Children* (New York: Columbia University Press, 1972); Martin Wolins and Irving Piliavin, *Institution or Foster Family—A Century of Debate* (New York: Child Welfare League of America, 1964); Gustav Jonsson, "Introduction to New Staff," *Children Away from Home—A Sourcebook of Residential Treatment*, ed. James K. Whittaker and Albert E. Frieschman (New York: Aldine Publishing Company, 1972).

3. Montreal Open Door Society Bulletin (Montreal, Sept. 1971).
4. James P. Comer and Alvin F. Poussaint, *Black Child Care* (New York: Simon & Schuster, 1975), p. 119.
5. Ibid.

Selected Bibliography

Adams, John E., and Kim, Hyung. "A Fresh Look at Intercountry Adoptions," *Children*, Vol. 18, No. 6, Nov.–Dec. 1971.

Anderson, David C. *Children of Special Value—Interracial Adoption in America.* New York: St. Martin's Press, 1971.

Bernard, Viola W., M.D. "Adoption," The Encyclopedia of Mental Health, Vol. 1. New York: Franklin Watts, 1963.

Billingsley, Andrew. "Black Children in White Families," *Social Work*, Vol. 13, No. 4, Oct. 1968.

Billingsley, Andrew, and Giovanonni, Jeanne. *Children of the Storm: Black Children and American Child Welfare.* New York: Harcourt Brace Jovanovich, 1972.

———. "Research Perspectives on Interracial Adoption," *Race Research and Reason: Social Work Perspectives*, ed. Roger Willer. New York: National Association of Social Workers, 1969.

Blauner, Robert. "Black Culture: Myth or Reality?," *Afro-American Anthropology*, ed. Norman Whitten and John Szwed. New York: The Free Press, 1970.

Boehm, Bernice R. "Adoption," Encyclopedia of Social Work. New York: National Association of Social Workers, 1965.

Bowers, Swithen. "The Child's Heritage—from a Catholic Point of View," *A Study of Adoption Practice*, Vol. II, ed. by M. Shapiro. New York: Child Welfare League of America, 1956.

Braithwaite, E. R. *Paid Servant.* New York: McGraw-Hill, 1968.

Branham, Ethel. "One-parent Adoptions," *Children*, Vol. 17, No. 3, May–June 1970.

Brooten, G. "Multiracial Family," New York *Times Magazine*, Sept. 26, 1971.

Brown, Claude. *Manchild in the Promised Land*. New York: Macmillan, 1965.

Buck, Pearl S. *Children for Adoption*. New York: Random House, 1964.

Carmichael, Stokeley, and Hamilton, Charles V. *Black Power: The Politics of Liberation in America*. New York: Random House, 1967.

Chambers, Donald. "Willingness to Adopt Atypical Children," *Child Welfare*, Vol. 49, No. 5, May 1970.

Chappelear, Edith, and Fried, Joyce. "Helping Adopting Couples Come to Grips with Their New Parental Roles," *Children*, Vol. 14, No. 6, Nov.–Dec. 1967.

Chema, Regina, et al. "Adoptive Placement of the Older Child," *Child Welfare*, Vol. 49, No. 8, Oct. 1970.

Chestang, Leon. "Dilemma of Biracial Adoption," *Social Work*, May 1972.

Child Care Association of Illinois, *Subsidized Adoption—A Call to Action*. Moline, Ill., 1968.

Child Welfare League of America. *Adoption of Oriental Children by American White Families*. New York: Child Welfare League of America, 1960.

Child Welfare League of America Standards for Adoption Service. New York: published by author, 1959; also rev. ed., 1973.

"Child Welfare League of America Statistics, June 1974, Compared with July–December 1973, Summary of Findings." Oct. 1974, mimeographed.

"Children Without Parents," *Trans-Action*, July–Aug. 1970.

Clark, Kenneth B., and Clark, Mamie P. "Racial Identification and Preference in Negro Children," *Readings in Social Psychology*, ed. T. M. Newcombe and E. L. Hartley. New York: Henry Holt and Co., 1947.

Comer, James P., and Poussaint, Alvin F. *Black Child Care*. New York: Simon & Schuster, 1975.

Council on Advocacy for Children, Proceedings of the Fourth North American Conference of Adoptable Children, Washington, D.C., March 1974.

Curtis, James. "Point/Counterpoint: Should Whites Adopt Black Children?," *Encore*, Dec. 1972.

Davis, Mary J. "Adoptive Placement of American Indian Children with Non-Indian Families," *Child Welfare*, Vol. 40, June 1961.

Deasy, Feila C., and Quinn, Olive W. "The Urban Negro and Adoption of Children," *Child Welfare*, Vol. 41, Nov. 1962.

DiViglio, Letitia. "Adjustment of Foreign Children in Their Adoptive Homes," *Child Welfare*, Vol. 35, Nov. 1956.

Doig, Ivan. "Interracial Adoptions: How Are They Working?," *Parents'*, Feb. 1971.

Dolliver, B. "We're the Lucky Ones! Child of Mixed Racial Background," *Good Housekeeping,* Dec. 1969.

Doss, Carl, and Doss, Helen. *If You Adopt a Child.* New York: Henry Holt & Company, 1957.

DuBois, W. E. B. (ed.) *Efforts for Social Betterment Among Negro Americans.* Atlantic University Publication No. 14. Atlanta, Ga.: The Atlanta University Press, 1909; reprint, New York: Russell & Russell, 1969.

Dunne, Phyllis. "Placing Children of Minority Groups for Adoption," *Children,* Vol. 5, Mar.–Apr. 1958.

Dywasuk, Colette Taube. *Adoption—Is It for You?* New York: Harper & Row, 1973.

Edgar, Margaret (ed.). "Some Experiences in Inter-Racial Adoption." An unpublished report of transracial adoptions by the Open Door Society of Montreal.

Edwards, Jane. "The Hard-to-place Child," *Child Welfare,* Vol. 40, Apr. 1961.

Encore. "Should Whites Adopt Black Children?" Jan. 1973.

Erikson, Erik. "A Memorandum on Identity and Negro Youth," *Journal of Social Issues,* Vol. 20, Oct. 1964.

——. "The Concept of Identity in Race Relations: Notes and Queries," *Daedalus,* Winter 1966.

—— (ed.). "Youth: Fidelity and Diversity," *Youth: Change and Challenge.* New York: Basic Books, 1963.

Falk, Lawrence L. "A Comparative Study of Transracial and Inracial Adoptions," *Child Welfare,* Feb. 1970.

——. "Identity and the Transracially Adopted Child," *Lutheran Social Service,* Vol. 9, No. 2, Summer 1969.

Fanshel, David. *Far from the Reservation: The Transracial Adoption of American Indian Children.* Metuchen, N.J.: Scarecrow Press, 1972.

——. "Indian Adoption Research Project," *Child Welfare,* Vol. 43, Nov. 1964.

——. *A Study in Negro Adoption.* New York: Child Welfare League of America, 1957.

Farmer, Robert A. *How to Adopt a Child.* New York: Arco Publishing Company, 1967.

Feinstein, P. "Report on Interracial Adoption," *Parents',* Dec. 1968.

Festinger, Trudy Bradley. *Why Some Choose Not to Adopt Through Agencies.* New York: Metropolitan Applied Research Center, 1972.

Fischer, Clarence D. "Homes for Black Children," *Child Welfare,* Vol. 50, No. 2, Feb. 1971.

Fowler, Irving. "The Urban Middle-class Negro and Adoption: Two Series of Studies and Their Implications for Action," *Child Welfare,* Vol. 45, No. 9, Nov. 1966.

Fradkin, Helen. "Adoptive Parents for Children with Special Needs," *Child Welfare*, Jan. 1958.

Fraser, C. Gerald. "Black Unit Finds Impact Is Broad," New York *Times*, Apr. 6, 1972.

——. "Blacks Condemn Mixed Adoption," New York *Times*, Apr. 10, 1972.

Fricke, Harriet. "Interracial Adoption: The Little Revolution," *Social Work*, Vol. 10, No. 3, July 1965.

Gallagher, Ursula M. "Adoption: Current Trends," *Welfare in Review*, Feb. 1967.

——. "Adoption Resources for Black Children," *Children*, Vol. 18, No. 2, Mar.–Apr. 1971.

Gallay, G. "Interracial Adoptions," *Canadian Welfare*, Vol. 39, No. 6, Nov.–Dec. 1963.

Gentile, Angela. "Subsidized Adoption in New York: How Law Works—and Some Problems," *Child Welfare*, Dec. 1970.

Glazer, Nathan. *Affirmative Discrimination: Ethnic Inequality and Public Policy*. New York: Basic Books, 1975.

Goldberg, Harriet L., and Linde, Lewellyn H. "The Case for Subsidized Adoptions," *Child Welfare*, Vol. 48, No. 2, Feb. 1969.

Goldstein, Joseph; Freud, Anna; and Solnit, Albert J. *Beyond the Best Interests of the Child*. New York: The Free Press, 1973.

Goodman, Mary Ellen. *Race Awareness in Young Children*. New York: Macmillan, 1964.

Graham, Lloyd B. "Children from Japan in American Adoptive Homes," *Casework Papers 1957*. New York: Family Service Association of America, 1957.

Grant, Maye H. "Perspective on Adoption: Black into White," *Black World*, Nov. 1972.

Greeley, Andrew. "Making It in America: Ethnic Groups and Social Status," *Social Policy*, Sept.–Oct. 1973.

Griffin, Barbara P., and Arffa, Marvin S. "Recruiting Adoptive Homes for Minority Children—One Approach," *Child Welfare*, Feb. 1970.

Grossman, Susan J. "A Child of Different Color: Race as a Factor in Adoption and Custody Proceedings," *Buffalo Law Review*, Vol. 17, No. 2, Winter 1968.

Grow, Lucille J. *A New Look at Supply and Demand in Adoption*. New York: Child Welfare League of America, May 1970.

—— and Shapiro, Deborah. *Black Children—White Parents*. New York: Child Welfare League of America, 1974.

Haight, Frances. "The Development of an Interracial Program (A Board Member Speaks)," *Child Welfare*, Vol. 32, No. 5, May 1953.

Hagen, Clayton. "Community Challenge," mimeographed paper, 1967.

——. "Interracial Adoption," paper presented to the Human Relations Council of Bloomington, Minn., 1966.

——. "Is the Hard-to-place Child so Hard to Place?," paper presented at Child Welfare League Midwest Conference, Des Moines, Ia., 1967.

——. *"Matching Values" in Mixed Race Adoptions*. Mimeographed paper, 1970.

——. "New Patterns in Adopting," mimeographed paper, 1969.

——, et al. *The Adopted Adult Discusses Adoption as a Life Experience*. Minneapolis: Lutheran Social Service of Minnesota, 1968.

Hawkins, Mildred. "Negro Adoptions—Challenge Accepted," *Child Welfare*, Vol. 39, Dec. 1960.

Heffernan, William, and Ain, Stewart. "Big Money, Little Victims: Kids in City Care Denied Homes," New York *Daily News*, May 13, 1975.

Herzog, Elizabeth, and Bernstein, Rose. "Why So Few Negro Adoptions?," *Children*, Vol. 12, Jan.–Feb. 1965.

Herzog, Elizabeth; Sudia, Cecelia; et al. *Families for Black Children: The Search for Adoptive Parents. I: An Experience Survey*. Washington, D.C.: U. S. Government Printing Office, 1971.

Heyliger, Fleur Conkling. "'The Answer' (to an adopted child)," *Saturday Evening Post*, Apr. 5, 1952.

Hill, Robert. *Strengths of Black Families*. New York: Emerson-Hall, 1972.

Hobby, Fred. "Transracial Adoption: A Political Threat or Social Movement." St. Louis, Mo.: Washington University, 1972, unpublished paper.

Isaac, Rael Jean. *Adopting a Child Today*. New York: Harper & Row, 1965.

Jaffee, Benson, and Fanshel, David. *How They Fared in Adoption: A Follow-up Study*. New York: Columbia University Press, 1970.

Jenkins, Alma. "Some Evaluative Factors in the Selection of Adoptive Homes for Indian Children," *Child Welfare*, Vol. 40, No. 6, June 1961.

Johnson, Charles S. *Shadow of the Plantation*. Chicago: University of Chicago Press, 1934.

Jones, Edmond D. "On Transracial Adoption of Black Children," *Child Welfare*, Mar. 1972.

Jonsson, Gustav. "Introduction to New Staff," *Children Away from Home—A Sourcebook of Residential Treatment*, ed. James K. Whittaker and Albert E. Frieschman. New York: Aldine Publishing Company, 1972.

Kadushin, Alfred. "A Study of Adoptive Parents of Hard-to-place Children," *Social Casework*, Vol. 43, May 1962.

——. *Adopting Older Children*. New York: Columbia University Press, 1970.

——. *Child Welfare Services.* New York: The Macmillan Company, 1972.

——. "The Legally Adoptable, Unadopted Child," *Child Welfare,* Vol. 37, Dec. 1958.

——. "Single Parent Adopters: An Overview and Social Research," *Social Service Review,* Vol. 44, No. 3, Sept. 1970.

Kardiner, Abram, and Ovesey, Lionel. *The Mark of Oppression: Explorations in the Personality of the American Negro.* New York: W. W. Norton & Company, 1951.

King, Helen H. "It's Easier to Adopt Today," *Ebony,* Dec. 1970.

Kirk, H. David. *Shared Fate: A Theory of Adoption and Mental Health.* New York: The Free Press, 1964.

Klein, Wells. *The Special Needs of Vietnamese Children—a Critique.* New York: International Social Service, American Branch, Sept. 1971.

Klemesrud, Judy. "Furor over Whites Adopting Blacks," New York *Times,* Apr. 12, 1972.

Kline, Droza, and Overstreet, Helen-Mary Forbush. *Foster Care of Children.* New York: Columbia University Press, 1972.

Ladner, Joyce A. *Tomorrow's Tomorrow: The Black Woman.* Garden City, N.Y.: Doubleday & Company, 1971.

——. "What 'Black Power' Means to Negroes in Mississippi," *Trans-Action,* Nov. 1967.

Lahner, U. C. "Easier Adoptions: Some Agencies Follow More Flexible Policies for Placing Children; Changes Help Single Person, Poor." *Wall Street Journal,* Jan. 9, 1970.

Lawder, Elizabeth A. "Quasi-Adoption," *Children,* Jan.–Feb. 1966.

Lewis, Hylan. "Agenda Paper No. V: The Family: Resources for Change," Planning Session for the White House Conference "To Fulfill These Rights," Nov. 16–18, 1965. Washington, D.C.: Government Printing Office, 1965.

Lyslo, Arnold. "The Indian Adoption Project," *Child Welfare,* Vol. 40, May 1961.

——. "Adoption for American Indian Children," *Child Welfare,* Vol. 39, No. 6, June 1960.

——. "Adoptive Placement of Indian Children," *Catholic Charities Review,* Vol. 51, No. 2, Feb. 1967.

——. "The Indian Adoption Project—an Appeal to Catholic Agencies to Participate," *Catholic Charities Review,* Vol. 48, No. 5, May 1964.

Maas, Henry S. "The Successful Adoptive Parent Applicant," *Social Work,* Vol. 5, Jan. 1960.

—— and Engler, Richard E., Jr. *Children in Need of Parents.* New York: Columbia University Press, 1959.

McCoy, Jacqueline. "Identity as a Factor in the Adoptive Placement of the Older Child," *Child Welfare,* Vol. 40, Sept. 1961.

McDermott, Robert E. "Oriental Adoptive Placements," *Catholic Charities Review*, Vol. 40, No. 4, Apr. 1965.

McWhinnie, Alexina M. *Adopted Children—How They Grow Up.* London: Kegan Paul, Trench, Trubner & Company, 1967; New York: Humanities Press, 1967.

Manning, Seaton W. "The Changing Negro Family: Implications for the Adoption of Children," *Child Welfare*, Vol. 43, Nov. 1964.

MARCH. *Adoptive Placement of Minority Group Children in the San Francisco Bay Area—A Study by MARCH.* San Francisco, 1959.

Marmor, Judd. "Psychodynamic Aspects of Transracial Adoptions," *Social Work Practice*, 1964. Selected Papers, National Conference on Social Welfare. New York: Columbia University Press, 1964.

Mech, Edmund V. "Trends in Adoption Research," *Perspectives of Adoption Research.* New York: Child Welfare League of America, 1965.

Mills, C. Wright. *The Sociological Imagination.* New York: Oxford University Press, 1959.

Mitchell, Marion M. "Transracial Adoptions: Philosophy and Practice," *Child Welfare*, Vol. 48, No. 10, Dec. 1969.

"Mixed Adoptions," *Newsweek*, Apr. 24, 1967.

"Mixed Race Adoptions—Report on the First International Conference on Transracial Adoption," Montreal: The Open Door Society, 1970.

Moe, Alice Y. "Reality Factors in Early Placements," *Child Welfare*, Vol. 37, June 1958.

Montalvo, Frank F. "Casework Consultation in Overseas Adoption," *Social Casework*, Vol. 40, Mar. 1959.

Morgan, Neil. "Computer with a Heart," *McCall's*, June 1971.

Morgenstern, Joseph. "A Mother's Love," *Newsweek*, June 21, 1971.

———. "New Face of Adoption," *Newsweek*, Sept. 13, 1971.

Neely, Mae. "Point/Counterpoint: Should Whites Adopt Black Children?," *Encore*, Oct. 1972.

Newman, William N. *American Pluralism.* New York: Harper & Row, 1973.

Nordlie, Esther B., and Reed, Sheldon C. "Follow-up on Adoption Counseling for Children of Possible Racial Admixture," *Child Welfare*, Vol. 41, Sept. 1962.

Novak, Michael. *The Unmeltable Ethnics.* New York: The Macmillan Company, 1972.

Nutt, Thomas E. "Adopting the Hard-to-place: System Change in a Public Service," unpublished Ph.D. thesis, Massachusetts Institute of Technology, 1973.

———, and Snyder, John A. *Transracial Adoption.* Cambridge: Massachusetts Institute of Technology, 1973.

Open Door Society. "Progress Report." Montreal, 1963.

———. "Historical Sketch of Interracial Placement Programme of Children's Service Centre, Montreal, and Formation of Open Door Society," mimeographed paper, 1968.

———. *Mixed Racial Adoptions.* Montreal, 1970.

Opportunity, *Survey of Adoption of Black Children.* Portland, Oreg.: Boys' and Girls' Aid Society of Oregon, 1968, 1970, and 1971.

PAMY (Parents to Adopt Minority Youngsters). *Final Report: PAMY's Progress (1957–1963).* St. Paul, Minn.: Minnesota Department of Public Welfare, June 1963.

Pepper, Gerald W. "Interracial Adoptions: Family Profile, Motivation, and Coping Methods," unpublished Ph.D. thesis, University of Southern California, 1966.

Pettis, Susan. "Effect of Adoption of Foreign Children on U.S. Adoption Standards and Practices," *Child Welfare,* Vol. 37, July 1958.

Pinkney, Alphonso. *Black Americans.* Englewood Cliffs, N.J.: Prentice-Hall, 1975.

———. *Red, Black and Green: Black Nationalism in the United States.* New York: Cambridge University Press, 1976.

Polk, Mary. "Maryland's Program of Subsidized Adoptions," *Child Welfare,* Vol. 49, No. 10, Dec. 1970.

Porter, Judith. *Black Child, White Child.* Cambridge: Harvard University Press, 1971.

"Position Statement on Transracial Adoptions," National Association of Black Social Workers, Sept. 1972.

Poussaint, Alvin F. "The Negro American: His Self-image and Integration," repr. in *The Black Power Revolt,* ed. Floyd Barbour. Boston: Porter Sargent, 1968.

Powdermaker, Hortense. *After Freedom: A Cultural Study in the Deep South.* New York: Viking Press, 1939.

Priddy, Drew, and Kirgan, Doris. "Characteristics of White Couples Who Adopt Black-white Children," *Social Work,* Vol. 16, No. 3, July 1971.

Pringle, M. L., et al. *Adoption Facts and Fallacies: A Review of Research in the U.S., Canada, and Great Britain, Between 1948 and 1965.* New York: Humanities Press, 1967.

Rainwater, Lee. "The Crucible of Identity," *Daedalus,* Winter 1966.

Rathbun, Constance, and Kolodny, Ralph L. "A Group Work Approach in Cross-cultural Adoptions," *Children,* Vol. 14, No. 3, May–June 1967.

Raynor, Lois. "Extending Adoption Opportunities for Negro Children," *Child Welfare,* Vol. 32, No. 4, Apr. 1953.

———. *Adoptions of Nonwhite Children—The Experience of the British Adoption Project.* London: George Allen & Unwin, 1970.

———. "Agency Adoption of Nonwhite Children in the United Kingdom," *Race,* Vol. 10, No. 2, Oct. 1968.

Roskies, Ethel. "An Exploratory Study of the Characteristics of Adoptive Parents of Mixed-race Children in the Montreal Area," unpublished Master's thesis, University of Montreal, 1963.

St. Denis, Gerald. "Interracial Adoptions in Minnesota: Self-concept and Child-rearing Attitudes of Caucasian Parents Who Have Adopted Negro Children," unpublished Ph.D. thesis, University of Minnesota, 1969.

Sandusky, Annie Lee, et al. *Families for Black Children—The Search for Adoptive Parents. II: Program and Projects.* Washington, D.C.: U. S. Government Printing Office, 1972.

Scyner, Lawrence A. "Looking Ahead to Youth and Adulthood," *Children Who Wait.* Proceedings of the Second International Conference on Transracial Adoption, Boston, 1970.

Sellers, Martha G. "Transracial Adoption," *Child Welfare,* Vol. 47, No. 6, June 1969.

Sharkey, Nora Clare. "White Parents, Black Children: Transracial Adoption," *Time,* Aug. 16, 1971.

Shepherd, Elizabeth. "Adopting Negro Children: White Families Find It Can Be Done," *The New Republic,* June 20, 1964.

Simon, Rita J. "An Assessment of Racial Awareness, Preference, and Self-identity Among White and Adopted Non-white Children," University of Illinois, 1973, mimeographed.

———. "An Assessment of Racial Awareness Preference, and Self-identity Among White and Adopted Non-white Children," *Social Problems,* Vol. 22, No. 1, Oct. 1974.

———. "White Parents of Nonwhite Children: An Analysis of Transracial Adoption," University of Illinois, 1973, mimeographed.

Skolnick, Arlene S., and Skolnick, Jerome H. *Family in Transition.* Boston: Little, Brown and Company, 1971.

Smith, Jean. "I Learned to Feel Black," repr. in *The Black Power Revolt,* ed. Floyd Barbour. Boston: Porter Sargent, 1968.

Social Planning Council of Metropolitan Toronto, *The Adoption of Negro Children: A Community-wide Approach.* Toronto: Social Planning Council, 1966.

Solnit, Albert; Freud, Anna; and Goldstein, Joseph. *Beyond the Best Interests of the Child.* New York: The Free Press, 1973.

Standards for Adoption (rev.). New York: Child Welfare League of America, 1973.

Standards for Foster Family Care. New York: Child Welfare League of America, 1959.

Suzuki, Ryo, and Horn, Marilyn. "Follow-up Study on Negro-white Adoptions," unpublished manuscript, Los Angeles County Bureau of Adoptions, Los Angeles, Calif., 1965.

Thompson, Era Bell. "The Adoption Controversy: Blacks Who Grew Up in White Homes," *Ebony,* June 1974.

U. S. Department of Health, Education, and Welfare, Children's Bureau. *Termination of Parental Rights and Responsibilities and the Adoption of Children.* Washington, D.C.: U. S. Government Printing Office, Aug. 1971.

——. *When You Adopt a Child.* Washington, D.C.: U. S. Government Printing Office, 1965.

U. S. Department of Health, Education, and Welfare, Office of Child Development. *Progress Report: A Three-year Plan for a Black Adoption Project.* Washington, D.C.: U. S. Government Printing Office, Sept. 17, 1971.

Valk, Margaret A. *Korean-American Children in American Adoptive Homes.* New York: Child Welfare League of America, 1957.

Wachtel, Dawn D. *Adoption Agencies and the Adoption of Black Children.* Washington, D.C.: Adoptions Research Project, 1972.

Watson, Kenneth. "Subsidized Adoption: A Crucial Investment," *Child Welfare,* Vol. 51, No. 4, Apr. 1972.

Weinberg, Martin S., and Rubington, Earl (eds.). *The Solution of Social Problems.* New York: Oxford University Press, 1973.

Westoff, Leslie Aldridge. "Kids with Kids," New York *Times Magazine,* Feb. 22, 1976.

Wheeler, Katherine B. "The Use of Adoptive Subsidies," *Child Welfare,* Vol. 48, No. 9, Nov. 1969.

Wolins, Martin, and Piliavin, Irving. *Institution or Foster Family—A Century of Debate.* New York: Welfare League of America, 1964.

Wylie, Evan McLeod. "ARENA Breaks the Adoption Barrier," *Reader's Digest,* Nov. 1970.

Yette, Sam. *The Choice—the Issue of Black Survival.* New York: G. P. Putnam's Sons, 1970.

Zastrow, Charles. "Outcome of Negro Children-Caucasian Parents' Transracial Adoptions," unpublished Ph.D. thesis, University of Wisconsin at Madison, 1971.

Index

25880

DATE			
MAY 12 '81			
MAR 24 '82			
APR 8 '82			
MAY 3 '82			
DEC 15 '82			
MAR 21 '83			
MAR 20 '84			

25880

© THE BAKER & TAYLOR CO.